"Threadbare, Seawolf three fiver and three six. Ammo expended. Get ready, we're coming in to get you. Stand by to load."

Well, we just can't believe it. We're certain that Seawolves are designed to carry like three or four people, and even split up, there are eight of us on the ground. . . . This ain't never gonna work, but beggars can't be choosers, so we move out into the open and drop down. I step forward and kneel on one knee, pointing the strobe light. I guide them in, bringing the enemy tracers with them. I can sense the bullets tearing up the ground around us, and I expect any second to get hit. As Seawolf three fiver's hood settles about ten feet away, the guys get up and run for them, with me right behind. . . .

WHATTAYA MEAN I CAN'T KILL 'EM

A Navy SEAL in Vietnam

Rad Miller Jr.

IVY BOOKS • NEW YORK

An Ivy Book
Published by The Ballantine Publishing Group
Copyright © 1998 by Rad Miller Jr.

Grateful acknowledgment is made to APPLESEED MUSIC, INC., for permission to reprint an excerpt from the lyrics of "ALICE'S RESTAURANT" by Arlo Guthrie. © Copyright 1966, 1967 (renewed) by APPLESEED MUSIC, INC. All Rights Reserved. Used by Permission.

www.ballantinebooks.com

Library of Congress Catalog Card Number: 98-93233

ISBN 0-8041-1766-7

Manufactured in the United States of America

First Edition: December 1998

10 9 8 7 6 5 4 3 2 1

To Jim Richards, our only casualty to date.
A good friend and a funny guy, gone way too soon.

Vietnam

I CTZ
(MR1)

II CTZ
(MR2)

III CTZ
(MR3)

IV CTZ
(MR4)

MAP 1

IV Corps, Detail

SOUTH VIETNAM

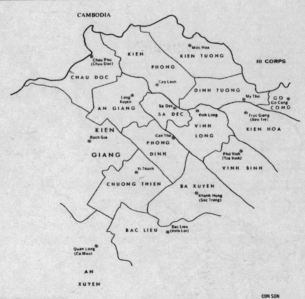

CAMBODIA

KIEN

PHONG

Moc Hoa

KIEN TUONG

III CORPS

Chau Phu
(Chau Doc)

CHAU DOC

Cao Lanh

DINH TUONG

My Tho

GO
CONG

Go Cong

Long
Xuyen

AN GIANG

Sa Dec

SA DEC

Vinh Long

Truc Giang
(Ben Tre)

KIEN

VINH

KIEN HOA

LONG

Rach Gia

PHONG

Can Tho

GIANG

DINH

Phu Vinh
(Tra Vinh)

Vi Thanh

VINH BINH

CHUONG THIEN

BA XUYEN

Khanh Hung
(Soc Trang)

Bac Lieu
(Vinh Loi)

BAC LIEU

Quan Long
(Ca Mau)

AN

XUYEN

CON SON

(Administered from Saigon)

0   25   50 Miles

0   25   50 Kilometers

MAP 2

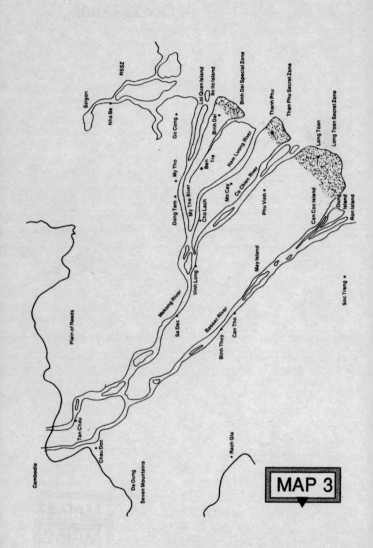

MAP 3

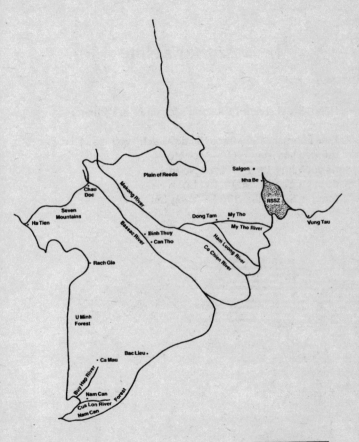

Saigon

Nha Be

RSSZ

Vung Tau

Plain of Reeds

Chau Doc

Mekong River

Seven Mountains

Ha Tien

Dong Tam   My Tho

My Tho River

Bassac River

Binh Thuy

Can Tho

Ham Luong River

Co Chien River

Rach Gia

U Minh Forest

Bac Lieu

Ca Mau

Buy Hap River

Nam Can

Cua Lon River

Nam Can

Forest

MAP 4

Author's Note

Echo (SEAL Team 1) platoon's locations in Vietnam:

Late February 1969 through late March 1969—Sa Dec
through late May 1969—Moc Hoa
through July 1969—Tuyen Nhon
through August 1969—Cat Lo
through September 1969—Vung Tau

Chapter One

I WAS HEADED STRAIGHT to hell in a handbasket. The Old Man had told me so several times. He was not happy at all about the way I was living my life, and he let me know it. Me, I couldn't figure out why he was so excited. It was 1965, I'd graduated high school in the spring, had a job as a grass-mower with a local nursery, and I was just about to turn eighteen. The Old Man, however, wasn't satisfied. He kept insisting that I should go to college in the fall. If not, I should get a "real" job with IBM, which was our major local employer.

"If you don't get your shit together," he said, "you're gonna get drafted and sent to Vietnam. Change your ways or get your ass shot off, it's up to you."

Ah, man, I couldn't see what all the fuss was about. Regular sex was available, I was partying with my friends, and I had a hot-rod Ford that kicked ass. I'd given some thought to college, mainly as a place to meet girls, but I was really sick of school. Besides, I was making good money, sixty bucks a week, for doing next to nothing. Since cigarettes were twenty-five cents a pack, gas was twenty-five cents a gallon, and beer twenty-five cents a glass, I only had to keep out thirty dollars a week for gas, cigs, and dating; the rest I put in the bank. As for getting drafted, hey, they had a million guys to choose from, they wouldn't bother with me.

Well, the Old Man kept bugging me, so I finally put in an application to IBM, scored high on their entrance exam, and I'll be damned if they didn't hire me. It was better pay, eighty-eight dollars a week, and there were lots of women around to hit on, but it was second shift, which really sucked. Doing second shift

1

was getting ready for work at 2:30 P.M., start work at 4:30, work until 12:30 A.M., and then party at a nearby bar until 2:00 A.M. Go home ("Your place or mine?") and sleep till 10 or 11, get up and eat, and it was time to get ready for work again! I didn't like it. I never seemed to have any free time, and I missed my friends—they were partying while I was working.

But on the job, it took me less than a month to become a hero to my boss. I sat by a microscope on the manufacturing line and checked the alignment of two small parts—with a foot pedal I'd stop and start each part under the scope. In no time at all I was a pro. I'd sit down at my station, start the line, and immediately fall asleep. Since my line never stopped, I achieved *huge* production numbers. At lunch and quitting time, I'd wake up with red circles around my eyes from lying on the scope. Amazingly, I got very few rejects. (Aren't you thrilled you owned that IBM mainframe computer manufactured in 1965?) I was a star! But I had only been working there a few weeks when I got an awful surprise. It was my letter from Uncle Sam, saying, "I want you."

Oh man, what was this? Although I'd been hunting and shooting all my life, I had no intention of hunting and shooting humans, and I definitely had no intention of letting anyone shoot at me. But what could I do? "Honor and Duty" called. You see, the Old Man had been in the Merchant Marine in WW II, and his stories about convoying to Northern Europe against the German U-boats were really scary. But he firmly believed that I should do my duty and serve, so I never even considered avoiding it. It's like family tradition, that sort of thing. But I ain't no fool. When I passed my induction physical in Poughkeepsie, New York, the man gave me a decision.

"You got your choice, pal, Army or Marines."

I quickly shook my head and said, "Lead me to the Navy recruiter!" Nobody shoots at sailors. I had to sign up for four years, but at least they guaranteed me a service school, and I was locked in. I was safe, man, I wasn't playing at no war.

My younger brother A.J. was like my twin. He'd always hung out with me, so he figured he'd quit school and enlist with me under the Buddy Plan. See, the Old Man had made it plain to A.J. up front that if he wanted to quit school, he must enlist in the military. A.J. didn't mind, he hated school, so he went up with me to take the entrance exam. And that's when I got my first taste of the military mentality.

A.J. didn't do very well on the entrance exam, so the Navy wouldn't take him. Ah, but all is not lost. While A.J. is waiting for me to finish up my paperwork, a Marine recruiter comes strolling by, and I saw him and my brother talking together.

He tells A.J., "I just happened to see your paperwork [sure] and you'd make a great Marine. The Navy's not going to do anything for you because of your low test scores, but the Marine Corps would see you got a high school equivalency diploma, plus you'd get a lot of other good training. The Army and the Navy, they're just ordinary, but Marines are stud dogs." And so on and so forth. Oh, he was looking good, this Marine, slim and trim in his sharp uniform, and he conned A.J. into signing up on the spot. By the time I found out what was going on, it was too late. So much for the Buddy Plan.

Chapter Two

So, JANUARY 1966, I go to Albany, New York, to get sworn in, and then it's on by bus to Great Lakes, Illinois, for boot camp. I keep to myself, because I'd never been out of New York State before. Hell, I'd never been anywhere before. I scanned the guys traveling with me, and they were a strange bunch. Most were a lot bigger than me. I was only five foot six and 125 pounds. Some of them, like me, were quiet, cooling it until they found out what was going on, some were friendly, but there were these four dudes from Scarsdale.* They were loud and

*A wealthy suburb of New York City, located to its north in Westchester County.

obnoxious, pushy. They had to be "city guys." I already knew I wasn't going to like this shit.

One thing I'll say about the military, they sure had it down pat. I didn't know my ass from a hole in the ground, so I played it quiet and followed directions, right on into recruit barracks. Oh my God, how I hated boot camp! I was cleaned, scalped, outfitted, and verbally abused right into the military mold. What I hated most was the loss of privacy. I mean, I couldn't imagine undressing and stuff among a hundred guys, but I had to do it. Racks (bunks) were three high and four feet apart, and guys were always coughing and snoring around you all night long. I never did get used to that.

The second day I was there we go to get shots, and I am terrified. They march us into this huge room where hundreds of guys are lined up in ranks, waiting. When it was my turn, I followed the line into the next room to run the gauntlet. You walked between rows of corpsmen (medical aides), and as you passed they'd stick needles in you, one after another. Left arm, right arm, and one in the ass. At the end of the gauntlet stood a guy with a silver gun, and he would shoot you in the arm. The sound of that thing hissing and blasting dried the spit in my mouth until I could hardly swallow.

I'm telling you, I was shaking like a leaf, my armpits were pouring, and my bladder was ballooning. I hated needles, and I wasn't sure I was gonna make it through. Somehow I did, and when I got to the dude with the gun, he was smiling. Uh-oh. As he pressed the gun against my arm I flinched, and the high-pressure liquid cut across my skin.

The dude snarled, "Oh, a pussy!" and shot me again.

Hey, that wasn't so bad. A corpsman gave me a cotton ball soaked in alcohol to put on my cut, which was bleeding slightly. When I pressed the cotton ball against my arm, streamers of alcohol-diluted blood ran down my arm, and I thought, oh boy, here's a chance to have some fun.

I pressed around the cut to get some more blood flowing in streaks, then I held my arm and staggered out into the big room full of men. *Thump thump thump,* down they went like tenpins. Fainting, man, it thinned the ranks right out. Then a corpsman ran up to me and hustled me right outside, cussing all the way. Me, I played Mr. Innocent, but my act mustn't have been very convincing; I had to spend the rest of the day picking up cigarette butts.

Boot camp turned out to be just bearable, but I tell you what, I hated every minute of it. This military thing was not my style. We took classes to learn the basic Navy stuff—you know, tying knots, saluting, and the like, and we did lots of marching and drilling with old M-1 rifles. Since I was a country boy who had been running the ridges for years, the physical stuff was no problem, and in fact I did well enough to be appointed First Squad leader. Big deal.

It was the mindless rigidity that I hated. Get up at this time. Wash, shower, and shave at this time. Eat at this time. Be a sheep and follow orders, don't you dare think. Some shit. The only way I could handle the regimentation was to click on my robot switch, stay low-key, and just exist. Get through it and get out, and don't fuck up. Resentfully, I followed the herd, trying to figure out a way to avoid all the bullshit, until I saw what happened to someone who screwed up. There was this one dude, he stuck his tongue on a rifle barrel on a dare, and they hung him out to dry.

Now you got to understand, this was Chicago in midwinter. It's 30 degrees below zero and windy, and the instructors had told us, "Don't touch any metal on your guns with your bare skin, 'cause if you do, it will freeze." This dude don't listen, and he takes the dare. He licks his rifle barrel and it hurts, so he yanks the barrel away, taking half his tongue with it. The guy is hollering and bleeding all over the place, and what do they do? First they fix him up so he can eat and drink through a straw. Then they give him a Captain's Mast, a lesser form of court-martial. The charge was: "destroying Government property." Can you believe it? The dude isn't even out of boot camp and already he's got a black mark on his record, plus they made him repeat boot camp!

I'm only there about three weeks and things start getting worse for me. I grow this red pimple on the end of my nose, and

one of the wiseasses from Scarsdale comes up with the nickname "Wartnose." I jump him, his three buddies jump me, and
after a futile battle I go down hard. Shit! I had to put up with that
lousy nickname for the rest of boot camp. You better believe,
though, that those assholes died the ugliest kinds of death in the
greatest of pain. Only in my mind, of course. Then one night a
guy who was sleeping in the top bunk got sick and vomited
"over the side." It was enough to roll my stomach, and I was
hurting the rest of the night. Naturally we named the guy
"Puke."

One thing that helped me get through boot camp was music. I
was a country guitar picker from way back, until I got hooked
on the Beach Boys. My mother had bought me "Surfin' USA"
for a birthday present, and did she ever regret it. I wore out that
album, playing it over and over and over. I quickly learned all
my favorite songs by heart, and I'm certain that I ruined my
voice singing falsetto along with Brian Wilson. I think my
mother was glad that I got drafted because she wouldn't have to
listen to any more Beach Boys.

Anyhow, someone had screwed up, and we were allowed to
have portable radios and listen to them while on remote watch.
Standing watches was fun. You guarded a door for four hours at
a time so that the enemy couldn't mount an assault on boot
camp. Good thing, too; I'd have surrendered it to them in a
second.

I was able to trade for a portable radio and "California
Dreaming" kept me going. It had it all—good beat, fabulous
harmonies, and of course, Michelle Phillips. Every guy I knew
wanted to jump her bones.

Somehow I stuck it out, and after a lifetime, boot camp
finally ended. I was now a Seaman E2, nearly the lowest rank in
the military, and I could wear two pretty white stripes on my
arm. We got our first liberty (free time off base) and I chose
Chicago. Sex? No one in Chicago would even talk to me, but I
did get a neat tattoo of a skunk on my arm.

Chapter
Three

OH BOY, I get my first thirty days' leave to go home. Home is Hopewell Junction, New York, a tiny little farm town on the Hudson River, close to West Point and Poughkeepsie. After my leave is completed, I will go right back to Great Lakes for electrician school. I take my first ever plane ride, to New York City (what a nasty place!), then hitchhike eighty miles north to my home. I figured that in uniform, I wouldn't have any trouble getting rides, and I was right. Only trouble was, they were queers, after my sweet young body. (Before you start busting my chops, remember that this is 1966, long before "gay.") The first ride was an old guy, maybe forty, and after I told him I wasn't that way, he was cool about it. The second ride was a college guy my age who was more persistent, and I had to show him my fist before he would let up. He did take me close to home, though.

I liked being home, so much so that I stayed too long. I was busy showing off in my neat little sailor's uniform, and people actually respected me for being in the military. (How things change. In later days, you wouldn't catch me in uniform at home, because that respect had disappeared.) I cut my travel time too close, and got back to Great Lakes two days late. Damn, I know I'm in trouble now, and I'm really sweating it. I report in, and lucky for me the sign-in person is a WAVE, and she ain't at all bad looking. I had thought all military women were dogs. So I give her a sweet smile and my best bullshit line to explain being late. I figured since she's female, I can get over on her, but she held up a hand and stopped me.

"Not bad. Not bad at all. That's the best story I've heard

7

today." She smiled. "Now get your ass on over to the barracks and count yourself lucky I'm a sucker for a pretty face."

Well now, I think that's mighty nice of her, so I lay out my best line for us to get together, you know, get better acquainted, but again she stops me. "Whoa! Don't press your luck."

I got out while the getting was good.

Chapter Four

$\mathbf{M}$E AND MY friend Dennis Szeba (we had been friends in high school, graduated together, and ran into each other at Great Lakes) were reading the bulletin board one day and he said, "Hey, you should try this."

I say, "What?"

He says, "They're looking for frogmen. They're gonna have a physical test next week, you know, push-ups, sit-ups, shit like that. You can do all that stuff, you were a big sports king in school. You should try it, just for kicks."

Now, while I knew he was just busting my ass, I was pretty proud of my athletic skills. I had won a trophy for wrestling in the ninth grade, and played freshman football on an unbeaten team until we played the reform school. (Those guys were all six-footers and had whiskers! They broke our halfback's leg the first play of the game, then pounded the rest of us into the dirt.) I had lettered each year in track—cross country, mile, and pole vault—and I had won all kinds of ribbons for long-distance running. See, I wasn't fast—a girl could beat me in the 100-yard-dash—but I could run all day. I think that came from the times A.J. and I had run down deer in the snow when we were kids. And I remember at one track meet, I'd taken the wrong trail and ran 10 miles instead of 2.5, pulling all the opposing runners with me. I was hardly winded when I finished, but it *had* seemed to take longer than usual. My competitors thought I did it on purpose, and man were those guys pissed!

My first love had always been football, but I was too small for varsity football. I was five foot four and 120 pounds, and they wouldn't let me play. That broke my heart.

Regardless, I think this frogman thing would be fun, so the following week Dennis and I go, he's just planning to watch. We get there and I sign in, and then I go "Uh-oh."

Dennis says, "What?"

I say, "Part of this test is swimming laps."

"So?"

"Well, hey man, I can't swim."

His jaw drops, he wide-eyes me. "What the fuck you mean you can't swim? I saw you diving out of the tree at Pells, and you were swimming then!"

"Well, I can dog-paddle good enough to get to shore, but that's it."

He shook his head. "Oh man, you are in a world of shit now. You'll drown for certain. Can I have your guitar when you do?"

I find out that I've got to do two laps of backstroke, two of breaststroke, and two of sidestroke. I think, what the hell, maybe I can fake it. I am sort of familiar with how swim strokes should be done, between watching Tarzan on TV and some of my friends swimming over the years, so I'll do something similar and see if I can get by. Since there are about forty of us competing, and only three or four monitors, it just might work.

Well, I have no problem with the sit-ups, push-ups, pull-ups, and timed run so I get all pumped up and figure I'm gonna make it through, until we line up at the pool. As I'm eyeing the six lanes (down and back for one lap) my pump-up starts fading, and the lanes look longer and longer. Can I really do this?

Pretty quick the pool is full of guys churning in every direction, and the crowd is hollering encouragement. When my turn comes, I jump in, and in no time I'm floundering. I'm moving out, but barely staying above water, because the other dudes are making these great big waves in the pool, and they're swamping me. Every time I suck a mouthful of air, I get water instead.

The monitor is watching us and his stopwatch, and I realize at that point that there's no way in hell I'm gonna make it, so I'll just concentrate on not drowning. But that doesn't work either, because I must have swallowed half the pool. Somehow I make it down and back doing one hell of a dog-paddle, then I quick switch to a sort of bastard sidestroke and nobody seems to notice. I get almost to the end of the pool and suddenly all is confusion. People are hollering and guys are jumping into the pool, so I hang on the far wall a minute to try to catch my breath and see if I can't figure out what's going on. That's when I see them pull a limp guy up over the side of the pool. That scared me. That's also when I say to myself, fuck this, I can't get it done. So I do my best dog-paddle back to the start and climb out, breathing like a bellows.

A monitor comes up to me and says, "You finished?"

I gasp, "You bet!"

He looks at his stopwatch, writes a time next to my name, and says, "Well done."

Man, I don't care, I'm dying. I just can't seem to get enough air in my lungs. When I have recovered somewhat, I go over to Dennis, and that fool is rolling on the ground laughing.

He says, "Man, you were right, you sure can't swim. I was just about to jump in and save your life."

I scowled at him. "Fuck you, man. That was hard. Besides, I made it, didn't I?"

He kept laughing. "Sure, if you count one lap of damn near drowning as making it. I thought a tornado had come up, all that air you was sucking in."

Well, there was no shutting him up until a couple of days later, when they posted the results on the bulletin board. I was in the top one-third of the qualifiers, especially my swim times.

I gloated, "See, I told you I was a hero."

Dennis came right back, "Man, you should be ashamed of yourself."

I strutted a bit. "Hey, I'm just good is all."

After that I bragged a bit for fun, but I put it behind me, glad that I was still alive. It had been doubtful there a few times during my swim pool adventure. The fun was over, however, and I went back to normal life: classes, meals, and occasional liberties.

While I think of it, I want to thank a small place called Fort Atkinson, Wisconsin, for the only decent liberty in the whole Great Lakes area. See, any large military base, it's a jungle out there. The military guys are the herd of zebras, and the local civilians are the lions, hyenas, and vultures. Chicago, and specifically Waukegan, Illinois (home of the Great Lakes Naval base), was about the worst I've ever seen. Sailors get paid very little money, but the local civilians were determined to get *every* penny of it. I'm telling you, when you stepped out of the gate into Waukegan, you were on your own. You'd be extremely lucky to walk back through the gate after liberty with even your clothes on. Every con game, scam, and trick was used to the max to clean the sailor out. And if those didn't do the trick, there were always head-busting, mugging, and outright robbery to get the job done. I mean, a sailor goes on liberty with only three things in mind: eat, drink, and sex. Mostly sex.

Young "Johnny," he's far away from home, family, and friends. Mom, Dad, and relatives, none of them are around to put a clamp on his behavior. Johnny can jump on anything that moves, he can drink himself blind, and nobody is around to frown on his behavior or remember it. He doesn't have to date a good-looking girl to impress friends and parents—hell, any warm body will do. And around military bases, it sometimes seems every other woman is a prostitute. I mean, the ugliest woman in the world (you look up "ugly" in the dictionary, it's got her picture) is Raquel Welch. Every woman has twenty dudes sniffing around her all the time, and the guys will pay and pay to get into her pants. It runs the gamut from "nice" local girls who get sailors to pay to entertain, wine, and dine them, to hustlers who steer sailors to gambling clip clubs, to the outright pros. The nice girls usually reward you with a set of blue balls. ("Oh no, I can't; I'm saving myself for marriage.") The clip-joint girls will leave you with empty pockets and a busted head, while the pros will leave you with a good case of clap or syphilis.

The only way to avoid the rat trap is to get as far away from the base as you can. I tried Chicago first, and that was no dice, they hated sailors there. Then I tried Madison, Wisconsin, a big college town, but they were used to sailors, and conditions were better, but not all that great. It wasn't until I stumbled onto a little town called Fort Atkinson (or Whitewater?), Wisconsin, that I found heaven. Whitewater State Teacher's College was located there, and since teachers were mostly women, that's who hung out in the bars, diners, and movies. I'd stopped at a roadside diner and had no sooner sat down than girls started coming around and introducing themselves. I'd only been there about ten minutes before my whole weekend was scheduled.

Wow! These were nice girls, it was just that there were so many of them, and so few guys for them to match up with. I wasn't even pretty, and all of a sudden I was Clark Gable, James Dean, and Cary Grant. And friendly? I must have lost twenty pounds that first weekend, but you know I was smiling the whole time. I'd found a home. "Chicago? Where's that? Waukegan? Never heard of it."

It wasn't all roses, though. Just before I finished school, five of us went out on a drinking run. I rarely went on these expeditions, but my friend Dennis convinced me to go on this one. We headed out to Madison, got wasted, and when we were finished we hitchhiked back to the base. A carload of guys stopped to give us a ride, I don't know, maybe three or four of them as I vaguely remember. Next thing I know we're out in the boondocks, everybody's piling out of the car, and there are a bunch of guys pounding on us. Daddy had never taught me the Marquis of Queensberry's rules, so I found me a piece of log and was pounding away with it. I was doing pretty good until my log broke and somebody hit me in the back of the head. And that's about the last I remember. Next thing I know, there's cops all over the place and lots of flashing lights. My friends are lying around me, and we're hurting. I was tonguing two broken teeth and all of us were bloody. The civilians? Hey, they were long gone. The cops told us that they were local guys who were upset about sailors chasing their women, and this wasn't the first time for this sort of thing. That certainly made me feel better.

The cops take us back to base, and we go right into the infirmary. We all got out the next day except my friend Robb, who had a crushed nose. Me, I'm walking around with two jagged stumps of teeth, and a few days later my gum is swollen into a huge lump. My lip is all pushed out, and I'm in incredible pain, so I am forced to go to the man I fear most in this world, the dentist.

He takes a look and says: "Infected! I'll fix you right up."

He gets me in his chair, picks up a scalpel, and says, "We might as well fix up those teeth while we're at it." Without warning, he whips up the scalpel and swipes it across my swollen gum.

Well, I tell you what! My body arched up like a bow and tears started out of my eyes. *Yeow!* Stinking juice poured down my chin and suddenly there was this incredible feeling of relief. He gave me some antibiotics and, after a week or so, a new set of caps. I was myself again. I bet that dentist, though, wishes that dentist chairs had seat belts and restraints for cowards like me.

Oh boy! I got my orders, and I'm going to a ship stationed in Hawaii, the USS *Falgout*. Surf's up, sun and fun, and all that good stuff. Dennis has grit teeth, because he's got four more months of school to do.

I bust his hump with pleasure, but all he would say was, "If ever I seen anybody step in the shit it's you. How come you luck out so much?"

Well, I have to rub it in. I double up my arms and give him a pose. "Muscles so big, body so beautiful. What can I say?"

He was disgusted. "Yeah, muscles so puny, body so ugly!"

I knew he was green, though. Great Lakes sure wasn't Hawaii.

Better yet, when I check my leave and arrival dates I discover that I got five extra days in between, so I figure I'll pop home for a couple of them, and away I go on the airplane. I say hello to everyone, hang out, spend a couple nights with my friend Babs, and then go down to New York City to catch my plane to Hawaii. Only one problem though, nothing's flying. Seems there's a big airline strike on, and no one's going anywhere. The terminal is jammed, lines are long, and everybody's pissed off. When I check with the airline woman, she tells me my flight is canceled and she has no idea when it's going to be rescheduled. My only choice is to go on military standby and hope I get lucky.

Well, it took me three days, but I finally got a flight. By then I was out of smokes, my white uniform was brown, and I was starved. Airplane food never tasted so good. Lucky for me the airlines were giving servicemen priority. I mean, they all wanted to cooperate with the government and get us to Vietnam as quickly as possible. When I reported in to my ship three days late, only one thought was in my head, here we go again. I'm getting pretty good at this shit, so I give them my best song and dance about my airline strike adventure, and amazingly, they buy it. It's one more close escape for me.

Chapter
Five

SHIPBOARD LIFE SURE sucks! I mean it's really horrible. The USS *Falgout* is a DER (Destroyer Escort Radar), a mini-destroyer. I had thought there was no privacy in boot camp, but this was much worse. Not only was there no privacy, there was no room! One thing I had always demanded in my life was my eighteen inches of personal space. I didn't like to be touched, and I especially didn't like being crowded. But on this ship, forget it! It was almost as bad as I thought a submarine would be. Our sleeping compartment (rows of fold-down aluminum and canvas racks with thin mattresses, on both sides of the walkway) was also a daytime passage and hangout. I was always being bumped, pushed, or crowded by other sailors, and I couldn't stand it. Every task was completely regimented, and there were no exceptions. It seemed as if the guys on that ship spent their entire Naval career on board, be it three, four, six, or twenty years. No one had ever gotten a transfer off, and they considered that as normal Navy life.

It's totally unacceptable to me. I knew at the end of my first week that I couldn't survive here. Remembering the UDT test I had passed at Great Lakes, I immediately wrote out a transfer request for the next class of UDT training, and SEALed my doom. I dropped my request at the Electrical desk, and it wasn't fifteen minutes later that I was called in by, of all people, my former roommate at school, Don! I grinned and started to shoot the shit, but he wasn't having any of it. He spent the next half hour telling me how my transfer request was a mistake, and that I should tear it up. I tried explaining to him why I couldn't hack it on the *Falgout*, but he wasn't listening.

Finally he said, "Look, there's no way they're gonna approve this transfer, and if you push it, the officers are gonna make your life miserable, and I won't be able to help you. Forget about the transfer, and I'll try to get you assigned to the Electrical gang as soon as possible. Normally it would take three months of crap duty before that happened."

But I was Dutch stubborn, I couldn't understand all the fuss. I mean, I was nobody. Why should anyone care what I did? You see, I still didn't comprehend the military mentality involved, but I was about to learn firsthand: Don't make waves. I was immediately assigned to compartment cleaning and other assorted crap duties, and the harassment started.

I sweep and mop the compartments twice a day. Although Don is officially my boss as the first class electrician petty officer, I really work under a third class chicken fucker (sorry, farmer) from Asswipe, Mississippi. His name is Thomas, and this guy is a real winner. He's six foot four, about 200 pounds, and has a third-grade education. He talks in an accented whine that can cut wood, and he never fails to raise my hackles. Third class petty officer (paygrade E-4, the equivalent of a corporal) is as high as he's ever gonna go, and he's in for as long as they'll keep him because there's no way he could cut it in the outside world. Alcoholic, vicious, and petty, his size and muscle have been his ticket through Navy life. He's my "shepherd" to guide me along the Navy way, and naturally nothing I do is right, so I end up doing things over and over and over under that grating whine of his.

"Jesus Chris' a'mighty, yer the poorest bag of shit ah ever see'd. Cain't ya do nuthin' raght?"

And the other sailors would grin because this was entertainment. I took it as long as I could.

Now, since I was a baby I've had a ferocious temper. As a kid I'd had kicking and screaming tantrums if I didn't get my way. When I was fifteen, I'd beaten my first car to death with a tire iron when a wrench slipped and I barked my knuckles. With my dad's help I had trained myself over the years to bury that temper deep, and thankfully, I'd only had a few relapses. There were just a couple of things that would free the beast. If you caught me by surprise you could set it free, but if you messed with my face, like slapping it, I was guaranteed to go berserk.

Thomas had boiled me several times, but somehow I'd been able to keep control. I figured that since I was a new guy, I should stay low-key until I learned the lay of the land. But old Thomas just wouldn't have it that way—he had his orders, and he was enjoying himself.

One day there were about ten guys hanging around, watching Thomas putting me through the paces. Judging by the amount of laughter directed at me, it was quite entertaining. I know I wasn't all that thrilled. Finally, Thomas, playing to his audience, pulled the mop out of my hand and stuck the business end of it in my face.

It was some shock when suddenly my whole world was gritty, wet, and stinking. I heard the laughter, and that's all she wrote. I grabbed the mop, snapped the handle with a good stomp, and proceeded to beat old Thomas to a bloody whimper. When the red mist finally cleared from my eyes, I just turned and walked away, trembling all over. Nobody was laughing. Well, I know it's the brig for sure, or maybe hang me from the yardarm, but strangely, not much was said. Too much paperwork, I'd imagine.

Regardless, I was quickly reassigned to the scullery, and

what a stinking hole it was! The scullery, where the food trays and eating tools were washed, was an eight-by-eight-foot room, dark, filthy, and superheated. When a sailor finished eating, he'd scrape his food tray into a fifty-gallon trash can and set his dirty tray on the conveyor belt. The tray would enter the scullery through a window, and I'd stack it with the others in a tray rack. When the rack was full, I'd run it through the steam-heated dishwasher that occupied most of the room. As the racks of "clean" trays came out the other end of the dishwasher, I'd let them sit for a few minutes to dry off. Whenever necessary, I'd run an armload of clean trays up to the beginning of the chow line. This duty is three times a day, seven days a week. At night, long after everyone else had knocked off and was relaxing if not on watch, I'd come out of my fetid cave drenched with sweat and stinking to high heaven. But I wasn't done yet. After every meal I had to haul the food trash can out to the deck, and the after-supper run was the worst. That son of a bitch had to weigh a hundred slopping pounds, and I could rarely handle it without getting nasties all over me. At sea, I could dump it over the side, but in port I was supposed to dump it in a Dumpster (unless there was no one around). Fun, fun, fun.

After a week or so of this nonsense, I suddenly realized I was going about this all wrong. I was stuck here, and scullery duty was the worst crap job they could give me, right? Well, it didn't have to be. What was wrong with this picture? First was my work location. The scullery was smelly, steamy, hot, and dark. Second was my time—I had no free time at all, and I was wiped out at the end of the day. Third, my end product: the supposedly clean trays were often greasy and spotted with dried food, and everyone was constantly bitching to me about that.

What was good about this picture? Absolutely nothing. Now wait a sec, that wasn't necessarily true. The one thing I did have was glorious, glorious privacy. Nobody would ever come near the scullery, much less go inside. *Eeyow!* I had to take advantage of the fact that I had my own private room. All I needed to do was make it comfortable to spend time in.

Okay. First thing I'm gonna attack is the ventilation—I need air. I pulled the vent grill, up near the ceiling, and what a nasty mess! There was a twenty-year-old greasy, gooey chunk of filth completely sealing the vent hole. Using an old worn-out mop and scraper, I cleaned out the vent pipe as far as I could reach. Uh-huh. Already I could feel a small movement of air through the vent hole. But it was pitifully slight. I needed a fan.

Between meals, I started searching the areas of the ship I was allowed in. The engine room gave up a small high-speed fan with a changeable filter, and in the Electrical storeroom I "found" light fixtures, switches, and wire. Finally I made a sneak-and-peek trip to the bosun's paint locker and liberated five gallons of white paint. Excellent! I installed the fan and filter, added two more light fixtures, and then started disassembling and cleaning the dishwasher, one section at a time. Like the vent, it was filled with greasy sludge, and the improvement was immediately apparent. The food trays started coming out clean, and I didn't have to run them through more than once, which meant less steam in my room. All right! Now for the big job.

Starting with the overhead (ceiling) I cleaned, scraped, and painted the room, down to and including the deck. Oh man, what a difference! The scullery was clean, airy, and bright. Previously, I'd always kept the door open to help vent the place, but now I kept it closed. I didn't want any company, thank you. Between meals I could read to my heart's content, sleep, or just sit and think. I was living high, so naturally it was too good to last.

I'd only been in the scullery a month and a half when we had a captain's inspection. This was the biggy, held once a year. I stand by my space for inspection, and here they come, the captain, the exec, and my boss, Cook First Class. The captain is chewing out Cook, apparently the mess line didn't do so good. When the captain glances in the scullery, he does a double take, then walks right in, while I stand at attention, sweating it. Out they come, and the captain starts questioning me. I stutter out answers, telling him about all the work I've done, and he nods and turns to Cook.

"This is a real Navy space, the kind I like to see. It hasn't looked this good in years. Too bad the rest of the mess space doesn't match it."

Cook gives me a scowl, and my heart sinks, because I know my good times are over.

Chapter Six

HALLELUJAH, I'M SAVED! My transfer request, although disapproved by all of my ship's command, is granted by the Navy Department. I am outta here! I will be attending the January 1967 class of UDT Training. There is a God, and now he smiles on me.

I don't really know for sure, but I figure between the transfer being a done deal and my good showing with the captain, the lifers gave up on me. I'm reassigned to the Electrical gang, working for Don. Now I'm just one of the guys again, no better or worse than the others. My scullery adventure followed me though, and I had to tell the story several times for the entertainment of the others. Don soon set me straight.

"You were lucky," he admitted. "If you hadn't gotten good marks with the captain, they would have hung your ass out to dry. You can't just go around taking gear whenever you want it. All that shit has to be submitted and approved on paper, and it never would have happened. The way it's supposed to go is that you trade off work and equipment with other departments. As it is, you're gonna have to do some payback for the gear you hooked." Seeing my apprehension, he said, "Don't worry, it won't be crap work. We'll figure something out."

Meanwhile, life ain't so bad. I finally get to go on liberty and see something of Hawaii. Each day after breakfast, we hang out in the shop for a while, and then Don assigns us our day's work.

I'm mostly partnered up with Jenkins. He's a Third Class, and he's training me. He's okay I guess, but a big talker. He never stops, and don't ever tell him anything you don't want the whole ship to know. It's all right, though, 'cause mostly I'd rather listen than talk.

And as you might guess, I had to go through all the rituals. I was sent to get a bucket of steam for cleaning, a left-handed spanner wrench, and because I was going to be a frogman, I was also sent to the bosun to draw diving gear and check the bottom of the ship. The bosun didn't see the joke, however, and chewed my ass good, just because I had hooked his lousy paint. What an asshole. I shrugged and took it all with a grin, though, because mostly it was just good-natured fun at my expense.

One thing perked up my ears, though. Jenkins, with a shit-eating grin, mentioned something about a "sea chicken" initiation but wouldn't elaborate. I figure if Jenkins ain't talking, it probably won't be good for me. I couldn't figure it out, but I knew damn well that any initiation figured to be lousy. I had never bought into initiations, and had never joined any organization that had them. They are always humiliating, usually violent, and sometimes dangerous. Any time pleasing a crowd is the object, there seems to be no limit to the excesses. Hanging parties, gangs and mobs, college sororities, they don't make for reasonable behavior. I clench my fists and grit my teeth, 'cause no one in this world is gonna humiliate me without paying a price.

But sure enough, one morning in the shop, out of the blue, the guys grab my arms and bend me over the workbench. The yell goes up, "Sea chicken time!" They've caught me by surprise, but I figure I'll go along and see what happens, so I don't struggle too hard. I figure maybe it's better to get it over with. Suddenly someone reaches from behind and pulls down my pants and shorts. It isn't fun anymore. I feel something round and slimy touch my buttocks and I lose it. Now I'm fighting for my manhood, and there ain't no holding me. I slung off my attackers, and started throwing punches at anyone I could reach, but I was hampered by my pants being down around my ankles so I grabbed a screwdriver and looked for someone to stick it into. The guys were spread out by my explosion, and the smiles were all gone. Jenkins was standing there with a limp hot dog in his hand so he was going to pay first.

Then Don's voice broke the tension from his desk, where he'd been spectating.

"All right, Miller, relax now; it's all over. C'mon, man, they were just funning. Cool down."

I threw down the screwdriver and yanked up my pants. I was crimson, and my expression dared anybody to make a comment.

Don said, "All right you guys, get to work. Miller, you stick around."

When the shop had cleared out he said, "You okay now?"

No, I wasn't okay, but at least now I had words. "What the fuck was all that?"

Don sighed. "Listen, for whatever it's worth, I apologize for them. It's one of those stupid traditions that bored sailors use to have some fun, and you know there ain't much of that on board this ship." He chuckled. "From the looks on their faces, you won't have any more trouble with them; they were shitting bricks."

Then he said, "Listen. Be cool and let it slide. You've still got to work with these guys, and this ship is too small to carry grudges." He added, "Besides, you'll be out of here in a few months, and you ain't got time for this petty bullshit."

Well, I was mostly over my mad by then, but I'm a Scorpio (we never forget), and I filed it under the "injuries to be paid back" column. Finally I said, "What would have happened had I not fought back?"

Don laughed. "Then you'd have been 'sea chicken,' and you'd never know when someone would try to stick you from behind with a different kind of hot dog."

I stared. "Are you serious?"

"There's all kinds in the military, some you'd never expect. You take men away from women for long periods of time— I mean, these guys come from everywhere, and some of the crackers, they been fuckin' their sisters, brothers, cousins, horses, sheep, hell, anything that moves."

I didn't quite buy it. "Get outta here. I never heard of stuff like that."

He grinned. "Mr. Innocent Country Boy. Nah, listen, that sort of thing is rare on a ship, but I'm telling you, I'd be mighty careful about dropping the soap in the showers. And definitely keep your young ass clenched tight on the beach."

I showed him my fist. "Anybody messes with me, they're gonna be singing soprano."

He laughed. "Well, we'll see. Meanwhile, you better work with Schnell for a few days, give Jenkins a chance to get his color back. For a minute there, I thought he was gonna pee his pants."

So, I was through another test. There were a few uncomfortable moments, but the episode was soon buried, and I got on with normal shipboard life. I still hated it, but I was getting by, looking to the future. Days I spent doing "on the job training" as an apprentice electrician, doing repairs, maintenance, and standing watch, stuff like that. Nights and weekends, when not standing watch, I hit the beach, where I found out that Don was right. On the beach after dark and hitch-hiking back and forth, seemed like every guy I met was after my young ass. It was extremely hard for me to deal with, because where I came from, that sort of thing was completely unheard of. Plus, I couldn't figure out how someone could compare a nasty old hairy-chested dude with a soft, smooth, pleasingly curved woman. It don't make no sense to me.

The problem was, even though I had earned a promotion to E3 in June 1966, I was only paid twenty-three dollars twice a month. If you took out for cigarettes, toothpaste, and the like, there was very little left to spend. So I had to hitchhike everywhere I went and sleep out on the beach at night. And no women. None! The Hawaiian girls, they were forbidden to fool around with sailors. And American girls? Forget it! I mean, they were everywhere around, to look at and drool over, but they would never lower themselves to even acknowledge the existence of sailors, and so Hawaii was a tropical desert for me. Although I guess if you had big bucks and could go to the right places you could make out. Money would buy you any woman.

Anyway, I did what I could. I "swam" in the shallow water and learned to surf, but mostly I roamed the beaches and did some climbing in the hills. In those days you could walk all the way around the island on the beaches, and I did it several times. I hear that now all the beaches are fenced off from the public and, if true, that's really sad.

Chapter
Seven

SEPTEMBER 1966 WE left Hawaii for patrol duty in Vietnam. I liked the open ocean, and thanks to Don, I got to spend a lot of time on deck, because he put me in charge of the small fanroom just below the bridge. I spent every spare moment up there, reading, sleeping, or checking out the ocean. Contrary to popular belief, the ocean isn't necessarily empty. There were flying fish, dolphins, and the occasional floating debris. Out in the middle of the trip we ran into a hurricane/typhoon/tropical storm, hell, I don't know what it was, but you should have seen those waves! My fanroom was just below the bridge, which is the highest point of the ship, and I was looking upward at those waves. Yow! I was nervous for a while, but the ship rode them like a cork. Man oh man, you should have seen all the sailors ralphing over the rail, though. I mean, those guys were green! I didn't get sick at all. Just lucky, I guess.

We stopped at Guam, but got no liberty because there's nothing there. Then we arrived at the Philippines, Subic Bay, and I'm on my first foreign soil. For liberty, we go to Olongapo City, and what a hole! You go out the base gate and cross over a small brown stream full of sewage. And stink? Man, you could cut the stench with a knife, but, unbelievably, kids were swimming in it, begging us to throw coins. Ugh!

We get into these small trucks called jeepneys, and they're pretty neat. They're all painted up with pinstriping and fancy designs and they got bench seats to sit on. We zip down the street, which is lined with bars, and everywhere we look there are women, women, women! Oh boy. They're real small, with brown hair, skin, and eyes, and not all that bad looking. It's party time now, mister!

I'm Mr. Cool, I've heard all the stories, and I was prepared to get my share. God, I was so naive. I mean, these women were pros. I was nineteen, looked sixteen, blond, blue-eyed, a real sacrificial lamb. A sweet little lady cut me out of the herd immediately. One hand is always in my lap. Her other arm is around my neck and her voice is in my ear. She's telling me, "Let's blow this crowd and do some serious screwing." I heard that!

So we hop into a jeepney and away we go. I'm a-pantin' and a-snortin', I'm more than ready. Then we arrive at her place, and Jeez, it's just a grass hut, but who cares? We go inside and I rip off my uniform, all I can think about is woman.

I'm Mr. Cool, and I'd heard all the stories, so I only had about nineteen dollars in my wallet, five of which was for her. I had another forty dollars safe in my sock. When she insisted that I take off my socks too, I was hesitant, but hey, I put them right next to the bed, where I could keep an eye on them. Well, after I finish up, she's bugging me, let's go, let's go, she's got to report back to her bar, or her boss will rain all over her. Ah, what the hell, so I get dressed, and I feel my forty bucks still in my sock as I put it on. We go back to her bar and she zips off, I guess to give the boss his share of her earnings. I don't see her again, but that ain't a problem, because there are plenty of others around.

Now that my edge is off, I'm hanging with the guys, drinking and bullshitting, watching the floor show. We move on to other bars, stopping along the way to eat "monkey-meat," strips of meat on a stick, and it's really good. One of the guys says it's really dog or cat, but we don't mind, it's tasty. Eventually my turn comes to buy a round, and I go into my sock to get the money to pay for it.

Jesus H. Christ! I can only stand there with my mouth hanging open. All I got in my hand is a couple of peso notes, worth about twenty-five cents each. I'm telling you, my heart went right through the floor. I have been fucked over good— Mr. Cool had turned out to be Mr. Sucker. I had to borrow money from Don to pay for the drinks, and those guys laughed and laughed. Laughed at me. Mr. Cool got out of there, my liberty was over.

When we go back to sea, I got some good laughs back. Several of the sailors had caught the clap in Subic, and you should have heard those dudes moaning and whining whenever they took a leak. I guess it burns a bit, because I'm sure I saw finger-grip prints in the urinal piping where they hung on.

Chapter Eight

WE'RE OFF THE southern coast of Vietnam on patrol duty, and I'm Mr. Cool again. My friend Binky Connors, he was a gunner's mate, he'd let me shoot a grease gun (.45 caliber World War II–era submachine gun) when they were practicing, shooting at floating cans and flying fish, never hitting any of them. But when it was my turn, I nailed two cans and one flying fish. It was million-to-one luck, but I wasn't telling anyone. You know how it is. Mr. Cool just looked wise and said there wasn't nothing to it for a hunter. Hey, those guys were really impressed, 'cause they asked me if I wanted to be one of the boarding party when we stopped a Vietnamese junk to search it. Well now, I wanted to back up a bit, but I asked myself, what would John Wayne do?

So I said, "Sure, no problem." I thought they were just joking, but next thing you know we got a couple of junks stopped, and I'm on my way across with the crew to board and search them. I didn't need the ammunition I was carrying, because I was sweating bullets.

The junks were big wooden boats with long rudder poles. At the top of the rudder pole was a small gas engine, and at the bottom end, in the water, was the propeller. One person drove and steered the boat just by dropping the propeller into the water and moving the pole around. Pretty neat. Some of the junks also had small sails. We board these boats and search them thoroughly for military contraband but never find anything illegal. I meet the Vietnamese fishermen for the first time, and they're little guys, all stringy muscle and bone. They're so meek and unassuming that it's hard to consider them dangerous. They don't sit, they squat on their haunches by the hour, and we tower over them. I got to tell you, it's something that I can't do, squat like that. My muscles don't stretch that far.

Regardless, in the next couple of months we stopped and searched about thirty of these junks, and twenty or so sampans, which are smaller paddle boats, almost like big wooden canoes. Man, these people have got some big balls to be riding these things on the ocean. You certainly wouldn't catch me doing it.

It's December 1966 when we pull into Kaohsiung, Formosa. No liberty for me, I'm all packed to catch a flight to San Diego, California, for UDT training, and I am out of here! Jesus, what a relief. I am a little nervous about leaving the known world of the ship for the unknown world of UDT, but I got no regrets at all, and I don't look back as I climb on the C130 with my seabag and guitar case. I've got a Fender Stratocaster in there, with all my paperwork—travel orders, personnel records, and such.

I'm on my way, and during the flight, I get to shooting the breeze with one of the aircrewmen, who had spotted my guitar case. We're talking guitars and music. He's a picker too, and admires my Stratocaster. It helps pass the time until we land in Japan. When we do, the crew chief comes back and tells us passengers that they are refueling the plane, and if we want, we can go get some chow. They'll send somebody to get us when they're ready to take off, and the aircrewman I'd been talking to said he'd come.

Sure. We ate, waited an hour or so, and went back to the

plane, only the plane was gone! So was all our gear and, Jesus Christ, my guitar and paperwork. Oh man, we were done for. We had the uniforms we were standing in, our wallets and ID cards, and that's it. Mr. Aircrewman, I don't know who you are, but may you rot in hell. Mr. Cool had been suckered again.

Well, what could we do? We complained, we whined, we cajoled, but nobody was listening to two dumbass sailors and one Marine. It took us three days to finagle a military hop out of there to San Francisco, then from Travis AFB I got another hop to San Diego. I was pissed. Finally I board a bus and travel out to Coronado Amphibious Base and walk into UDT training prepared to explain my situation. For once, things go right, and they're expecting me. A First Class sits me down and explains how everything works. He stresses that I can quit at any time, all I've got to do is say so, and they'll ship me right back out to the fleet. Hmm . . . not hardly. No way I'm gonna go back.

"The training is difficult," he says, "but not impossible. The thing to do is listen to your instructors, learn all you can, and then you might make it."

Might? Gulp. What had I gotten into? Well, I was soon to find out, since I would start class the following week. I was now officially a member of Class 40.

Chapter Nine

Basic Underwater Demolition School, previously called UDT training, is the toughest training in the world. So say all the rumors flying around while we're waiting for our class to start. I must have heard a hundred stories, and none of them were encouraging. I got pretty nervous, and finally I had to sit myself down and say, "Look, you're a stud dog, you're in good physical shape, and you ain't no dummy. This is just another trial and can't be that big a deal. Other dudes have made it, and so will you. Besides, John Wayne wouldn't quit." Boy was I in for a rude awakening.

I have to get used to a whole new world. First thing, all the sailor clothes get packed away. We get uniforms of Army greens, a couple pairs of black boots, and a green plastic helmet liner. I've got nothing "sailor" to pack away, so that's not a problem. What is a problem is money. I've got none, and since I lost my pay records I can't get any, but I will need stuff, like shaving and washing gear and cigarettes.

"No way," says the yeoman after I tell him my sad story. "No paperwork, no pay. I applied for copies, but until they arrive, you're shit out of luck."

Hmm . . . I'm beginning to feel a little desperate.

Then this wiseass standing by listening says, "This one's a loser. Might as well get rid of him right now."

What the fuck! Who is this fool? His nametag says "Olli-vera." He's about five foot six, he can't weigh 150 pounds, but his legs and arms are all knotty with muscle. He's wearing dark shades and chewing on a nasty old unlit cigar stub. It looks just like a dog turd. He's also dark as an Indian and wearing green shorts, for God's sake! Loser, huh? I start to glare a bit, but he just chuckles and walks away.

I look at the yeoman and I say, "Who the fuck is that?"

He laughs. "Oh, that's Ollie, the lead instructor. You'll get used to him if you're around that long."

Well, maybe. But I sure ain't liking his tone. Then I move out, 'cause I got work to do.

I need stuff, and if I can't buy it, I've got to "find" some. I scout all the heads (bathrooms) I can find, and come up with some good stuff. First I find a couple of used bars of soap. Then I find a toothbrush that ain't snaggled too awful bad, several almost empty tubes of toothpaste, a nasty old razor, and several rusty discarded razor blades. Finally I go into the Boat's head, and a couple of guys are in the shower. I figure they're rich, so I liberate a can of shaving cream and a towel. On the way back to UDT, as I walk by a parked jeep, I spot a couple cartons of cigarettes on the seat. Nobody is around, and *flash!* I'm gone. Salems, yuck. But cigarettes are cigarettes and I'm on my way. Later on, however, when things got really desperate, I had to get a loan from the Red Cross to get by. Thanks, guys, you really saved me.

Chapter Ten

HOLY SHIT! I'M a couple weeks into training, and it's a killer! We do runs on the beach in loose sand, wearing full uniform. Ollivera leads, and while our sweat is pouring, he doesn't even breathe hard. The rest of us blow and pant, and try to keep up as best we can, but there's an awful lot of gagging and puking. We do swims in the ocean, and let me tell you, that water is freezing! Where oh where is the warm California water that I'd heard the Beach Boys singing about? We've got an obstacle course that's guaranteed to make a grown man cry, and through all of this, the instructors are constantly encouraging us to quit. That's all we hear, what pitiful wrecks of "Tadpoles" we are, why don't we just end the struggle and quit. Some of the guys listen to them, and we start losing people. One day they're there with us, and the next day they're gone, never to be heard from again.

I can do well in the runs; I'm usually within sight of Ollie. The obstacle course is tougher, and I'm just fair at it. The swimming, however, is killing me. First of all, I'm afraid of the deep water, I'm never comfortable, and I dread each swim. Second, I hold the distinction of being the slowest swimmer in our class. I've never been last at anything in my life, and this sure tears me up inside. Thank God UDT uses stealth swim technique.

Stealth swim technique simply means that nothing ever

breaks the surface except your head, and that is kept as low in the water as possible. The breaststroke is done with the arms pulling outward under the water, and the legs doing a frog kick. Backstroke, arms pull inward, but with legs doing a flutter kick. Sidestroke, you put one arm out in front to steer and trail the other. Your legs do a flutter kick. No crawls or flashing arms permitted.

The instructors teach us these new strokes in detail, and while the other guys are bitching and moaning, I'm all ears and practicing hard, and no one seems to realize that I'm just learning to swim! There's only one thing that gets me by—I float. My body has positive buoyancy in salt water, and this keeps me from drowning, although I come awful close at times. But I'm as slow as a turtle, and the instructors lay the abuse all over me. I just have to grit my teeth and take it. I have to keep telling myself, "I can do this! I just gotta try harder." It's not that easy, though, because no one wants to be my swim partner.

Every water operation is conducted in pairs, for a couple of reasons. First, of course, is safety. If anyone gets in trouble, and it does happen, his partner is right there to help or to call for the instructors. Second is teamwork. A lot of the things we are asked to do require both men working together to accomplish the task. Third is learning. If I can't do something, or I don't know how to do it, my partner may be able to, and I can watch him and then get it done myself. Finally, and most important to me, morale. As an individual, when things get tough, I can convince myself quite easily that I can't hack it. I will say the hell with it, and quit. But under the eyes of my partner, my pride forces me to play the John Wayne role. I'm failing, or I'm really suffering, and I say the hell with this, I can't go on. But my pride won't let me quit, because I would have to acknowledge to my partner (and to the other guys) that I'm a quitter, less than him, and that just ain't gonna happen. In other words, I can easily justify failure in my own mind and come up with a hundred excuses for it, but under the eyes of others, especially people I respect, my excuses are meaningless to me. I must dredge up the physical or mental courage to keep going. And this kind of pride is what will carry me and others through all hardships.

In fact, that's how most men get through combat. Most of us are big chickens and scared shitless, because nothing in our civilian lives has prepared us to kill or maim others. Actually, it's just the opposite. We've been told a million times that "Thou shalt not kill." But under the eyes of our fellow team members, patrol members, squad members, or company members, we must do whatever is necessary to keep their respect and approval, even if that sometimes means violating our basic beliefs.

In later years, Arlo Guthrie made a joke of it: "I wanta kill! I wanta see blood and guts, get veins in my teeth. Burn women and houses and children, eat dead burnt bodies. I wanta kill! I wanta kill!"

That kind of thing is always good for a laugh, but dudes will do all kinds of shit so that they don't lose the approval of their group mates and lose their position as "one of the gang." I'm not trying to justify atrocities, but if you ever wonder why when they happen almost everyone takes part, this is the reason. Naturally, there are always a few exceptions, cold-blooded killers who just don't give a damn. But they are extremely dangerous, both to the enemy and to the members of their group.

Everywhere we go, we carry an IBS on our heads. An IBS (inflatable boat, small) is a six-man rubber boat with paddles. It's black with fat rubber tubes for sides and rear, two cross-member tubes, and a rubber sheet for a bottom. It's got to weigh three hundred pounds and the tube sections constantly leak air, which means we spend a lot of time pumping ours back up. I swear carrying that thing around on my head made me a couple of inches shorter. The IBS goes wherever we do, and it's a strange but common sight for the Base sailors to see a dozen IBSs lined up outside the chow hall while we are inside eating. We learn to carry our IBS into the surf, jump in, straddle the tube like you would a horse, and paddle like crazy, hopefully in unison. We carried those damn IBSs fifty miles, but I bet we paddled them hundreds more.

Living with the IBS definitely taught us teamwork, but always kept us wet. Launching and paddling the IBS several times a day left our uniforms and boots soaked with salt water, and when we fucked up, which seemed to be every five minutes, the instructors would march us out into the ocean or bay, there to stand neck-deep, singing, shivering, and shaking. The California air was warm, our blood was thin, and once we were in the cold water, our heat loss was rapid. Rumor says that the Japan Current coming down from Alaska and flowing along the California coast is what keeps the water cold. I didn't know and I didn't care what the reason was, all I knew was that I froze my nuts off. Often, when we'd come out of the water, we were made to roll in the sand so we'd be "camouflaged." Miserable, that's the proper term. Sand don't mix well with human skin.

By the end of the first couple of weeks, everybody had a bad case of crotch rot. The combination of salt, sand, and friction quickly removed the top layers of skin on our balls and inner thighs. We all walked everywhere straddle-legged. We quickly threw away our underwear shorts, never to be worn again, and we loosened our belts so that the crotch of our pants hung as low as possible.

We didn't know it, but the instructors were purposely breaking our bodies down physically (and in some cases mentally—more faces disappeared) so they could rebuild us. The culmination of this physical breakdown is called Hell Week. We hear that we will sleep for the last time on a Friday night, and then not again until Sunday, a week later. But the instructors need their sleep, so they work us in relays, and every minute of every day and night the students are kept on the move. We run all over the base carrying our IBSs, we run on the beach, we do the obstacle course, we're in the water, on the water, under the water, out of the water, and under constant abuse. Of course, it's all in good taste, 'cause we can end it at any time by quitting, as our instructors keep assuring us.

Huh! John Wayne be damned! Sometime during the first day of Hell Week I clicked on my robot switch and became a zombie. Don't analyze, don't reflect, don't hope, just do and survive. Most were like me, but some weren't, thought it over, and were gone.

If we stopped for a minute, we were immediately asleep, standing, sitting, it made no difference. Meals were the hardest.

There must have been a special arrangement with the chow hall because, thank God, we always had hot food and plenty of it. And we desperately needed that food to replace the energy we were burning up, so we sucked it down in huge quantities. The big problem was staying awake long enough to get it down. During every meal the instructors were constantly in our face, waking guys up. I didn't have to take a shit for the whole week, because my body used every particle of food and left no waste.

Naturally, no one can go for a week without sleep, so the instructors gave us some. Occasionally they'd tell us to knock off, hit the showers, and then hit our racks. We'd go racing inside, almost crying with relief, strip off our filthy, sodden uniforms, and jump into the incredible pleasure of a warm shower. Most of us never made it out of the showers, me included. There'd be bodies all over the floor or propped against the walls, sleeping peacefully in the spray. The instructors knew, however, that too much sleep might not be healthy for us, so after we'd had half or three-quarters of an hour of snoring bliss, they would come charging in, screaming and kicking us to our feet and out onto the grinder (concrete assembly pad). Almost always we weren't fast enough to suit them, so they would march us out into the ocean to wash the sleep from our eyes. Or, we would go out on the sand for PT (because we were weak and puny) and lay on our backs for sit-ups. Ollie didn't want to mess up the shine on his boots, so he would walk around our circle on our stomachs. Man, that was an experience!

Ollie was always hassling this guy we called Boomer (I can't for the life of me remember his real name) because Boomer was the slowest runner, that is, when Ollie was taking time out from hassling me for my slow swimming. About the fourth day, Boomer just can't keep up, even though we all help him. But he's like me, he refuses to quit. Ollie has run us up and down Mount Suribachi (a large sand mound) several times, and finally Boomer is down crawling on his belly, he's that wasted. Ollie is standing over him, laying on the abuse. But Boomer is hardcore, and still refuses to quit. After that, Ollie just gave up, and gave him less hassle.

Well, a year later the week finally ended, on Saturday noon, and there weren't very many of us left. The instructors took us into the barracks, congratulated us, and broke open a case of beer. Beer? Oh boy! I could drink the whole case myself. I eagerly pop a top and take a good slug, draining about half the can. *Ahhh . . .* sweet nectar.

Chapter
Eleven

Oʜ Gᴏᴅ, I know I'm a dead man, but it don't matter, my whole body still hurts. I'm lying on the floor fully dressed, I'm wet and smelly, and there's bodies all around me. Phew! The whole place stinks to high heaven, but by God, I'm still clutching my warm can of beer.

I'm telling you, it took me ten minutes to force myself to my knees and then to my feet. I'm whining and whimpering like a girl, and every muscle screams with pain. Then I notice a couple of the other bodies are also starting to stir, with moans and groans. Finally I'm swaying on my feet, trying to get the courage to take a step, when Dashper comes in out of the showers. He's bright-eyed and bushy-tailed and whistling. (What an asshole!)

I croak, "What happened?" Jesus, even my tongue hurts.

He says, "It's all over, man, we made it through."

I grunt. "What time is it?" (I'd never owned a watch.)

He checks his wrist. "It's six o'clock Sunday night."

I blink at him stupidly. Somewhere I've lost a day. Then, ignoring Dashper's laughter, I stagger the ten miles to the shower and turn it on full. After a couple minutes the hot water stirs me to action, and slowly, with many groans and curses, I strip off my uniform. I try my boots, but I just can't undo them, the water-soaked knots are impossible. I plod out to my rack, it's the top one about a mile above me, and there's no way I'm gonna make it up there. The hell with it. I fall down into Fang's rack and die.

Ow! Next thing I know Fang is shaking the shit out of me and yelling, "Wake up, asshole! Up and at 'em! Rise and shine!"

Oh man, leave me alone, I can't do this. But I summon all my willpower and climb out of his rack, and that's when I realize I still got my boots on, my feet are burning up. As I move around a little I feel better, but my body is still stiff and sore.

"What time is it?" I ask.

"Twenty-two hundred. C'mon man, have you got your shit together?" Fang is grinning, 'cause he's my friend. Fang (his real name is Fooshee) is cool. He used to be a member of the Rocking Rebels, you know, the ones who did the song "Wild Weekend." We call him Fang 'cause he's got a broken tooth.

"Yeah," I say. And suddenly, I do. My mind clears, the robot switch clicks off, and I'm alive again.

Fang said, "Hurry up and get dressed, we're going to Tijuana to eat and get laid."

I think about it and shake my head. "Nah, you guys go ahead. I still gotta get these boots off, and my feet are real bad." I glare at the offending boots.

"Well, okay man," he says, and then he's gone. I pull on my swim trunks and prepare to remove my boots. Should be interesting.

Five minutes later, I'm getting nowhere. The knots are welded together, and I reluctantly use my K-bar knife to cut them free. I try working the first boot off and it's no go. My foot is burning up with pain and the sweat is beading on my forehead, this is just not working. So I pull the laces completely out and loosen the boots as much as possible, then I hook the heel on the edge of a step and yank. Without pausing, I do the same for the other boot, and then I've got to sit down real quick. Red flecks are floating in front of my eyes, and I almost pass out from the pain and the incredible stench that rises from my feet. Man, that really hurts. I look at the wrecks of my boots that have been on me for a week, and they're throwaways. Then I look down at my poor abused feet, and it looks like most of them came off with the boots. Blood is pooling on the floor, and I leave bloody footprints behind me as I hobble into the shower.

Chapter Twelve

Hell Week is a turning point, and things change for us considerably. The torture has broken down our bodies to tendon, muscle, and bone, and the time has come to start rebuilding them. Now all the physical training is designed to develop muscles and bodies that will suit UDT operations, so we start bulking up. Our brains are working hard, too. We have classroom time every day, learning diving, explosives, boat operations, and basic weapons. There's still harassment, and it won't stop until graduation day, but it's nowhere near as severe. I mean, how can anyone ever hurt you again after you've gone through Hell Week? We alternate each day, doing beach runs (they're getting longer, building to the sixteen-mile final), obstacle course (faster and faster), and timed ocean swims. Suddenly I am in serious trouble. I'm about to flunk out, not because I can't hack it, but because I'm such a slow swimmer, and nobody's giving me any sympathy. The swim jocks, shit, they're just breezing through. (One of the guys, Tanaka, is the Hawaiian swim champ, for God's sake!) The rest of the guys are getting it done and out of the way. The problem is, we must make the times to qualify for our swim fins, so that we can continue on through training. I've improved enormously, but so has everyone else, and I don't gain on them. They're all leaving me and my unfortunate swim partner way behind. Finally Ollie calls me into his office. I make sure he's sitting, not standing over me.

He tells me, "Wednesday is the qualifying swim for fins, and there's no fucking way you're gonna make the times. Maybe it's best if you gave it up now. We'll move you over to Mainside and you won't have to see any of the guys. What do you say?"

It took a minute to sink in. I was appalled, then furious. "You mean quit? Absolutely no way!"

He tried more convincing. "Look, a Frog lives in the water. He's got to be completely comfortable there or he can't do the job. As training goes on, you're gonna spend more and more of your time in the water. You really think you're gonna cut it?"

But I was adamant. I looked him right in the eye and nodded my head. "I'll make it!"

"All right," he said. "It's your funeral. Get your dumb ass back to class."

I really couldn't pin it down, but I had the feeling I'd said the right thing.

I went out of there talking to myself, however. Man, I just had to do this! By God, even if I had to stuff an outboard motor up my ass, I was gonna make the times. I was long past just staying off a ship. This shit is personal now.

Wednesday's here, and I'm the only one that seems to be nervous. The other guys are laughing and joking, but I'm not. My teeth are grit, and I'm determined to get it done, one way or another. Uh-oh. Fang has been assigned as my swim partner, and he's really pissed.

He tells me, "Motherfucker, you better churn that water! If I don't get my fins because of you, I'm gonna kick your ass up between your shoulder blades!"

Since Fang is one of the fastest swimmers in our class and a lot bigger than me, I figure he means it. We climb on the boat and head out past the surf, and I am trembling. I'm freezing, but that ain't the reason I'm shaking. It's pure fear of failure. Somehow I got to do this!

We're off, and although I'm putting out maximum effort, we quickly get left behind. I'm breaststroking with a flutter kick to gain time, rolling over to a sidestroke when I just can't stand it anymore. Fang is easing alongside me in backstroke, and he's screaming bloody murder, but his verbal abuse is pulling me with him. I'm quickly lost to waves, cold, sky, and water, my whole world now is pain. Pain in my body, because I am putting out maximum effort, and the cold water has already killed my muscles. Pain in my brain, because I'm afraid I'm gonna fail. I pray, help me, God, but he ain't listening.

My whole existence is concentrated, forcing my exhausted body on and on. My arms quickly become useless, so I trail them, and my struggle is centered in my burning legs, punctuated by Fang's yells. Kick kick kick. I'm long since out of gas and air, but I must still kick my legs. My muscles don't work anymore, my brain is dead, I can't do this! But still I kick, my stubbornness won't let me stop, until suddenly it's all over. I just can't do any more. I go dead in the water, Fang grabs me, and then I'm hanging on the rail of the instructor's boat, puking my guts out. There isn't enough air in the whole world to fill up my lungs, and it really hurts to breathe. My throat is raw, my legs are just a mass of pain, and I'm as helpless as a baby. They have to tow me to shore, and I'm just about crying with disappointment and shame. Well fuck it, I sure tried. Fang is helping me up because my legs won't support me, and he's talking up a storm.

"You did it, man, you did it! You made the time!"

Suddenly the sun is shining again, and I got a stupid grin plastered on my face. Can't hurt me now! Then Ollivera comes over and brings me right back down to earth. He's shaking his head and he ain't smiling.

"Pitiful. Absolutely fucking pitiful. You got to be the worst swimmer I ever saw. I'm gonna keep my eye on you, and the first time you slack off, I'm gonna kick your ass right out of here!"

Well, I'll be goddamned! I made it, didn't I? I'm filled with resentment, and I determine that I'm never going to give him an opportunity in the future to bust my ass. But back in the barracks, Fang quickly sets me straight.

"Ollie called me in and told me to do whatever it takes to get you qualified," he said. "That's why I was doin' all that yellin' and screamin'. He didn't want you to drop out." Then he laughed. "Man, the way you were suckin' air out there, it sounded like a vacuum cleaner. Didn't you do any swimming in New York?"

This is Fang, so I say, "Nope, never learned," and his jaw dropped a foot.

"Are you shitting me? Whatever possessed you to try out for UDT?"

"I want to be a Frog," I say.

And suddenly I realize that that's the real truth. I did want to be a Frog, in the worst way. The challenge had been thrown down, I had grabbed it by the balls, and I was damned if I would ever let loose. Ollivera has given me another chance, and by God, I'm gonna make sure he never regrets it. After all these years, Ollie, thanks for that second chance.

Chapter Thirteen

My WHOLE WORLD has changed again, and I'm a new man. When you swim with fins, all you need are powerful thighs, and I got 'em! Nobody leaves me behind now. Well, that's not really true, but I can hold my own and get the job done. My body is changing, my muscles are building, and physical training is no problem at all. Surprisingly, we don't build up big pads of muscle like Charles Atlas. Rather, since we are building up the "long" muscles, we are slim and trim, and what we get is rock hard. (Hear that, ladies?) Actually, the only real hardship left is the water temperature. Lord, is it cold! We all dread going into the water, and each time we get briefed for a water exercise, we hold our breath waiting to hear about wet suits. You see, we had been custom-fitted for wonderful, warm, thick, lovely foam rubber wet suits, but the instructors were determined that we not wear them out. Rarely do we hear, "wet suits optional"; almost always it's "You won't need your wet suits today," and everybody moans. Survival to us is defined as hitting the cold water and peeing in your wet suit for the welcome warmth. I promise myself (along with everybody else) that after graduation I will never again in my life get into cold water, even the shower, without a full wet suit.

Training continues, and one of the new things we learn is our main job, beach reconnaissance. The way it works is that the Navy has split up the areas of responsibility. The ships, of course, have all the deep water in the oceans. Small boats have rivers, streams, and canals, UDT has offshore water up to the high water mark on the beach, and SEALs have everything else. (What the hell is a SEAL? You mean the "arf arf" kind?)

Frogs approach a proposed landing beach from the ocean, drop off a small boat at either low speed or high speed, and swim shoreward, mapping the landing area as they go. For low-speed drop we use a motor launch with an IBS tied alongside it. Basically the launch parallels the target beachline with the IBS on the side of the boat away from the beach, so it can't be seen from shore. We crouch in the launch, roll over the side of the launch into the IBS, then roll out of the IBS into the water, one swimmer every twenty-five yards. Man, when we plunge into the water wearing only our swim trunks, face mask, and fins, the breath is shocked right out of us, and it's all we can do not to yell in protest. Immediately your body heat starts to dissipate, but you tread water until everyone's dropped and the line starts to swim shoreward, pausing every twenty-five yards to take a sounding (depth reading). As you go you note and record useful information about what you see in your path. If you spot anything unusual such as a clump of weeds or rocks or whatever, you freedive down and check it out. Then you record it.

What we're after, when all the swimmers' info is combined, is an accurate picture of the underwater approaches to the landing beach and the beach itself: the gradient (slope of the bottom up to the shore), depth of water (at measured intervals), type of bottom (sandy, rocky, muddy), water currents, and any obstacles seen, natural or man-made. Our accurate info will save many lives, just ask any Marine who's ever done an amphibious landing. It comes down to a matter of the Marines landing on the beach and getting wet to the knees, but moving quickly to do their job, or the Marines stepping off the boat into deep water, having to struggle ashore or maybe drowning right there. That's some big difference! If you ever watch the Normandy landings in WW II on TV, one of the most terrible sights you will ever see is all the bodies floating offshore. Many of them drowned when the weight of their gear pulled them under before they ever hit the beach. That's what we want to prevent.

Rarely, when the training recon is really lengthy, we are allowed to crawl up on the beach. Our lips and nails are blue and our muscles are dead, and it may take five or ten minutes to get to your feet and move out. More commonly, when the recon is done, the line swims back seaward to the pickup point. Then the motor launch will come down the swimmer line at speed and the pickup man kneeling in the IBS hangs out a large rubber loop which is roped to the boat. When your turn comes, you tread water and stick one arm up in a "hook." The pickup man guides the rubber loop onto your hooked arm and swings you up into the IBS, and you immediately scramble up into the launch. If you are slow, the next guy who's picked up may be thrown right on top of you—I've seen dudes piled two and three deep. If anybody screws up and gets left in the water, the launch must make another run, which is dangerous for all concerned. It takes precision, timing, and lots of practice. I tell you, that damn water was so cold, I'd never miss a pickup. What I wanted most was to get warm, warm, warm. Somebody once told me that the water temperature was 40 degrees, and that don't seem possible, but brother, I sure believed!

We only did a few of the high-speed drops, and they were murder. We used a faster boat, and they would kick it up to top speed, fifteen or twenty knots if I remember right, and one at a time, we'd jump off the rear of it into the prop wash. It was just like hitting a brick wall—man, is that water hard! We got lots of sprains and wrenched muscles from these drops, and lost a lot of equipment that got torn off us by the impact and turbulence.

We've learned everything on paper about explosives. We know how to blow up underwater obstacles of any kind—bridges, roads, buildings, vehicles, and people. We also learn that if we can't get conventional explosives, we can make our own from homemade ingredients, one of which is fertilizer!

On paper we learn about basic U.S. small arms, and although the subject is really interesting to me, all the technical stuff puts me right to sleep. I need those weapons in my hands to get really comfortable with them, and I can't wait.

They teach us diving, using both open (SCUBA, which releases your exhaled breath into the water as air bubbles) and closed (MARK VI, which is completely self-contained) rigs. I will come to love diving better than anything so far, but since it's in the water, first I have to do some suffering. The instructors get us in the pool, we dive down to the bottom wearing our scuba tanks, and then they attack us. They rip off our face masks, turn off our air, pull out our mouthpieces, yank off our scuba tanks and swim away with them, and just generally make us miserable. We must recover from each attack while remaining underwater, and I do it, but it sure ain't easy, especially when Ollie takes my face mask and swims away with it. I never was able to catch him, and had to complete the exercise bare-eyed.

But somehow I get through it, and then we go out to the ocean for our first dive. I'm telling you, that was the most fabulous experience of my life! We dive in the protected game preserve in San Diego Bay, and what an incredible new world. It is a completely silent world, except for the sound of my own breathing. The colors are sun-gilded to a gorgeous blue-green with shafts of gold, and there is life everywhere. The bottom is just packed with every kind of plant and animal, there are fish swimming all around us, and a million huge lobsters backing away from us into cover. There are also bunches of these shellfish called abalone clinging to rocks, and since we've been briefed by the instructors that there are far too many of them for the area, we gather lobsters and abalone into burlap sacks. These sacks we will tie to a rope trailing over the side of our boat, and tow them into harbor, so that if the Conservation guys stop and search us, they won't find them on board. Once we are on shore, the instructors will see that they get properly used. (Naturally we won't get any of them until we actually become Frogs and get our own on "training" dives.)

When we've absorbed all this good knowledge, we get scheduled to go to San Clemente Island and put into practice what we've learned. San Clemente is an island off the coast that is used as a target range for aircraft, and one end of it belongs to UDT operations. Everybody's first question: "Does that mean we might get blown up?"

Meanwhile, a big storm blows up in San Diego, and the instructors are running around "chortling with glee." We can't figure out what's up, until we get briefed to do a night landing on the rocks near the Del. Our training beach area is located right next to the Del Coronado Hotel, and there is a big pile of huge boulders which separate the two. It may have been a breakwater at one time, but now it was just a mess of barnacle-covered rocks. Well, we don't worry too much about it, because after all, we're almost Frogs. The instructors' chortling makes us nervous, though, because anything good to them is sure to be bad for us.

You betcha! We head out to the beach at dusk, and it's much worse than we can imagine. The surf is booming, it's ten feet or more, and solid white water. We launch our IBSs and immediately our boots and uniforms are drenched. Nobody's cold, though, because we're just too scared, and our adrenaline is pumping full force. We're finding it damn near impossible to get out past the surf. Most of the boats capsize, some of them several times, and each time it happens you must start all over again. Finally, we all get out past the surf line, our boats gather together to prepare for landing on the rocks, but it's hard to stay in a group because the waves are so big. The only way it works is, we grab each other's lines and hang on. The instructors have mounted a large searchlight on the rocks to guide us in, and when it comes on, we can barely see it. I mean, it's pitch-black, howling wind, spray, and booming surf. Our hearts have plummeted right into our boots.

But here we go, we're riding a huge roller coaster of water, and since an IBS, like any other rubber boat, has no keel (a rib on the bottom to help steer the boat), we're paddling like crazy to keep the IBS straight to the rocks, and we're not having too much success. *Wham!* We hit the rocks, and instantly it's a turmoil of capsizing boats, flying bodies, and screams of terror. Somebody whacks me in the mouth with a paddle, our boat flips over, and my body is banging among the rocks. I've got hold of a line, though, and I'm hanging on for dear life.

Somehow—I don't remember much—we got our boat righted, and the four of us that were left fought the boat back out to sea. Holy mother! What an experience. After regrouping what remained of the boats, we paddled down the beachline and surfed to a landing on the beach. There, thank God for small favors, the instructors trucked us back to the debrief. Good thing, because we couldn't have marched it on our own, we were some sorry bunch.

When we arrive at the base, it's 4:00 A.M., and we're all banged up, bruised, and waterlogged. Our uniforms, boots, and hands were torn up from the barnacles on the rocks, and so were our IBSs. I was missing my two front teeth again, and my hands were just raw meat. I also had a badly wrenched right arm and a bruised knee, and it appeared that I was the worst injured. Just lucky, I guess. Incredibly, no one had any broken bones, and everybody was still there and alive. We could hardly believe it, although I think the instructors were thrilled. A quarter of our guys had been left stranded on the rocks, and we figure they were the lucky ones.

Chapter
Fourteen

THE PAPER INSTRUCTION is behind us, we're on San Clemente Island, and it's pretty interesting. We're blowing stuff up every day, land and water shots. We also get to shoot some of the weapons we've learned about (that's the part I like) and, fabulous, we get to wear our wet suits for every exercise. Since our wet suits make the cold water bearable, the only real discomforts we have left are salt sores. During training, if you get any kind of sore or break in your skin, the continual immersion in salt water will keep it from healing up. Salt sores are very painful, continually leak pus, and keep getting larger and deeper. Most of us have them, and some, like Bosun Campbell, have them real bad.

The bosun is quite a guy, and we're all impressed by him. He's an old man, got gray hair. He must be in his forties. Everyone's got the utmost respect for the bosun, because he's still hanging right in there with us. I mean, we're all eighteen, nineteen, twenty years old, even the officers. Bosun is twice our age, but the instructors haven't cut him any slack. Jeez, the salt-water sores on his legs are looking really nasty. They're like an inch deep and big as silver dollars. I don't see how he stands it.

Some of us (naturally, me included) have trouble blowing up the water obstacles. The obstacles are different kinds of steel and concrete nasties designed to tear out the bottoms of landing boats. The way it works is that you and your swim partner take turns freediving twelve feet down to the obstacle and attaching explosive charges to it according to a prescribed method that we've been taught. When you're done, you patch your detonation line into the main trunk line. Then, when everyone has swum to shore or to the boat, the shot is detonated with a "hellbox" (a hand-cranked detonator) either all at once, or in a time-delayed sequence, one obstacle after another. Woe unto you if your obstacle doesn't blow; the instructors will roast you. I was good, all my shots blew, but I ran into trouble loading up the obstacle with explosives. By now I'm confident in the water, and the freediving is really not that difficult. My problem is that I'm a big air hog, a problem no one else seems to share. I just can't stay down long, so it takes me twice the number of dives to load my obstacle as compared to the others, because they can stay underwater longer. Shit. I find I have the same problem with scuba diving. We use a military rig, two bottles of ninety cubic feet of compressed air, which is twice the size of any civilian rig. But it don't matter. I can suck out a set of twin ninety tanks in no time at all and have to come back up, which doesn't make my swim partner very happy. The other guys stay down forever compared to me. I figure maybe it's because I got big lungs. I told Fang, "Big lungs, big dick." I don't think he buys it, though, 'cause he gives me the finger.

As I mentioned, with my new confidence, any fears I had about the water have gone. I could float and swim for a week if necessary, and we just don't even think about danger from the denizens of the deep. Does familiarity breed contempt? I don't know, but we've been taught all about sharks, barracuda, jellyfish, and sea snakes, and we don't consider them dangerous. One incident at San Clemente, however, made us do some heavy contemplating. Now, the instructors don't pull Tadpoles out of the water for anything, ever. Rain, storm, wind, sharks, all that stuff is just part of the deal if you want to be a Frog. One day, however, we're loading water obstacles, and all of a sudden the instructors go berserk. They're jumping and hollering and waving their arms at us. They want us out of the water, and they want it right now! So we swim to shore, we don't know what the hell is going on, but then the word comes around—killer whales! And soon we see them, swimming along offshore on the surface, maybe six of them, and they are huge. When you see them on the TV, you get no conception of their size. We sure do. They swim behind our motor launch, which is a thirty-footer, and we can see their heads and tails past both ends of the boat. Well, so what? Whales are harmless, right? Sure, we're told, unless you happen to look like a seal, which is their favorite snack. And guess what we look like in our black wet suits? Mm-hm. You got it. Makes you think.

We've just about finished up at San Clemente, and only have a few things left to do. One of them is the seventy-five-foot free-dive. This one worries me because I'm such an air hog, but if I don't do it, I won't graduate. What happens is they anchor in seventy-five feet of water, then you jump off the boat and free-dive down to the seabed. There you must grab a handful of bottom and bring it back to the surface to show the instructor. As usual, the instructors swear there's nothing to it, and as usual, we don't believe them. We're nervous, me most of all.

Damn. There *is* nothing to it! I hyperventilated and dove hard for the bottom, so hard that I rammed my head into the sand. Then I grabbed a handful and drove for the surface, expecting to run out of air on the way. Surprise, surprise, I had plenty, and could have stayed down longer. What happens is, if you breathe several big breaths and load your lungs with oxygen (hyperventilate), then take a final lungful of air, it compresses as you go down. As you come back up it expands, and you never get that panicky feeling of empty lungs. It's no sweat at all.

The final op we had to do was a night ten-mile ocean navigation course in the IBS. Sounds easy, right? Ha, this is UDT. Our friendly instructors wait for a storm, and then send us out. We paddle for hours before we stop, and we have no idea in the world where we might be. All the IBSs are tied together, we're roller-coastering on the waves, and of course it's pitch-black, but that doesn't matter; there isn't anything out here to see anyway. We figure we'll end up drifting all the way to Hawaii, and that's if we don't get run over by a ship. Some shit. But we're lucky, I guess. The officers have been steering the course by compass, and for once they didn't screw up. At first light we're close enough to get a sight of the island, and we paddle on in. The instructors figured it was skill, so we didn't disillusion them.

One other thing happened at San Clemente that was kind of

cool and kind of scary and made me do some thinking. I found a sunken boat! It was off-time and we were fooling around on the rocks when out of the corner of my eye I caught a strange discoloration deep in the water. (Did I mention I've got the world's biggest curiosity? Well I do.) I look and look, but can't make out what I saw until I turn away, and then it appears again. I swear it moved, and regardless of all the flak I'll get from the guys, I've got to check it out. The water off the rocks is about fifty feet deep, so I dive off, followed reluctantly by my partner, Sonny. I kick over and dive, and I go down only about twenty feet when I turn and shoot right back to the surface. It's a big fishing boat, maybe a thirty-footer, it's laying on its side, and the thing is moving. "I ain't lyin'!" I tell Sonny, so he kicks over and we both go down again but stay shallow. Sure enough, we take a good look, and the thing is floating, not lying on the bottom. The ground swell is nudging it against the rocks about thirty feet down, and it is very spooky. We come back up, and soon all the other guys join us. Some of the guys, (not me) dive down to it and take a closer look. They say it's got a big hole in its bottom. After all our curiosity has been satisfied and I gloat a bit in the spotlight of fame, we ask the instructors about it, and they are very interested. They go check it out with SCUBA, then they call the Coast Guard, and they also dive down with SCUBA. It's a pretty big deal and very interesting. Finally our instructors tell us that the boat had been missing for over a month, and so were the four crewmen and captain. That really gave me the shivers. Five dead men. Wow. It took away a little bit of the comfort I had in living in the ocean, that's for sure.

Chapter
Fifteen

Back in San Diego, we are ready to finish up, and they schedule us for mud flats submarine training. Huh? We can't figure this one, but we might have known. We truck out to the mud flats, and they turn out to be a sewage waste disposal plant. We see all kinds of spectators gathered there, wives and girl-friends and some Frogs, but we don't see any submarines. Then the instructors march us out into the mud field, and we realized that once again we'd been had. This field of "mud" is solid waste which has been treated (God, I hope so!) and pumped into this field so the liquids can evaporate. The mud is chest-deep, and it's like standing in warm glue.

Ollivera struts forward. "All right troops, for today's exercise, you are all submarines." Ollie looks up at the sky and yells, "I see enemy aircraft. Dive! Dive!"

Well, we just can't believe it. But then the other instructors start shouting, and reluctantly, under we go. We pop right back up, but the damage is done. Shit (literally)! I can't see, I can't hear, and this crap tastes horrible! It's in my ears, eyes, and nostrils, and I'm spitting and rubbing, trying to see. As soon as I get some of the stuff cleared out of my eyes, under we go again. And that was the drill. We had to play submarine for over an hour, plus a few other inventive games dreamed up by the instructors. The spectators were rolling on the ground laughing, but eventually everyone got laughed out, and they trucked us back to base. What a mess we were. Well, we washed each other off with saltwater hoses and jumped in the showers to finish the job, but I found traces of mud in or on me for a week afterward. Fun and games . . .

We're finished! The torture is over, and I am now an official U.S. Navy Frogman, assigned to UDT Team 11. I can hardly believe it, and I can't shake the queasy feeling that someone will realize they have made a mistake and tell me I have to do it all over again. I get my gear ready to leave, and I still have almost nothing—shaving and shower stuff, a couple cartons of cigarettes, and that's about it. My green uniforms are rags, as are my boots, and except for what I'm wearing, I throw them in the Dumpster. (Later I have to go retrieve them and turn them in—this is still the Navy.) A couple of T-shirts and some socks are still usable, but underwear shorts are gone for the duration, and I'll never wear them again in my lifetime—too restricting.

I take stock of myself, and physically I'm a totally different person. I came into training at five foot seven, 130 pounds, but I'm leaving at five foot ten, and 180 pounds, and there's not an ounce of fat on me. My body is solid muscle and bone, and I'm pretty proud of it. Even John Wayne fears me.

Mentally I'm not even on the same planet. I've got confidence, confidence, confidence! I'll look you right in the eye, tell you exactly what I think, and I don't back up for anybody. There's nothing I can't do, and if you get in my way, I'll leave footprints across your chest. Drive on, mister!

Chapter Sixteen

We WALK OFF the Amphibious Base for the last time, right across the road to the UDT/SEAL Base. There we get issued a shitload of equipment, and it's like Christmas. I get new Corcoran jump boots, new green uniforms, swim trunks, blue & golds (two-layer T-shirts), coral shoes (canvas and rubber sneakers), and a bunch of other goodies. Oh boy! This is great! I'm just like a kid opening presents.

I spend my first week as a Frog preparing my gear so that I can stand tall and look good. My boots have to be layered with polish and spit-shined, and my greens must be tailored, heavily starched, and pressed. I had finally gotten duplicate records halfway through training, so now I can buy blousing bands for my pants, Frog patches, and nametags, and have them sewn on. It all takes time, but I get it done, and soon I'm strutting around in my new "wears." Except for my missing tooth, I am pretty!

Damn! I'm only here a couple of weeks, and I'm assigned to a Vietnam tour as a member of Detachment Bravo. It's reality time. I go to draw out my tour equipment, and I need a truck for it all. It's Christmas again, but this time with a shadow. I get swim fins, weight belt, and other diving gear, and a nylon parachute bag to put it all in. Uh-oh. I also get a flak vest, helmet, and a 9mm Smith & Wesson pistol, which I have to leave in the armory until we depart. Then we get two solid days of briefings, lots of shots, and a military ID card. Am I really ready for this? You bet. They can't hurt me.

Chapter Seventeen

WE CLIMB ON the airplane, and June 1967, we land at the Subic Bay, Philippines UDT base, and start intensive training for Vietnam. But first of all I must prepare for urban guerrilla warfare, because I'm back at Olongapo City, and it's sure different from what I expected. The Frogs (UDT Teams 11 and 12) have been stationed here since after WW II, and in Olongapo they have already reconned the water and secured the beachhead. Unlike the rest of the military, we don't have to pay for sex.

The way it works, you find a girl you like and make her your steady. Turns out it's high status to be the girlfriend of a Frog. Especially a boyfriend who can provide them with physical protection and do them favors, like getting them PX goodies. Radios, jewelry, and clothing from the PX are U.S. goods, high quality, and are obtained for ridiculously low prices by their boyfriends. Some good deal. Plus they get to spend nights in a hotel room with their boyfriends, instead of with the other bar girls. Naturally Frogs have permanent overnight passes. Hey, we deserve them.

What a life. I would roll into the UDT base for 0700 muster, do my day's training, whatever, and then knock off for the day at 1600. By 1630 I'm through the gate in civilian clothes. I go see my girlfriend first, and share her day's earnings with her. Then I eat supper and drink in our favorite bar, the Rainbow Club. The bars are great, they have house bands that play American rock music, which they learn note by note from jukebox records from the States. The bands are excellent, and one of them, "De Amazons," is an all-girl group. They are five cuties, and really popular. We all try to make them, but they're not whores, and they're not having any of us. Too bad . . .

At 10:30 P.M. I pick up my girl and we get a hotel room for the night to beat the military's 11:00 curfew. I get some loving, do some sleeping, and next morning start all over again. The only time my girlfriend is not available is when a big Navy ship is in port, and the girls suck up all the business they can, while they can. Throughout their working years the girls save up their money, and eventually retire away from Olongapo City to live out the rest of their lives. Some will retire early, but some enjoy the life and stay in it. America has completely bastardized this country with U.S. dollars, and that makes me feel bad, but I suppose it's probably the same in other places.

I go to jungle survival school, one of several that I will attend during my enlistment, and it's really interesting. I learn which plants to eat, how to live with the jungle, and how to travel through it. Turns out I like the jungle a lot, you know, the greenery and the huge amount of life that lives there, stuff like that. As a training tool we are each given a bolo, a small, heavy machete with a caribou-horn handle and a monkey-wood scabbard. The Filipino locals make them from ground-down truck springs, and they're pretty neat. We also get the privilege(?) of eating some pretty exotic stuff in the jungle. Flowers, roots, and (rarely) fruits that we find are not bad at all, and since I'm a veggie king, I really appreciate them. We caught a couple of snakes (ugh!) and ate them both cooked and raw. They're okay, but it's a tiny meal. When I complained, the instructor explained to us that the first week is when you are most hungry, especially us fat Americans, but as time passes your stomach will shrink, and it takes less and less to fill you up. That makes sense to me. Then the instructor shows us bugs, snails, grubs, and slugs that are edible. I listen and learn, but I don't eat.

The fifth day we're learning how to obtain good fire-starting material, and it's surprisingly hard to find in a tropical jungle; everything is soaking wet. While we're hunting around, a troop of monkeys come down low in the trees to check us out, and man, are they noisy! I finally got pissed and threw a chunk of wood at them.

Well, I about died, because one of the monkeys fell out of the tree and landed on the ground close to me. It was stunned, and without thinking I ran over and gave it a whack in the head with my bolo. Did those guys look at me! I played the role, you know, Mr. Cool, the Jungle King, and the guys started yakking it up, because that monkey was meat on the table. I tell you, outside I'm playing unconcerned, but inside I'm feeling awful guilty. The poor little thing. I felt like I'd just killed Cheetah. However, once I get it skinned out, that was all for me. The carcass looks just like a human baby body, my stomach is rolling and I ain't eating it. I ain't touching it again either. But I'm the Jungle King, so I don't say anything.

The instructor is thrilled, he's pleased to be able to teach this material, and he shows us how to cut it up and use every scrap. Then we start a fire to cook it up, and I edge to the rear of the group. What am I gonna do now? The Filipino guide is eyeing me and he's grinning—I bet that son of a bitch knows how I

feel! Well, I'm here to tell you, once that meat starts cooking
and the aroma spreads, I edge back up front, because it smells
awfully good. Then I taste it. Hmm . . . not bad, but it needs a
little salt. I make sure, though, that I don't look at the skull or the
hands.

While I am at Subic Bay, training, I use the opportunity to
commit one of the bravest actions ever noted in the annals of
military history. Completely disregarding my own well-being
and safety, I go to the dentist to have my front teeth replaced,
and lo! I volunteer to have several cavities repaired, which
eventually resulted in five root canals. It was worse than four
Hell Weeks, and I figure I should have been awarded at least a
Silver Star for bravery and sacrifice far above and beyond the
call of duty. My girlfriend called me a big coward, but what
does she know, she's got no teeth.

Chapter
Eighteen

WE DON'T STAY long at Subic before we're assigned
to the USS *Hermitage* (known to one and all as the *Hurtin'
Herm*), an amphibious landing ship, and we sail to Chu Lai,
Vietnam. Day after day we practice amphibious landings with
our Marines, and then we head to Dong Ha, right below the
DMZ, for the real thing, which they name Operation BEACON
GATE. One thing fills us with pleasure. Vietnam water is warm,
warm, warm! We won't even need our wet suits, which we had
all so carefully packed and brought with us. But being green,
we are kind of nervous, because we just know the enemy is
gonna shoot us up. We're Frogs, though, so we grin and try to
ignore it.

Just before first light we do a low-speed drop, swim very

low and cautiously in the water, and conduct a beach recon. It's my first taste of real combat conditions, and although I'm scared, I'm also fired up. I mean, this is what it's all about, and we are where we belong, out in front of all the other forces. In the quiet predawn darkness broken only by the luminescence in the disturbed water, visibility is surprisingly good.

The drop goes without a hitch, and as we tread water in our swim line, we hold until the light increases enough to make out details. No cold water? Hell, take as long as you want. As we swim slowly toward the shore, absolutely nothing's happening, and we soon relax and enjoy. The water is warm, the beach is all white sand with a smooth gradient, and there are no obstacles. There are a shitload of sea snakes, though, hundreds of them. It must be mating season. But we don't bother them, so they don't bother us. After we complete the recon, we swim back to sea and get picked up. Everything has gone smoothly, and it's skating time. Once we're back on board, our info gets fed to the planners. They like what they see, and the landing is scheduled for next morning.

It's 0300 and everybody's up and moving. The first-wave boats load up and away we go in the darkness, to lie offshore in a holding pattern until everything's ready. At 0500 our boat heads in, and we drop and swim to shore, staying in neck-deep water. We line up carefully, and at 0600 we face seaward and turn on our strobe lights to guide the first wave in. Strobe lights are a little bigger than a pack of cigarettes, battery-powered, and have a very high-intensity flashing light. They were originally designed to be clipped to shipboard life jackets so that personnel in the water (men overboard, shipwrecks, sinkings, etc.) could be easily located. We've installed hoods on ours so that the light can only be seen from one direction, and we use different-colored lenses to signal different things. They make excellent guide lights for the landing craft (later, in SEAL team, we will use them to guide in choppers) and if used properly can't be seen from the shore, which is nice, since it means we don't get a bullet up our ass. That I like.

In come the Amtrac personnel carriers between us, and they make an unopposed landing. The landing craft follow them, and the first part of our job is done. While the troops and equipment disappear inland, we hang out on the beach and get some rays, but shortly after the troops have left the beach, we hear the war. Off to the left flank there's a huge volume of small arms fire. After a half hour or so it slacks off and then stops. We scratch our heads, because out front, where the main assault force had gone, there was only desultory firing, with occasional bursts of automatic weapons.

Man, it's friggin' hot, and we are roasting! We didn't think to bring any drinking water, so we spend part of the time on the beach and part of the time swimming and freediving offshore to cool off. Me and Sonny Sanders play with the sea snakes, chasing them and stuff. They're not aggressive, in fact they try to avoid us, but you can bet I'm not fool enough to grab hold of one. I hate snakes with a passion, but these are more like fish than snakes. Besides, we've got nothing better to do.

The following day the troops come back aboard the ship (it's been a minioperation) and we get to touch base with our Marine friends and get the real skinny on what they ran into. With the exception of a few John Wayne types, all the jars are happy, because they hadn't had to do any fighting. As usual (so they tell us) the enemy had melted away in front of them, and the firing we'd heard was just for fun or for reconnaissance.

"Except for the ROKs," a corporal said. "Those fuckers fired up a ville."

That got our attention, and we wanted to hear the story. We'd seen the ROKs (Republic of Korea soldiers) before the landing and were pretty amazed by them. Where the jarheads carried one or two bandoliers of M-14 magazines, the ROKs staggered under huge loads of ammunition and grenades. They appeared to be serious about their fighting.

The corporal said, "We swept back through the ville (village) on the way out, and there wasn't anything left. I mean, they had leveled it! Seems they drew some fire from the ville as they were sweeping in, so they killed it. The ville, I mean. They shot everything that moved or was alive. Pigs, chickens, buffalo, dogs. Man, I even seen some birds lying there. Then they burnt it flat to the ground. Christ, anything that wasn't burnt was right full of bullet holes. Looked just like Puff had made a couple runs through there."

"Yeah, I saw those dudes on the beach," another jar said. "They didn't have one round of ammo left among them." He shook his head. "Those dudes are deadly."

"What's Puff?" Adams asked.

"Puff the Magic Dragon is a plane loaded with Gatling guns in the windows, and after they make a firing run, even the grass is mowed flat. Down south they call them Spooky. Man, they do some number on the gooks."

Well, we wanted to know a lot more, at least I did, but none of us was gonna speak up, for fear of appearing foolish. We were hot-shit Frogs, but we were also still noncombatants, and the jars knew it. They were friendly toward us, but condescending. My curiosity was aroused, and at that point, I decided to spend a lot more time with them and keep my ears open. I mean, I was still no fighter, but I had changed a lot from the draftee who had every intention of avoiding the war. These Marines talked about combat with casual confidence and familiarity, and that intrigued me. Besides, I had always wanted to know everything about everything, and I absolutely hated it when I wasn't "in the know."

And that's what I did. In between ops for the next month I spent most of my free time with the Marines, especially with one dude called Spiff. He was from Brooklyn (God, how I hate the New York City accent), and he was constantly talking a mile a minute. His accent made me wince, but I sucked up the info as fast as he put it out. Since the Marines loved to gamble, and they had plenty of time and money, I took advantage of this to spend time with them so it wouldn't appear that I was fishing for combat info.

"After all," Spiff said, "what else am I gonna spend my money on? You can't buy pussy on the ship or in the bush, so the bucks just mount up on the books. Easy come, easy go."

The married guys, of course, were forced by the Corps to send their money to their wives. Many a military wife partied up a storm while her husband was on tour. (Not *all*, okay? Give me some slack.)

Although I wasn't a skilled gambler, I started winning a lot of money from those guys. I wouldn't touch the dice; I only played poker and blackjack. I'd play a very conservative poker game, rarely trying to fill flushes and straights, and if I had a garbage hand, I'd fold early. In blackjack, I always stayed on sixteen. Even playing conservatively, I was able to win a little over $3,000, but some of the sharks (both Marine and sailor) won a lot more. Spiff was always losing, but he didn't care. He'd just shrug and keep on playing.

I picked up a lot of knowledge from these guys, and I was pretty happy about it. The M-14 and ammo (7.62mm/.308 cal) was very heavy but extremely reliable, and would definitely knock the enemy down. The M-16 and ammo (5.56mm/.223 cal) was superlight, so you could carry more ammo, but according to the Marines, it was a total piece of shit. It was always breaking or jamming, and unless hit in the head, a gook shot with an M-16 rarely went down and stayed down. All you'd find would be blood trails. The jars didn't much care, as long as the enemy couldn't shoot back, but their officers were so gung ho about body counts that they would run more and more ops just to get the numbers, thereby putting their grunts at high risk.

Anyway, gooks (or slopes) were skinny little dudes, always sneaking around, and rarely fighting pitched battles. When the Marines ran ops, the gooks would just fade out of their way, occasionally giving the Marines harassing fire. They'd wait until the Marines set up camp, and then they'd let them have it with mortars, rockets, and sniping fire. "Charlie" (from radio phonetics "Victor Charles," which was short for VC or Viet Cong) loved the night, however, ambushing the patrols and assaulting the Marines' fixed positions. Charlie would spend his days fishing or working his rice fields, and at dusk pick up his rifle, mortar, or rocket launcher and do a number on U.S. troops. Worse, even women and children could be VC, and you never knew who might shoot at you. Children, of course, were too young to be militarily motivated, but they would certainly follow directions given to them by elders who were. So look out, dude.

It was when the Marines mentioned NVA, though, that their tone changed to one of respect. NVA or "Mr. Charles" (North Vietnamese Army) were full-time soldiers who were excellent fighters, and they just wouldn't back up. The Marines didn't like to run into NVA, because when they did, Marines died.

The thing the Marines hated most, though, were booby traps. There were sharp punji stakes stuck in the ground which would pierce your feet and ankles, and since in the tropics any wound infected almost immediately, punjis were bad news, especially if they had been dipped in shit. There were trip traps, which were grenades and mortar rounds set up with trip wires. Those were especially dangerous on night patrols, because you couldn't see the trip wires. Then there were the big guys, mines. All the way from cigar box size up to big box mines, they were set off by trip wires, pressure detonators, or by a gook with a hand detonator ("command-detonated"), waiting for the right moment to do the most damage.

Punjis or trip traps could take out anywhere from one to five jars, and mines could take out a whole patrol or vehicle. I soaked up all the info, and filed it.

Chapter Nineteen

ONE THING THAT Frogs excelled at was demonstrating to the regular Navy forces how vulnerable a ship was to night stealth attacks. Ships were usually well guarded against assault from land, but were almost helpless against "sapper" attacks from the water. Every so often our officers would challenge ship commanders to an exercise, and without fail the Frogs would capture and/or disable the victim ship.

First the rules would be set up—no live ammunition and no actual physical violence. Then we'd do a daytime runby of the target to get a general physical layout of the ship, method of boarding, and approach and drop-off points. If the ship was anchored (in open water) we might be able to climb the anchor chain. If the ship was tied up to a dock or pier, we could climb the mooring lines or use muffled grappling hooks to get on deck. Occasionally there might even be stray lines hanging over the side, and if so, we'd use them. If the ship was isolated (anchored), lighting was minimal; just right for us. If the ship was moored at a pier, the additional dock lighting could be more of a problem. Sometimes we'd use a scuba approach, following compass headings underwater, but more commonly we would just surface-swim to the target, climb on board, and neutralize sentries, either by grabbing them and saying "you're dead" or sneaking by them. Then we'd capture the bridge or quarterdeck and, except for the debrief, the exercise would be over. A few times we even sneaked on board, observed all we needed, sneaked back off, and later gave a detailed reconnaissance report to the ship's commander. Naturally we had "mined" the ship while we were there, and it was a goner.

Those demonstrations were good training for ship's officer personnel in that it made them aware of their vulnerability. The sailors weren't too thrilled, however, because heads would roll after we had captured or disabled the ship. (You know, shit flows downhill. . . .) We, of course, immensely enjoyed all the sneaking and peeking, and being able to put one over on the regular Navy, especially the officers.

While on the *Hermitage*, we got to run several of these exercises, and they were a lot of fun. I got a big kick out of these games, because I could use my best skills to good advantage. I soon discovered I had excellent night vision, better than most, and I found that swimming in to the target was no problem. Naturally we used the UDT strokes, which simply meant that nothing broke the surface except our heads, which were kept low in the water at all times. We only had to be careful that our face masks didn't reflect light. We would trail our arms along our sides and use leg and swim fin power in a flutter kick to close the distance to the target, then we'd switch to underwater breaststroke to maneuver up close to the assembly point. The assembly point would be a patch of darkness, or a place up against the side of the ship where we couldn't be seen. I've had sentries look directly at my location in the water and never see me, even though they knew we were coming. The only problem we ever had was harbor refuse in the water—oil, fuel, sewage, and floating garbage.

Once we arrived at the assembly point, we would remove our fins and mask and hang them on our web belts behind us. Then we'd climb up the chain, lines, or whatever, and that was the hard-work part, but I had good arm strength to my body mass, so it was not really a problem for me. We'd slide onto the deck and crawl to cover, then pause momentarily while our breathing slowed back to normal. That recovery time was used to find and observe the sentries, if any, and note their locations. The deck of a ship was no mystery to me, so I'd plot my way to the objective, and when ready, sneak to it.

I had great fun and I learned a lot. A mobile attacking force has all the advantage over the fixed defensive force. Approach, method, execution, these were all my decision, not theirs. It was nearly impossible for them to detect their attackers, because half the time they had no idea what to look for until it was too late.

The sapper's best friend was boredom. The sapper was moving, thinking, planning, he had no time to be bored. A defender, even when expecting attackers, could only stay highly alert for about fifteen minutes, fully alert for about thirty minutes, and from that point on it was downhill all the way. Even the John Wayne types who dreamed of foiling and capturing attackers lost their effectiveness the minute they started daydreaming—their minds were already dulled by their thoughts.

Probably the most interesting lesson I learned was that the night was my friend, and I could better understand why Charlie loved to operate during darkness. The daylight world of many sights, sounds, and sensations being recorded by my brain was compressed in the darkness to my own small pocket of heightened awareness. My sight, restricted by the low light, made me much more focused on what I could see, and my motion detection seemed to be at its highest pitch. My hearing, bombarded during the day by a million sounds, was highly sensitive at night because there were so few sounds to be analyzed. My awareness of smell, physical sensation, and even taste went way up at night, because my brain was better able to perceive and record them. It was an amazing learning experience, and was to serve me well later on.

I know one thing for sure. I'd have given my right nut to do a real attack on enemy ships. I told Mr. Winant half-jokingly, "Send me to Hai Phong harbor. I'll wipe out the enemy's shipping in less than a week!" It's a real shame I never got the opportunity.

One morning in Da Nang harbor we suited up for a dive. Officially we were going to do a bottom search of some of the ships, but in reality we would treasure-hunt the harbor bottom. You could find all kinds of stuff underwater simply because nobody ever went there. It was our world, and nobody else's. We're just about ready, when all of a sudden one of the guys points up to an old chopper that seems to be in trouble. Its engine was missing, backfiring, and smoking badly. Next thing we know, it comes autorotating (more about that later) down and *splash!* into the water not twenty-five yards from us. Oh boy, a rescue! We quickly turned on our tanks, went over the side, and dived down to the chopper at high speed. We spot it, about fifty feet down, swim to it, yank open the doors, and pull out the two pilots. One's conscious, and one of the guys offers him his mouthpiece, but the pilot breaks free and kicks upward, he's panicked, and his highest priority is getting to the surface. The other pilot appears to be dead, so we drag his body up. As we break the surface, Danny compresses his stomach, and incredibly, the pilot starts to gag and cough. He's breathing again. Then he vomits, and all of us move away quickly so we don't get any on us. The *Herm*'s boat arrives about that time, picks up the two dudes, and speeds for the ship. A couple of our guys go with them to bask in the glory—the ship's rails are lined with people watching the action, and hey, who knows, we might get a medal. The rest of us, being more realistic, dived back down to the chopper to see what goodies we could find. But we're out of luck; we found nothing worth fooling with. We'd heard that chopper pilots carried .38 revolvers and other personal weapons, and that was what we were after, but nothing doing, the cupboard was bare. The next day we dived back down to the chopper and hooked a cable to the rotor shaft. A huge Chinook hovered down, connected to the cable, and lifted the downed chopper up and away. It was a pretty interesting sight and it drew a big crowd. It sure was great for our egos, what with being the center of attention and all, and a UDT recruiter could have done well that day. Later on they did give us a Commendation Medal, along with a nice write-up from Da Nang command and the *Hurtin' Herm*.

One of the other fun things we get to do as Frogs in Vietnam is to ride shotgun on the riverboats—PBRs, Swift Boats, LCPLs, and such. I volunteer to do a lot of this work because I want to see some action, but I always hate the thought of being a sitting duck. On the one hand, it was great fun for me to ride the boats and handle various weapons, but on the other hand, it turned out to be extremely dangerous. The gooks just loved to ambush riverboats, and since most of our boats were made of fiberglass, bullets and rockets would go right through them. If your body got in the way of the bullets, it pierced even easier and would leak all over the place. I was lucky, I guess, because I never got shot, but a few times I got fiberglass splinters in me, and they would itch for days.

It was really weird. We would be booking along on a river, and all of a sudden you'd hear the *snap* and *crack* of slugs hitting the boat, your eyes would glimpse bullet dimples appearing, splinters flying, and only then would you hear the firing of the weapons from on shore. Nighttime was much worse, because I could see the tracers coming out, and they always seemed to point straight at me. I quickly learned to sit either all the way up front, or all the way to the rear, because the gooks would always aim at the boat driver, or at least at the middle of the boat where he was. The thing that scared us the most was a weapon called a B-40 rocket launcher. It looked like a stream-lined bazooka, and the three times that one was fired at my boat scared the shit out of me, because it was at night, and I could see the trail of fire that the rocket made as it arced out from the shore and swooshed right by us. Then I was shown an iron-hulled ASPB (Assault Support Patrol Boat) that had been hit with a B-40, and the entry hole in the steel was like a foot wide. They tell me it exploded inside the hull and splattered three dudes.

Riding the riverboats brought me in closer contact with Vietnam and its people, the sights and the sounds and the smells were all different from what I was used to. One of the sights that would always crack me up was churning by a ville and seeing six or a dozen bare asses hanging out over the water; the Viets used rivers and canals for toilets. With such good targets around, I always wished I had a slingshot.

Other than the potential danger, I really liked riding with the "River Rats," the small-boat guys, and I made a lot of friends because they were mostly enlisted men, with the occasional junior officer who was generally human. These guys were very independent, much like us, and they pretty much lived on their boats, in their own small worlds. Even so, they made me wel-come, and I never felt like an outsider or extra baggage. I was really surprised that their morale and unit pride was so high because this was a risky business, being a sitting duck target, but they never seemed to care. I guess it comes down to what you're used to.

The smells and sounds of the Vietnamese were of course totally foreign to me. A herd of Viets talking at a distance sounded just like a herd of ducks, and was just about as intelli-gible. The smells of Vietnam were at first rank and disturbing, and then as I got used to them, just different. It was a real shocker for me when a Viet crewman told me that we smelled foul to them. I mean, I took showers and stuff, so I thought I smelled okay, but this Viet told me it was the different diet that made us smell so bad. He made me damn uncomfortable for a while, until I realized there wasn't anything I could do about it. Then as I thought more about it, I said to myself, "Fuck him"; he didn't smell that choice himself.

Finally, after a couple of close calls on the Qua Viet River, I came to realize that I was a fool to continue to play "target." I needed a new trade; this one could get me killed.

Chapter Twenty

I T'S SEPTEMBER 1967, and life sure sucks. We've been reassigned to the USS *Carpenter*, a destroyer on patrol duty off Vung Tau. Gone is the comfortable roominess of the *Hurtin' Herm*, and gone are the Marines; we're back in the regular Navy now and at sea. They've got us crammed into a little space (room) belowdecks, and the only area we can roam is the fantail (rear deck). All of our activities are conducted under the eyes of the ship's officers, and they don't like us at all. They say we're completely undisciplined—a bunch of rowdies. Hey, we're Frogs, not blackshoe pukes. Our two UDT officers, Mr. Winant and Mr. Parrott, spend most of their time buffering between the ship's officers and us, and it's a thankless job. The ship's officers' irritation with us stems from their egos. We pretty much ignore them, and that drives them crazy.

You have to understand the military mentality to appreciate their frustration. The academies tell their students that if you wear the gold (the stripes on the cuff of the officers' uniform jacket), you are God to all the enlisted types. You are always right, and they are always wrong. The UCMJ (Uniform Code of Military Justice—the law of the military land) guarantees and enforces this attitude. Nonacademy officers are also taught this doctrine. To be fair, respect for an officer's authority is a necessary part of military discipline, but difficulties arise when you're dealing with special operations forces. Spec ops people are taught—and expected—to think on their feet. Step up to the challenges, then solve and execute them for the good of the group, as (sometimes) opposed to the good of the service. That's the confidence factor for us. But it don't work that way in conventional forces, because they want sheep, not rams. Put in a different way, it's like asking a heart surgeon to make hospital beds. Certainly he's able to do it, but it's an incredible waste of his skills and talents. Conventional forces officers are first bewildered, then irritated, and finally furious when they have to deal with Frogs. And SEALs and Green Berets and LRRPs and Force Recon. I mean, we're not hoodlums or anything. We wouldn't dream of tantalizing them for fun, would we?

Our own officers we treated with utmost respect, because they had earned it. They had survived the same training, they thought like us, and they had the same skills and potential. We had no martinets, no foiled egos, and no incompetents in our officer corps. We respected, and in most cases, admired them for their leadership.

One case in point was our sleeping and living arrangements on the *Carpenter.* On deck, anyone on the ship was welcome to stroll among us, watch us at work or play, and shoot the shit with us; we didn't own the deck space, we shared it. Our sleeping place, however, was inviolate—stay the fuck out unless invited. Our officers were always welcome, as were the ship's medical personnel, who provided medicinal alcohol and fixed our various cuts and bruises. Also welcome were some of the ship's supply people, who provided fruit juice to mix with the alcohol and various other food goodies. Naturally we always kept a good supply of trade goods on hand to take care of our friends.

Anyway, the ship's enlisted people knew better than to violate our space, but not the officers. They were determined to bring us under their command. Since we didn't stand watches, clean shitters, chip and paint, or do other normal ship's duties, the ship's officers couldn't use those tasks to control us, so they tried the only other avenues available: reveille, musters, and inspections. Hey, they forced us to quickly disillusion them. Ship's reveille was at 0600, but we disconnected our announcement speakers and ignored it. Therefore, we also didn't make 0700 muster.

Sailors slept in shorts and T-shirts, Frogs slept naked. Sailors wore uniforms—black shoes, denim pants and shirts, with white hats. We wore coral shoes, no socks, swim trunks, and occasionally blue and gold T-shirts. Hats? Rarely, and then only to display our rank if we wanted something. Anyway, after several mornings of ignored reveille and musters, a young lieutenant was sent down to conduct reveille on us. ("Sorry, sir, our speakers don't work.") Robbie was awake and told us the story after it happened.

He said, "The lights come on, and this boot lieutenant comes walking in to do reveille. The Frog sleeping closest to the door is still asleep, and you know what he's dreamin' about, because he's lying on his back, naked, and visibly aroused. When the lieutenant sees that, he turns bright red, but he's got to do his duty, and he ain't givin' up.

"He shakes the Frog by the shoulder and yells, 'Reveille! Time to get up!'

"The Frog opened one eye and told him, 'Get the fuck outta here.' "

Robbie's cracking up while he's telling us this. "Well, that did it. The lieutenant zooms outta there, fuming and fussing."

We all laugh loud and long at the story, but we knew the shit would hit the fan. Sure enough, they call Lieutenant Winant on the carpet and chew him out. Pretty soon he comes down to see us.

"All right, you fuckers, you got my ass roasted. Some big changes have got to be made!" Then he grins. "Which one of you is guilty of lewd behavior?"

We all laugh, and tell him the saga of the Frog's hard-on, and what the Frog said to the guy, and he laughs along with us.

Lenny Horst asked, "So what happens now, Mr. Winant?"

Mr. Winant looked real serious and said, "Well, I was forced to make a deal to get you guys off the hook."

We all thought, uh-oh, here it comes.

He continued, "I told the captain we'd clean up our act, so from now on, you guys wear your jammies when you sleep."

He grinned at the Frog. "And no more hard-ons. Think clean thoughts or something.

"Seriously," he goes, "you guys aren't blackshoes, but try to get along with these people as best you can. I had to promise the captain we'd spend a lot more time working (groans from us), so we'll start doing a lot of ops off the ship—some dives, boat operations, shit like that (cheers from us). The less time we spend on the ship, the better."

Hey, that was great news. Our biggest gripe was being cooped up.

And that's what I mean about our officers. Mr. Winant could have taken the easy road and knuckled under to the ship's officers. Instead, he'd stood up for us, and actually gotten us a better deal. That's what it's all about.

And now life turned bearable. We did several dives, something we all enjoyed, because conditions were perfect. Water temperature was in the 70s and the water was as clear as crystal, and you could lay on the surface and see details on the bottom fifty feet down. Man it was nice! We found a couple of wrecked ships to check out, and on one of them I had a close call when I got tangled in some ship's cables eighty feet down. I was low on air (so what else is new?), and I had to control my panic and work myself free. Very tricky, but also very interesting.

Once we found a bed of giant clams. Me and Sonny pried a couple of them loose and brought them up, but once we reached the surface, we discovered they were too heavy to lift into the boat. They were like eighteen to twenty-four inches wide, but I swear they must have weighed over a hundred pounds. We were real disappointed to have to drop them back to the bottom, but the clams probably breathed a big sigh of relief.

Although diving was the second most pleasurable thing I had ever done in my life, I soon discovered I had yet another problem. Not only was I an air hog, which I had learned to live with, but I also had trouble with pressure in my ears. In reverse, goddamn it! Why am I always ass-backward? Humans have two opposing pressure chambers to deal with. One is the tiny air chamber surrounding your inner ear, relieved only through the nasal passages, and the other is the huge outside air chamber that we live in. These two air chambers are separated by the flexible eardrum, but it don't flex all that far without causing pain. If the outside air pressure gets less, like if you go up high in an airplane, the inner-ear pressure pushes against the eardrum, until enough pressure is released through your nasal passages so that the inner-ear pressure matches the outside pressure. That's when your ears "pop." Same thing happens in reverse when the plane comes down to land. The outside pressure gets higher, pushes against the eardrum until inner-ear pressure is increased, and your ears again "pop." But if your nasal passages are blocked with mucus (like when you have a cold), the pressure can't release, and the eardrum stretches farther and farther, until you feel pain, ranging from mild discomfort to absolutely unbearable. The pressure difference that your eardrum can handle in the atmosphere has a wide range, but in the water, that pressure range is tiny. Try diving to the bottom of your swimming pool and you'll know what I mean. You can manually increase your inner ear pressure by holding your nostrils and blowing gently through your nose, or relieve the pressure by not holding your nostrils and swallowing several times until your ears pop.

All the other Frogs had problems, if any, clearing the pressure in their ears as they dived downward. Coming back up to the surface, no sweat. Me, I could go down like a stone, but once I had been down for a while, I couldn't get back up, and my swim partner was always wondering what the hell I was doing dawdling below the surface. It would take me several attempts to clear the pressure in my ears before I could come all the way up. It was always painful, and I was disgusted with myself. Well, as you might guess, eventually the shit had to hit the fan.

On one dive we'd been down quite a while, teasing a bunch of moray eels in a ledge. There must have been twenty, and we had fun poking at them with our knives to make them retreat back into their holes. Since I'm always completely aware of how much air I have left, I check my Seawolf watch, and it's time to go up. We get up about six feet below the surface, and I can't go any farther, the pain in my ears is too intense. I try and try, but I just can't do it, and I'm not liking this at all. I sign to Mike Bennett, my swim partner, what's going on, and he stays close, but all of a sudden I run clean out of air. Shit, this is getting serious. I flip on my reserve, now I got about five more minutes of air, but I'm starting to worry a bit. What am I gonna do now? I keep trying to go up, but the pain is just too unbearable. Looks like I'm gonna drown right here.

Suddenly my air is gone and so are my options. Survival takes over, and I kick up, screaming into my mouthpiece. I break surface right on the edge of passing out, mucus blows out my nose, my ears pop, and unbearable pain is replaced with unbearable relief. But my eardrums didn't rupture; they must be made of rubber. But as you might guess, that was my last deep dive—one more pleasure down the tubes.

Chapter
Twenty-one

ONE DAY I get a telegram from my brother A.J. He'd been wounded, and was recuperating at Cam Ranh Bay hospital. He's saying why don't I pop over, and we'd suck down a few brews? Sounded mighty good to me. With tears in my eyes, I told Mr. Winant that my only brother was all shot up and at death's door, and he let me have five days of emergency leave. I jumped ship at Vung Tau and caught a supply chopper to Saigon, and then on to Cam Ranh. Man oh man, it was just like Hawaii! Landward the place was all uglied up with military stuff, but the water was this gorgeous blue-green, bordered with a pure white sand beach. Heaven in the war zone. I hunt up A.J. and he's sitting in a beach spa drinking beer with a dog (Army guy).

I say, "What's happening, man?"

First he laughs long and loud at my clean, neat, starched uniform, then he grins and moans and holds his right biceps.

"Aw, I'm in terrible shape, man, and need more time to heal up."

We all laugh, and then he tells me his story. He's been over for several months with the Fifth Marines, almost continually in the bush, and he's a gunner, the M-60 man. Higher-higher kept putting them out as bait for the enemy, and they finally got their wish. Dying Delta, A.J.'s company, had been overrun by NVA and mostly wiped out. A.J. said the NVA got pissed off because Delta had moved into their freshly dug fortified positions while the NVA were gone, so when the NVA returned, they kicked Delta's ass. A.J. had taken an AK round in the arm, and had to hide up for ten hours until the enemy left.

Jesus, was I pissed! Typical Army/Marine maneuvers in Vietnam: send your troops out to draw enemy fire, and when they did, call in air strikes to get a big body count. Hey, ignore your own casualties, they're just grunts and there are plenty more where they came from. I get so goddamn mad every time I run into this kind of thinking that I want to frag every officer above captain. And you can bet that they're not out there with their troops, oh, no way! They're sitting back in air-conditioned Command Center giving each other medals. Bastards. Risking my brother on their stupid maneuvers.

I hardly heard A.J. through my rage as he continued. "I'm telling you, man, the wound hardly hurt," he said. "But when I got here the nurses almost killed me with shots. I musta got forty of 'em. Just think, almost killed by friendly fire." .

We soon had a little bullshit party going there, maybe ten or twelve of us shooting the breeze about the Nam. I pretty much kept my mouth shut, playing Mr. Wise, and acting like I knew what they were talking about. I heard all about gooks, mamma-sans, pappa-sans, baby-sans, water buffalo, Cs versus K rats, jungle rot, AK-47s and booby traps. The Mattel toy (M-16) really sucked, it was a muzzle-loader, only good for about five rounds before you had to clear a jam with your cleaning rod. The fucking lifers weren't sending enough food and supplies out to the bush. All the officers should be made into line grunts—see how they liked it! And, of course, many "short" lines, describing their time left in country.

"Man, I'm so short I can sit on a dime and dangle my legs!"

Or, "I'm so short I can walk under an ant and squeeze his balls!"

Although John Wayne was nudging me from the rear, and I was eating this shit up, it was clear to me that none of these guys wanted to be there. The heat, humidity, the incredibly poor leadership displayed by their officers, and being used as cannon fodder had really disillusioned them, and they had developed an actual hate for the country, the people in it, and everything attached. Esprit de corps? What's that, man, never heard of it.

One of the dogs, when he heard we were brothers, said, "Hey, man, you can't have two brothers in the combat zone at the same time. One of you could go back to the World—I heard it from a headquarters REMF" (Rear Echelon Mother Fucker—noncombatants in the combat zone).

I told A.J., "I'm gonna check this out, and if it's true, we'll get you outta here. I'm in no danger, so it's no problem if I stay."

A.J. looked at me with hope in his eyes. "Oh man, if you only could, I'd kiss your ass at high noon on Main Street!"

The conversation around us continued, and I asked A.J. about his nurses, were there any we could jump, and all the dudes said the same thing—No way! According to them, all the "round-eyes" were making big bucks banging the officers and rich civilians, and even the uglies were getting rich. (Ow! I can feel my ears burning.) Naturally no ordinary grunt was going to get any attention from these women. Hmm . . . where had I run into that before? The women had even come up with a nifty way to keep the money they made at the trade. They would deposit their earnings in the American bank office there in Cam Ranh and just have the account transferred back to the States when they left.

Well, five days' good times is five minutes long, so we soon say good-bye and I'm back on the *Carpenter.* First thing I did is start an inquiry about this brothers thing. Oh boy, it's true, so I put in the paperwork, and get a quick answer. Shit! I should have known better by now. Yes, it was agreed that they didn't want only-brothers in the combat zone at the same time (something about the Sullivan brothers in WW II, five of whom were lost on the same ship), so they would send me back, not A.J. That figures. I sent the bad news to A.J. and we agreed not to pursue. Turns out later we made the right decision. A.J. had already served seven months of a thirteen-month tour, and if he had cut short, they would have sent him back for another thirteen-month tour after I had gone.

Chapter
Twenty-two

OCTOBER 1967, MY tour is almost over, and we're gonna head back to the States. We're bored stiff until Mr. Winant comes through again. A nice R & R for the platoon in Formosa, but first a volleyball game at some POW island—Con Son or An Thoi, I forget which. We hadn't played much, but hey, nobody was gonna beat Frogs. Boy did we get surprised! They may have been VC POWs, but when we arrived, our opponents had real athletic uniforms, a regular volleyball court, and a huge crowd of spectators. When we saw the place was packed, we got our first intimation that we might have to work at it to win.

With our big egos, we hadn't considered "face." Hell, we didn't even know about face then. Face, a form of pride, is an aspect of Oriental life that is not well developed in Western countries, and I still don't really understand it, but it has to do with how you treat other people. Americans are boisterous, loud, familiar, and straightforward, but this kind of behavior is foreign to the Orientals, who tend to be reserved and quiet, and who follow a whole set of rules governing their dealings with others. While Orientals are rarely too familiar, we Americans will walk right up to strangers, talk to them, shake their hands, grab their arms, or put our arms around their shoulders. This is taboo behavior to an Oriental, I guess that's why the Japanese bow instead of shaking hands. But the really hard thing to understand was the smile.

Westerners smiled to show they were friendly, and the more comfortable they became, the more they smiled. Westerners laughed easily, at most anything, because it displayed their friendliness. Orientals were just the opposite. Meeting strangers, they were grave and reserved, and only smiled if they were nervous. The more they would smile and laugh, the more nervous they were. I don't get it, but I hear this behavior is different only when they are with family or intimate friends, and that I can buy. I learned what little I know about this behavior later on, when I was friendly with our Vietnamese scouts, and it helped me a lot then, both in dealing with friendlies, and especially dealing with hostiles. More about that later.

It turns out the prisoners had their families there with them, so they needed very little guarding. I think they were mostly political prisoners put there by the South Vietnamese government, but still, they seemed to be living well. Since these Vietnamese prisoners were performing in front of their families, and because of "face," they were determined to win.

Well. I'm telling you, they kicked our ass! At first, it was great fun for us, then we bore down and concentrated, and it made no difference at all. They were a well-oiled machine and just massacred us, with the spectators cheering (I hope it was cheers) like crazy. What can I say, we hadn't played much volleyball, and the heat killed us. From the beginning of the game these guys were giving us rice wine. It was warm and tasted like Kool-Aid, but the devils gave us as much as we wanted. I still think they cheated, because several times I saw two or three balls coming at me instead of just one.

After the games were over, we commenced to do some serious singing and partying, fueled by more rice wine. We were having a great time, and the prisoners seemed to get a big kick out of us, because they were crowded all around. I remember looking at my watch, it was like 1500 in the afternoon, and I was feeling fine. Next thing I know, I wake up in my rack on the ship.

Huh? My whole body is sore—what the hell? I'm bruised and battered, I got skin missing, and I hurt all over.

I groan and say, "What's going on?" as I fall to my knees out of my rack.

D'Angelo yells, "Hey, it's alive! Man, I thought we were gonna have to get you a body bag."

Hmm . . . a smart-ass.

It takes some time and a lot of abuse, but I finally get the story. I'm still not sure they told me the truth; those guys are all big liars, and did they laugh and laugh. Seems that around 1600 yesterday (yesterday?) I decided my partying was over, and it was time to go back to the ship. Since nobody else wanted to leave, I picked up our outboard motor from the IBS and, pulling the start cord, started wading out into the surf. I was gonna motor out to my rack, I was tired. They tell me it took five of them to take away my motor and tie me to the IBS until they were ready to leave a few hours later. Then, when they were carrying me back on board the *Carpenter,* I came to. I was rested by then, and I wanted to go back and kick some ass.

Mike said, "Man, we had some time getting you down the ladder and tied in your rack, that's where you got all the bruises." Sure. I bet.

But I had to hang my head, because I didn't remember any of it. I wasn't buying their story 100 percent, though, because I knew these guys too well. I figure somebody ambushed me. For the next several days I was known as "the outboard king," and "the human boat," but I didn't think it was all that funny.

Chapter
Twenty-three

THE CARPENTER SAILED to Kaohsiung, Formosa, and the whole ship prepared for extended liberty. We're gonna be there for two weeks. Naturally, the Frogs are the first off the ship, and we stampede right through the gate into town. Kaohsiung, Formosa (Nationalist China), is the greatest liberty port in the Pacific if you've got money, and we had plenty. I had earned a promotion to E4, third class petty officer, a few months before, so my regular pay plus diving pay plus combat zone pay, all tax-free, made for a tidy sum. We tell our cabbie to take us to the best hotel in town, and he does.

"Chiang Kai-shek stay here," he says.

"Oh, that's uh . . . interesting," we say.

Sonny says in my ear, "Who the fuck is Chiang Kai-shek?" and I tell him.

We rent the best rooms they have, and Robbie and I end up in the Presidential Suite.

"Chiang Kai-shek stay here," they say.

Well, maybe he really did; it sure was luxurious enough. We dump our gear and immediately head for the best bar in town. Oh boy, the bar girls here are really beautiful. I mean, absolute knockouts! First we do a recon, buying drinks and talking with servicemen who are stationed here.

"This place is completely different from Po City," they tell us. "You better treat these women nice; they got feelings and everything. Pick one out and take her for dinner at a nice hotel, and you won't be sorry."

Well, we may be young, but we ain't no fools, so we look around. I want to grab the first one I see, but Robbie says be patient, wait for the best. He's Mr. Smooth-dog from L.A., so I listen, and eventually he hooks up with a real sweetie. (Hey, man, I saw her first!) I grit my teeth and start asking around. I'm determined to find a girl who's even better. I keep hearing about a girl named Snow—she's supposedly gorgeous. Sounds like my kind of woman. I hunt her up, and she's everything they say, but she ain't interested in me at all; she's so popular. I work my ass off giving her my best lines. Finally, to get rid of me, she names her price at $100 a night, which is top dollar for Kaohsiung. I say yes, and away we go so I can show her off to the other guys. She's far and away the most beautiful woman I've ever had. The group of us hang out for a while, go to our hotel for dinner, then go see a show. Finally it's off to bed. And it was good.

We sleep until noon and spend the rest of the day partying, but that night when it's time for loving, she tells me no, she's too sore. I was pretty disappointed, but in my mind I strutted a bit. What'd she expect? I'm a Frog! I tell you what, that was some two weeks, my best ever. I spent a shitload of money, but so what, I'd had the time of my life. I know one thing. I should have married that girl, brought her back to the States, and made her my sex slave.

When our two weeks ended, we were off to Taipei, Formosa, to catch a plane back home; our tour was over. We took a train up to Taipei, and the train was clean and modern, with stewardesses, just like planes. When we arrived at Taipei we headed for the nearest club, because the trip had made us thirsty. I drink Chivas and water, but this one doesn't taste just right, and all of a sudden I am sick as a dog. I streak for the door and zoom outside, bumping some guy and his girl on my way to the bushes. Man, that was painful. Uh-oh, I see the guy I'd bumped walking toward me (Have mercy, mister, I'm really hurting).

He says, "Jesus Christ, boy! All that noise out here, I thought I was hearing a banzai charge!"

Shit. It's my brother, A.J., here on R & R! What are the odds of meeting like this—maybe a million to one? We go back into the club and I do the introductions, and the guys are all amazed. After I take way too much verbal abuse about my weak stomach, A.J. and I get to talk, and I find out what's going on with him. The news is not good, and inside I'm really worried. He's been in almost constant action with little resupply. He's worn out two M-60s, and because the M-16s are such pieces of shit, A.J.'s down to fighting with a .38 revolver and whatever weapons he can find during battle. Fuck me! This ain't right. But there's nothing I can do about it, except make a run out to our equipment box at the airport and get him a can of .38 ammo. I am very upset, but A.J. shrugs it off.

"Hey man, I'm so short my balls drag on the ground when I walk."

Huh. That don't make me feel any better. A.J. tells me he'll meet me in California when he gets back, right after Tet, the Vietnamese new year, and we left it at that. Footnote: If we'd only known what Tet 1968 was gonna be like, I'd have kidnapped A.J. right then. Tet 1968 was the major enemy offensive in South Vietnam. Some of the hottest fighting that A.J. experienced was during Tet, when Dying Delta had to recapture Hue City from the VC. A.J. got to be a TV star, though—that's him you see firing an M-16 over the stone wall in the popular Vietnam documentary.

Chapter
Twenty-four

It's DECEMBER 1967 in San Diego. I've got an apartment on the beach, and life is excellent, although I'm slightly bored. As soon as we got back to San Diego I went on thirty days' leave, and it sure was good to get back home with the family. It was weird, though, everyone had changed. (Or was it me who had changed?) My high school friends were all gone, either in the military or married, which was the same thing, and some of them were already divorced. I was forced to hang out with much younger people, and the young guys couldn't relate to me; they were living a different lifestyle. I didn't have the same problem with the younger girls.

In between partying, I take my old car down off the blocks and ready it for the trip back to California. I got a 1955 hot-rod Ford convertible, black accented with brown rust patches. The springs are jacked up so that it sits about three feet off the ground, and it's got no top, but who needs a top in California? Not me, man, not me.

I've had the car on blocks for three years, and after I kick out the snakes, mice, and bees, everything still works, but it just won't start up. What the hell is going on? The motor won't turn over, so I check the oil, and find that the oil pan is right full of rusty water. Son of a bitch! My wonderful rod is dead. But I'm a Frog, so I never say quit.

I've got a spare engine tucked away, a Police Interceptor 312-cube full house Mercury, and that should do the trick. I yanked out the ruined motor and slid in the 312, and it started right up. All right. I give it a good tune, and I'm ready to rock and roll.

I figure at speed, I can make the trip easy in four or five days, but since I've got six days' leave left, it should be no sweat. My tires are kind of bald, so I throw a few spares in the backseat, a couple of fan belts and, just for luck, a two-gallon gas can. Hey, you never know, right? Finally I make sure the radio plays nice and loud, put on my lucky Budweiser sweatshirt, adjust my sunglasses, and depart New York forever.

Things go fine for several hundred miles, but at the western border of Pennsylvania, the old car starts to spit and sput. I've got an awful sinking feeling in my stomach, so I start giving my rod encouragement.

"C'mon, baby, hang in there, and I promise I'll give you a new paint job when we get to California. I'll even buy you some new mag wheels and tires." You know, things like that.

Well, she seems to hear me, and we struggle into Ohio, but that's it, and as she dies, I coast onto the shoulder. As the traffic is whizzing by at high speed, I do some checking, and I find

I'm getting good spark, but no fuel to the carburetor. My gas tank is three-quarters full, so it looks like I've got a blockage somewhere in the fuel line. I crawl under the car and start disconnecting the line from the carburetor backward, and sure enough, there's crap in the line; it looks like granular resin. What could it be? I don't know, but I clean out the line as best I can with a piece of wire, and then blow into it until it's clear. I reconnect everything, squirt a little gas into the carburetor, and away I go. Ah, I feel a lot better now.

I'm heading for Missouri and old Route 66, but I don't quite make it before my Ford dies again. It's the same problem. Phew, that gas tastes nasty! But I think I've figured out now what's going on. Fresh gas in the tank and the motion of driving had freed the gunk that had settled to the bottom of the tank while I was away, and my problem would continue until I cleaned out the gas tank or replaced it. Since I had only sixty dollars with me for gas for the trip, I couldn't pay to have the tank repaired. I could only shrug my shoulders. I'd have to do the best I could with what I had.

I was already filthy and greasy from lying under the car and repairing it, but that was no big deal. I wasn't gonna be appearing in public except at gas stations. I had a shopping bag full of sandwich stuff with me, so I didn't have to do restaurants and stores, and I'd do my sleeping right in the car. I could pee anywhere at all, I wasn't modest.

And so it went. I'd go a few hundred miles holding my breath, climb under the car and clean the fuel line, prime the carburetor with gas, and take off again. I did have a good night's run through Missouri. It was freezing cold and that seemed to help the fuel flow, because I was able to keep my speed at ninety all night long. But eventually I just couldn't keep my eyes open anymore, and had to stop for some sleep in Oklahoma. After I got about four hours of good Zs, rain woke me up. With no top to protect me, I figured I might as well be wet and cold and miserable while I was driving, so I started out again, and finally drove out of the rain into Texas.

I couldn't make much distance during the days, what with all the repair stops, but I did a little better at night, although never again as good as the Missouri run. As I crawled through Texas (would the damn state never end?), New Mexico, and Arizona, things got progressively worse. Now I was traveling through the desert, and it got really hot—maybe over 100 degrees. I was only getting about twenty or thirty miles between repair stops. I was filthy dirty, and man, did my body stink! The fumes rising up made my eyes tear. If that Viet crewman could smell me now, he wouldn't just grimace, he'd faint. My sandwich stuff looked kind of green and didn't smell too good either, but I ate it anyway. I finally made the California border and heaved a big sigh of relief. I was almost home. I stopped for the agricultural inspection and the inspector was asking me a bunch of questions until I noticed his nose start wrinkling up; then he let me right through.

Finally, about twenty miles from San Diego, it all ended. I ran out of money, food, and gas, and as the final fumes sucked through the carburetor, I coasted onto the shoulder of the road for the last time. I got out and stuck out my thumb, and two hours later I walked into my apartment. (A Mexican dude had given me a ride in the back of his pickup truck, but for some reason he wouldn't let me up front.) I was hungry, tired, and four days late on my leave. The 4,000-mile trip had taken me eleven days, and I was in deep shit. About all I had was a good tan—I was as brown as Ollivera. Well, forget that. When I showered and washed up good, my deep tan ran right down the drain, and I was my regular old white self again. I called the base and reported in, and then I got a good night's sleep, because I knew it was all over for me.

Sure enough, at the end of muster the next morning, the word comes out. "Miller! Report to the captain's office on the double!"

I go in and stand at attention, and butterflies are swarming in my stomach. Here we go again. It's obvious the captain is not happy. He says, "All right. Give me your story, and it better be good."

So I tell the captain about my epic struggle, and all about how I almost had to carry my car across the country on my back, and how I deserve a medal and all. I go on and on until he stops me abruptly. "That is absolutely the worst goddamn story I ever heard! It's so bad it's probably true, but that isn't getting you off the hook."

I think, uh-oh, here it comes.

The captain glares at me. "Mr. Winant swears you're a good Frog, but I can't imagine why. I'm not impressed."

Then he looks at the exec and says, "Restricted to base for two weeks, but scrap the paperwork." Whew! Am I ever relieved. No black mark on my record.

He looks back at me. "You can thank your lucky stars that Mr. Winant went to bat for you. Don't you dare make him regret it! Get out of here!"

Man, I went. My car adventure was over. How much longer could I stay lucky?

Chapter
Twenty-five

LIFE AS A Frog has become routine. Each morning I drive to the base for 0700 muster, and then do my normal physical workout, day one—one-mile ocean swim, day two—five-mile run, day three—obstacle course, and then repeat. Afternoons we fool around with equipment or just hang out. At 1600 we knock off and head to the Tradewinds, our team bar in Coronado, or down to Mexico. Mostly it's Tijuana, with occasional runs to Ensenada.

Tijuana (or TJ) is our kind of town, since it's just like Olongapo City. Low-down and nasty, you can find about anything you want there, and all the stories you've ever heard are true. But like Po City, you had to know what you were doing if you wanted to keep intact.

On the way back from Mexico, we'd always make sure to

stop just before the border to buy tacos. There was this little old Mexican, he stayed open all night long, and he sold the best tacos in the world. The bacteria count was probably in the billions, but we didn't care. We'd each eat two or three on the trip back, and they were so hot my bottom eyelids would sweat. Good stuff, guaranteed to put lead in your pencil.

Regardless of where we went, we'd party until late and then head home—either UDT barracks or our apartments. I share my apartment with Robbie and Jim, not related but both Andersons, and it's not unusual to have five or six other guys crashing in our living room. I tell you though, it sure is great to walk out our back door, down a flight of steps, and step right out on the beach, where we hang out a lot trying to meet women.

We sun and swim and pursue, and when storms come up, we bodysurf in the big breakers. In fact, one time I damn near drowned in these storm breakers. I was bodysurfing and I got rolled under by the surf until I lost my sense of direction. I was under an awful long time until my feet brushed the bottom, and I was able to kick to the surface. Scary. Earthquakes were pretty interesting too. Being right on the beach, we felt them all, even the little ones. Our second-floor apartment would get to shaking and swaying until we'd get a little queasy from our loss of balance.

A.J. is back. One morning he comes strolling into my apartment, happy as a lark because he'd completed his thirteen-month tour and was still alive. I didn't realize how much that meant until he told me that only he and two other guys out of his original company had made it out of the Nam whole. I say, "Thank you, God." Then I have to give him first aid, because one of his boots is filled with blood. Seems his last night in country, the airport had been rocketed, and A.J., sleeping on his bunk, had gotten a chunk of shrapnel in his foot.

I say to him, "So why didn't you get it treated?"

He looks at me like I'm a total fool. "Are you shitting me? They would have held me over on a 'medical.' No way I'm gonna spend an extra second in the Nam!"

What he said made sense, so I bandaged him up, and sent

him on his way home. One of the Killer Millers had made it through.

Chapter Twenty-six

ALTHOUGH OUR BASE was shared with SEAL Team 1 (they had half, UDT Teams 11 and 12 had the other half, separated by a concrete wall), we didn't mix during working hours. We did party together though, especially at the Tradewinds. Frogs were good, and didn't hesitate to let anyone know it, but SEALs were in a class all by themselves. They were warriors, and had a mystique about them that said: "Don't fool with me, I'll tear you a new asshole."

As usual, to be in the know, I had done my research on SEALs to find out what they were all about, and at the Tradewinds, over many a beer, this is what I learned. SEALs play sneak and peek in the bush, shooting or capturing Charlie whenever they find him, and just generally kick ass. Nobody is as good as a SEAL, and their shit don't stink. To be a SEAL you had to be nasty, cunning, and smart. You must be able to walk a hundred miles, swim fifty, see like an eagle, and have at least a twelve-inch dick. Hmm . . . okay, but I don't know if I can swim fifty miles.

And SEALs carried themselves with a manner of quiet competence, sort of the ultimate "Mr. Cool." I have to admit, I was attracted and impressed, especially since I had been doing some heavy thinking, balancing the pluses and minuses of a change. On the one hand, being a Frog was fun, I could get by in the military aspects (if I really worked at it), there were no chicken-shit duties, and UDT was a known quantity, so I'd get no major surprises.

On the other hand, there were also no real challenges ahead, even though I'd started training for the space program— something about retrieving space capsules after splashdown. Also, I wasn't forgetting that I could no longer do deep dives because of my ear problems, although no one knew about that except me. Hmm . . . my thoughts are driving me crazy.

John Wayne is whispering in my ear, "Do it, mister, take a step up to the very best."

But I'm answering him, "Jesus Christ, man, I'm a big old chicken, I don't want to get my dick shot off. Besides, what if I can't cut it?" Wow. Safety and security versus challenge and status, I just couldn't make up my mind.

Then two things happened that tipped the scales. First, we did a submarine exercise. This adventure is where we go down in a sub to fifty feet, crowd into this tiny little dive chamber with the instructor (in swim pairs as always), turn a valve, and let in the ocean until the chamber is full. Then we open the hatch, swim out, and ascend to the surface to our boat. While ascending you must blow out air as you go, otherwise your lungs will expand until they explode. As you might imagine, the air hog didn't like to blow out what little air he had in his lungs; he was worried about drowning. On the surface, we wait until everyone has made it up, then we reverse the procedure. For me, it turns out to be an absolute nightmare, from beginning to end.

I'm claustrophobic! Although I don't let on, the minute I go into the sub I am panicky. When I climb into the diving chamber I am terrified, and as the chamber fills with water I am right on the edge of losing it. Naturally my ears are giving me intense pain as the pressure changes. (The sub is at surface pressure but the chamber pressure must be increased to water pressure at fifty feet deep so that the chamber hatch will open.) I reach the point of absolute panic, go past it, and still the torment doesn't end.

Finally (thank you, God!) the chamber is full of freezing water, the pressure is equalized, and I push open the hatch. I go out so fast I leave meat on the sides. Jesus Christ, don't get in my way! Once outside the sub I cool down a bit, and I ascend properly to the surface, breathing out air all the way, so I don't blow up my lungs. But one thing I know. Ain't no fucking way I'm going back down there. I won't do it! I can't do it!

Well, I do it. I'm a Frog and I got my pride, but I promise myself, never never again. I got my limits. But wouldn't you know it, the exercise doesn't go well, so they decide to do it again the next day. Among other catastrophes, Gore breaks an eardrum, and blood runs out of his ear. That certainly made me feel more comfortable.

Are you shitting me? All that night and the next morning, I think, nope—no way, even as I get my gear prepared, and we truck from the base to the pier. Impossible, I say, as I climb onto the sub. All I can do is pray, "God, give me a break, get me out of this one, and I'll go to church every Sunday from now on!"

I get a miracle! God hears me, and when our pickup boat arrives they're short a crewman. Can they borrow a Frog to comply with Navy regs? I scream in my mind, and Gore says, "Miller and Emerson. You two [can't leave a man without a swim partner] have just volunteered for boat duty." I give some big sigh of relief, but I play the game and act real disgusted and disappointed. My partner acts the same way, but it is all settled, and away we go. Boy, I sure lucked out this time. (Uh, listen, God, about the church thing—I'll have to catch you next time.)

We spend a boring but safe day floating on the ocean until the exercise is completed, then God gets me back. I'm scanning the ocean and I spot a floater. I should have kept my mouth shut, but like a fool, I point it out to the guys. The body is floating on its back, and she's been out there a while—birds have eaten her face off. Ugh. It's really gruesome. We get on the radio, and there's nothing for it but to get the body in the boat and take it back with us. Hey, we might get a medal. You never know . . .

What a nasty job that was. Me and Mike get into the water, and when I touch the body's arm, the flesh dissolves. Yuck! All we can do is get a basket stretcher and maneuver it under her. It takes a couple of attempts, because neither one of us wants to get near her face, and we keep pulling each other back and forth. Finally we do it, swim it to the side of the boat, and the stretcher is lifted up and in. By the time we get back to the harbor, the body is smelling pretty ripe in the hot sun, but those coroner dudes with their rubber gloves bag up the body and carry it right away—it don't even bother them. Another interesting day.

So now I know I can't do sub ops, and I definitely can't do long dives. I'm some poor excuse for a Frog. Then the clincher occurs that will change my life.

I was hanging in the area filling dive tanks when I saw a platoon of SEALs all geared up for a training exercise. They were wearing camouflage greens, their faces were all painted up, and they were just bristling with weapons. All in all, a fearsome sight. John Wayne gives me a final shove, and I go to the office and submit a transfer request. The rest of that day and all that evening I got butterflies, I'm having all kinds of second thoughts. What have I done now? But it's too late. They need SEALs for Vietnam, and my transfer is immediately approved. I have become an official member of SEAL Team 1. God help me now.

Chapter
Twenty-seven

BUT I DON'T get much time to worry, because my training starts immediately. First I turn in a lot of my UDT gear, and then get issued a whole bunch of SEAL stuff. Camo uniforms (neat!), web gear, jungle boots, M-16, and 9mm pistol. (Oh boy!) I get assigned to communications, and I wonder why. Because I'm an electrician? Or because I resemble a pack mule? But I am actually pleased to be a radioman, because that was what my dad was in the Merchant Marine during WW II.

PRC 25 is the basic patrol radio, but it's already being upgraded to the PRC 77, which has longer range and less power draw on the battery. Both are designed to be carried on a man's back, but they're bulky and heavy. My boss assures me, though, that the radio is the lifeblood of any operation. It is the one piece of equipment that allows extended patrol operations, and of course that's what we'll do for a living.

"In any firefight," he tells me, "you keep your body between your radio and the bullets. Protect your radio at all costs." (He's joking, right?)

"Of course," he continues with a grin, "you realize that the radioman is the first one the enemy shoots at?"

Hmm . . . makes sense to me. You know, I bet I'd make one hell of a point scout. Or a rear guard, or anything else.

I am assigned to Echo platoon. Some of the guys I know, but most are strangers. It doesn't matter—I will get to know them all, very well indeed. There are two officers—Lt. Arch Woodard and (all right!) Bosun Campbell—and twelve enlisted—Tom McDonald, myself, Ray Wilkins, Mike Emerson, Gil Espinoza, Roger Cochlin, Bill Noyce, Lou Hyatt, Jim Richards, Larry D'Angelo, Louie McIntosh, and a corpsman, Doc Lin Mahner.

We start basic training immediately—we need to become a well-oiled machine before going to the Nam. Since any one of us might lead a patrol, regardless of rank (and as far as I know, this is unique to SEAL teams), we all learned all there was to know. We start out with basic weapons handling. We learn all the technical stuff, but the real education is our hands-on training. I learn to handle my weapons expertly. In this case, familiarity breeds confidence and skill.

Then we are taught basic patrol maneuvers. These are based on standard infantry methods that as SOP (standard operating procedure) have been modified to fit SEAL teams' special needs. Our key will be mobility. We must be able to move great distances quickly and quietly, over any kind of terrain, both going in to a target when we are fresh and eager, and more important, coming back out when we are tired or hurting.

The perfect SEAL op is deceptively simple. Sneak in to the target undetected, do our thing, and sneak back out, again undetected. When done successfully, it is physical and psychological guerrilla warfare at its best, and is only made possible by the top-notch physical and mental condition of the SEAL members. For the first time I can understand why my UDT physical and mental torture and training had been so difficult. It had created a never-quit, go-for-it attitude, and my body could do any task that was asked of it. I was in perfect condition to do my new job.

As the instructors take us through our troop movements, we quickly learn that there will be no guessing—every move is choreographed to provide 100 percent efficiency. We spend a shitload of time learning all these maneuvers, until they are as instinctive as breathing. Since our normal seven-man patrols will usually be outnumbered by the enemy, we never "charge that hill" or "hold that valley at all costs!" And we never patrol to draw enemy fire, because that's not what we're about. SOP for us is at the first shot, get on the horn (radio) and call in extraction. Sounds excellent to me!

Well, would you believe it, I am appalled to realize that I've finally found my home. I eat this shit up, especially when I find out I'm good at it—that's a real confidence-builder. But what happened to the smart-ass combat avoider I always thought I was? I guess he died somewhere during UDT, after I had gained a new level of confidence. I am still a big chicken, of course, so I'll have to walk careful while holding up my end of the job. I also quickly erect a mental block about what will happen when I actually enter combat. I know it's there on the horizon, but I make sure to ignore it.

Back during my UDT tour, when we were on the USS *Carpenter*, I'd been scheduled to attend Jump School at Fort Benning, Georgia. We'd been initiated (yes, even in the teams), our heads shaved, and we'd been loaded up with all the horror stories that the veteran jumpers could invent when, to our great disappointment, the class was canceled. Now I am delighted to find out that my first school as a SEAL is Jump School. We fly to Fort Benning, where they break us up, assigning one or more SEALs to each jump platoon, the rest of the platoon being dogs. I find out that, as in other conventional forces schools, the instructors like to have SEAL/UDT students. Their morale is always excellent and they tend to pass that on, carrying the other students along with them.

Well, in my new role as Mr. Super-SEAL, I'm afraid I was gung-ho obnoxious. I paid strict attention to the instruction, and I was flat-out disgusted whenever I didn't perform perfectly. When my jump platoon did their physical training, I whipped it out effortlessly, and on the conditioning runs I would break ranks and run circles (literally) around the moving platoon. The dogs were resentful; they were having to work at it, but of course they weren't gonna mess with a SEAL.

Turns out that parachute jumping is not at all difficult, except for the fear of falling and smashing yourself into jelly. For some reason, I didn't have that fear. In fact, I was impatient to get the training behind me and get into the air, but no shortcuts are allowed, and my training continued.

I learn that parachuting is a simple matter of dressing in your jump rig properly (a big main chute, a smaller reserve chute, and the web gear that holds it all together), flying up to a selected altitude, hooking your chute-pulling line to a steel cable in the plane, jumping out the door using a prescribed body position, and after your chute opens, steering yourself to the landing spot, then landing using a specified method of body position. Nothing to it. So with the rest of the students, I practiced the parachute landing fall (PLF) in which, as soon as your feet touched the ground, you collapse your body and roll on your side. This dissipates and redistributes the shock of hitting the ground so that you don't drive your legs up into your belly and become a midget. They used all kinds of rigs to hang us in a jump harness so we could learn all the body positions. These rigs were real hard on the testicles, since the harness crosses between the legs. (I hope I can still have babies!)

Finally, after you have learned all the basic goodies that you need to know, you climb into a hanging parachute rig with an open chute that is hooked to a cable. They pull you 250 feet up to the top of a big tower, then release your chute, and you float to the ground, making sure you steer yourself away from the tower so you don't crash and burn. I loved it, and wanted to do several more, but you only get one shot.

As training completes, and the big day of our first jump arrives, I am fired up. I'm not gonna run out of air, I'm not gonna have ear pressure problems, and I'm not gonna be claustrophobic. I can do this! When we go up in the plane, I stand in the open door, because I want to be the first to go. As I look out, it's not as exciting as I thought it would be—at 2,000 feet you can't see much detail below. Finally the red light turns to green, the jumpmaster slaps my ass, and out I jump. It's a momentary weightlessness, then a solid tug as my chute opens. So far so good. But when I look up, I've got a partial "Mae West"—my chute is not completely open and has ballooned up around the tangled risers. Shit. As I had been trained to do, I yank furiously on the lines, and soon my chute pops out full. Oh boy, I am in business now. I whip out my trusty camera, and about that time I see my platoon sergeant go plummeting by me trailing a streamer, a deployed chute that hasn't caught the air. Looks like I'm gonna have a flat platoon sergeant.

My ride is absolutely glorious, but it's way too short. I do an acceptable PLF, gather up my chute, and I'm ready to go again. Hey, that was great! Then I am amazed to see my platoon sergeant limping around. How in the devil? But he tells us that by working hard, he'd finally gotten a partial opening of his chute, and by doing an excellent PLF, had saved his legs. Goes to show you the cadre know what they're talking about. We did four more jumps with no problems, and then we graduated. Man, I wore my silver wings on my chest with pride!

The training for a SEAL never stops, there's so much we need to know. I learn map reading and compass work—how to plot a course and follow it. As radioman and potential patrol leader (gulp!) I have to pay special attention because I will be guiding patrols and calling in supporting fire. And I must get good at it, because I will want to hit the enemy, not us.

Ah yes, supporting fire. It will be our equalizer, and make up for our lack of numbers on operations. It will also save our ass in times of trouble. I learn to use my radio and maps to call in artillery, naval gunfire, helicopter gunships, and jets—both strafing and bombing. I do well, but I'm very nervous, because it's one hell of a responsibility, and I'm not sure I'm up to doing it under combat conditions. All I can do is hope I never get any-body killed. I may lack full confidence in my ability to use maps and coordinates to call in supporting fire, but I sure love the results. I can't wait to play God and blow the enemy to red mist.

One part of training I don't like much, and that is medical. It's bad enough that this training brings home the fact that we might get blown up or shot, but a piece of the action is injecting morphine, and that part gives me the shivers.

The way I had been brought up by my father, doctors and medicines were for hypochondriacs. If I became ill or injured myself, he'd taught me to just ignore it and go on about my business until my body cured itself. Oh sure, for serious illness or injury, get medical help, otherwise, let nature and my natural defenses do the job. And I agreed with his viewpoint com-pletely. I'd had and survived all the regular childhood diseases, but without the help of medicines, my body had built up strong defenses against both illness and pain. I hadn't had five head-aches in my life, I rarely caught colds or flu, and I'd developed a very high threshold of pain. About the only serious medical problem I'd ever had was painful earaches when I was a kid, and they had eventually disappeared. It's not real complicated or anything, I just don't get sick.

And luck. Man did we have it! My family, that is. My father had gone through WW II without injury, he'd walked away from major car wrecks and many other injurious situations without a scratch. Both A.J. and I had done the same thing—the Millers just didn't get seriously hurt. The only persons in our family who had died were my grandfathers (one in his sleep at eighty-five, the other struck by lightning at eighty-three) and one uncle who was killed in WW II at the Anzio landings; but he was an in-law, so he didn't count. Good health and luck seemed to be part of our heritage.

So now I was introduced to the world of wounds, injuries, pain, and sickness, and it was a world I was not familiar with. It was also a world I didn't like. Well trained by TV and movies, I had it in my mind that combat for the good guys was clean-cut. Wounds were minor and never messy. Oh, occasionally one of the good guys might get killed, but of course it would always be the other guy, not me. It was always the enemy who got all torn up, lost body parts, and bled all over the place. If the good guys did get wounded, it was always a flesh wound, and you would just grit your teeth and carry on. Now I find out that there are very few places on the human body to get a "flesh" wound without breaking bones or hitting vital organs. This wasn't the kind of news I liked to hear.

I had to learn everything from scratch and it wasn't easy, especially the part where I had to stick a needle in someone's body and inject morphine. Needles? Drugs? Yow! We will all carry a good medical kit, one that also contains morphine syrettes, so the man tells me I must stick a practice syrette into my own thigh. I ask him if he is nuts, but he doesn't listen, I've got to do it. I'm telling you, that was the hardest thing I ever did, and it taught me a valuable lesson—I don't ever have to worry about being a drug addict, 'cause there's no way I could shoot myself up. Needles? Brr . . .

When we have completed the medical training, we talk it over. Rocky Cochlin has been enjoying my discomfort, and busts my ass.

"So Miller, now that you're a hot-shot corpsman, you know how to save my life, right?"

But I ain't letting him get away with it.

"You bet. If you get hit, I will stick you with a knife. If you holler, I'll figure you're worth saving and will give you medical help, for a price. If you don't holler, I will be sure to strip off all your gear and sell it on the black market. Then I will raise a beer in your memory. How's that?"

Rocky mutters for me to go fuck myself, but we laugh.

I also attend Escape, Evasion, and Survival School, where I learn to escape without being shot, avoid the enemy while I'm making my way back to friendly forces, and keep myself alive while I'm doing it. This is a real good school, very straightforward and informative, and I pay attention. I can't imagine any scenario in which I am gonna allow the enemy to capture me, not while I got two strong legs that work good, but you never know, and I want to be prepared for all contingencies.

We receive very detailed training in mission behavior. This is where we do our thing once we have arrived at our objective. Our primary responsibility as SEALs will be reconnaissance. We will always be the first to arrive, and we must obtain detailed information about terrain, approach, danger points, enemy personnel, fortifications, and weapons. In other words, we must be the unseen eyes of conventional forces that will determine how various combat tasks can be accomplished. A good example would be aircraft. If you want to do detailed bombing or strafing, first you need to select a valuable target, and then you need an exact location and description of that target, so you don't waste men or equipment or materiel. That's the kind of information SEALs provide. Or, as an infantry company commander, you may want to run a sweep or a search and destroy mission in a particular area. Send in the SEALs first and you will have an excellent idea of what you will face.

Aggressive military forces feed on intelligence, whether they are large or small. Throughout the ages, scouting parties, recon patrols, and individual scouts, agents, or partisans have fed valuable info to conventional forces so that they can operate efficiently. And smart commanders utilize their intelligence sources to the max to get the job done. If you know an AO is hot, loaded with the enemy, you go into it forewarned and anticipating action, and not wasting your troops or supplies. You take enough to get the job done—not too many, and not too few. By the same token, if you know that an AO is cold, you will not devote a lot of manpower to it, rather you will allocate your troops to where they can be most effectively used.

The small recon units—SEALs, LRRPs, Force Recon, and others—provide an extremely valuable tool to obtain area intelligence. But sad to say, in Vietnam, many of them were terribly underused, or worse, misused. Military commanders with poor or insufficient training, such as ground troop officers in the Army and Marines, often pushed their own troops out into the bush, hoping to draw fire so that retaliation could then be made, usually using air or artillery supporting fire. This method was very costly in both lives and materiel, and was entirely ineffective. Since the enemy was a guerrilla, he rarely massed enough troops to justify the huge expenditure of bombs, arty shells, and manpower that were used against him. The enemy? Hell, he was smiling the whole time, because he was doing successfully what a guerrilla force was made for: pinning down large numbers of conventional forces and gnawing away at those numbers piecemeal, at little cost to him. The U.S. troops? They were employed as cannon fodder. That was cruel and unusual punishment and needlessly wasted many lives.

You're asking how I can make such a statement, and I'll tell you. We regularly offered our services to both the Marines and the Army in our areas and were turned down cold. "We have our own people" was the reply. What a shame that was. We could have saved many lives.

I learn what it is like to set up a recon post. Based on the terrain, it may be a circular, in which the men of the patrol will lie in a circle, feet to the center, so that we have 360 degrees of observation, and also 360 degrees of fire protection in case we get attacked. This one works well when you are in open, flat terrain with little cover.

It may be a linear, where we will set up in a line alongside a terrain feature, such as a stream or a trail. Either one man will be facing the rear as guard, or every other man is facing the rear. This one can get tricky, and we use it carefully, but it works well in broken terrain where visibility is limited. It will turn out to be our most common formation in Vietnam.

Recon can also be conducted on the move. We will sneak quietly through an area gathering info as we go. This is the most dangerous method for us, both because of booby traps, and because if you're not careful, you could walk right up on anything or be ambushed by an alert enemy. The instructors tell us that it will certainly ruin our day if we walk up on a battalion or company of enemy, or stroll unwittingly into one of their base camps.

Our secondary responsibility will be action. Unlike the passive role of recon, we may be called upon to conduct ambushes, personnel snatches, ville searches, or sabotage. This sort of mission appeals to the John Wayne in all of us, but certainly fires up the adrenaline when we think about the potential consequences.

I want to kick ass and take names, but I don't want new holes in my body. The ones I already have work fine, thank you.

But the instructors make no bones about it. Regardless of what we will be called upon to do in combat, we must do it well, and it will usually be done as a squad, which means seven men only (eight with a Viet scout). We will be in enemy territory, we will be alone, and we will be a long way from help. Get your shit together, and keep it that way at all times.

To sum it all up, I listen carefully, I pay full attention, and I lock the new knowledge in my brain. Forget all that horseshit about Semper Fi, God and Country, mom and apple pie. I have one simple goal, and that is to do a good job, don't let my team members down, and bring my young ass home, alive and in one piece.

Chapter
Twenty-eight

SINCE SEAL TEAM operations and activities are classified Top Secret, we must attend a Prisoner of War School. It sounded dry and boring to me, but it turned out to be a real motherfucker. Me and Sonny Sanders go together, and we are prebriefed. We will do two days of survival training, during which we will not eat, then with empty stomachs, will allow ourselves to be captured and interned in a prison camp, so we can experience what it's like to be a POW. Hey, we think, this might be fun after all.

"I'm telling you, it's like the real thing," the briefer told me. "They will beat the crap out of you, use some really nasty interrogation techniques, and because you're a SEAL, will single you out to make your life miserable, 'cause they know you can take it. And as a SEAL, we expect you to be outstanding, and set an example for the other troops."

We are told that the class will be about 125 students, mostly conventional forces that handle sensitive documents and materials, or people who have duties that will make them potential POWs (aircrew, for instance), and anyone else that has or will have a secret or higher clearance. Then I learn that there are special instructions that kind of confuse me.

"You will not, no matter what the provocation, attack or strike the instructors. If you do, you will be immediately failed, and have to repeat the school. Two failures, and you're out of SEAL team. Fail academically, and you're out of SEAL team."

Well now, that's food for thought. But the other guys give us the real scoop that night in the Tradewinds, so we make some special arrangements.

The POW School starts with classroom—a history of POWs, how to handle yourself as a POW, and our military responsibilities. It's name, rank, and serial number only, and never anything else! We listen, but we're cool, you know. We're SEALs. That shit will never happen to us.

Next day is classroom for escape, evasion, and survival techniques. Then we go to the shore of the ocean, and are shown the "cafeteria" of edibles, and sample some. Seaweed sucks, it's really horrible-tasting and lays in your gut like a stone. The crawlies in the tide flats are nasty-looking and nasty-tasting, but for some reason, even though they're slimy going down, they're more acceptable to me than the ones I saw in jungle survival school. For one thing, this is now the real deal. I just think of them as raw clams, which I love, and down they go. I'm garbage gut, so I figure if I get hungry enough, I will eat almost anything.

After leaving the ocean, we head out into the desert for survival training, and learn that there ain't shit out there to eat. But we don't really care. That night after dark, Sonny and I sneak out the access road. Sure enough, my girlfriend Ginny is there waiting for us as planned. She's got a couple of pizzas and two sixes of beer, and we party down. Best meal I ever ate. When we sneak back to the class, all the troops are bitching and moaning about how hungry they are, because they've never missed a meal in their lives. Me and Sonny are grinning, burping and farting, and no one can figure it out.

Next morning we do an evasion exercise, at the end of which we get "captured." What a rude awakening! I mean, Sonny's a SEAL, I'm a SEAL, we're old friends, and we've already been through the mill. How tough can this school be? Well, we soon find out. We meet our captors, and some of our attitude quickly disappears. They are all big burly guys, and they start man-handling us like we're children—kicking, shoving, and slap-ping us into trucks for transport to the prison compound. They are "Communists," wearing the red star on their hats and talk-ing with exaggerated foreign accents. But we don't do any laughing, because these guys aren't fooling around. I raise one eyebrow at Sonny. We may have to make some adjustments to our plans, as we'd already had to do with our attitudes.

Well, screw it. We know what we want to do, and start look-ing for opportunities immediately. We can't jump the trucks because they're going like a bat out of hell, and the minute we arrive at the compound we are surrounded by guards and herded on hands and knees into the "pigpen," which is a three-foot-high barbed-wire enclosure. The head guard tells the pris-oners to strip down to their shorts—we will hand our clothes through a small door to be searched before we crawl into the prison proper. Since Sonny and I don't wear shorts, we strip naked, and the guards make a big fuss—throwing dirt at us and calling us perverts. We don't pay attention, though, as we are looking around hard for escape potentials. We edge out to the side of the pigpen away from the guards, and when I glance at Sonny, he nods and crawls out through the barbed wire. I follow him quickly, and we both leave some skin and meat on the barbed wire, but as we flop down in a little gully, we are out and undetected. All right! Successful escape number one.

In the classroom, we had been informed that after a suc-cessful escape was made, we were to go to a small shed outside the camp and call in our names and serial numbers. Then we would be rewarded with a bologna sandwich and a half-hour rest before returning to the camp.

Hell, we never got the chance. Two more trucks pull up loaded with prisoners, and we're caught dead nuts. Seeing two naked prisoners in the ditch, the guards are momentarily confused, then really pissed. Oh man, did they ever thrash us. Slaps, kicks, and shoves forced us out into the open and back into the pigpen. We crawled in, retrieved our discarded uniforms, and passed through the entrance into the camp under the watchful eyes of a specially detailed guard. Scratch escape number one. We dress, and they chain Sonny and me together. (Holy shit! Chains?) The rest of the prisoners are already lined up in ranks waiting for us to join them.

I say to Sonny, "We gotta get out of these chains somehow, or we're helpless."

He nods, and we do some quick thinking, and then he laughs. "Since we're stuck in these things," he says, "let's use them to have some fun with these jokers."

He flaps a limp wrist and puts his arm around my waist. "Follow my lead."

I laugh too. I think I know what he's planning. Oh boy, this should be fun. Since the chain binding our ankles is very short, we have difficulty walking anywhere and we look ridiculous trying, which is the whole idea. Hah! Watch this. So we stroll out to ranks tight together, my arm is around Sonny's neck, my hand is down inside his shirt, and our other wrists are limp and fluttering. Man, the whole place breaks up. The prisoners are rolling on the ground laughing, and even the guards are grinning. Then they recover and go berserk. See, we had violated the main theme of the prison camp—break down the prisoners mentally and physically, which will make them ripe for interrogation. The pigpen, name-calling, hunger, and manhandling were all designed to do this. Laughter and defiance had no place in their plan, so they tried to negate what we had done. They pummeled us pretty good until all the laughter was gone, but at least they did remove our chains. We were free to move, but unfortunately we were marked men. Maybe that's not so good.

The POW camp was no mock-up. It was a bare dirt yard devoid of all vegetation, surrounded by barbed-wire walls and gun towers, and the POW barracks were some dirt caves. No beds, no blankets, nothing. I walked the place over looking for possibilities, but the situation looked pretty grim. To me, the only potential area of escape seemed to be the main gate, a wooden swinging door about ten feet tall. They were moving prisoner groups in and out for interrogation, and the prisoners were allowed to mill around fairly close to the gate. I sauntered over to give it a better look, but decided it was pretty iffy. Suddenly I was forced to react. Two guards, one in front, one in the rear, hustled out some prisoners, and on cat feet, I simply followed them out, cut a fast right turn, and *flash!* I was gone.

Taking my own sweet time (Mama didn't raise no fool), I strolled up to the escape shed, contemplated for a while, then called in. A guard comes for me and escorts me to the office, where I claim my reward. I was really surprised: that sandwich tasted great! You can imagine how good it would have tasted to the other prisoners who hadn't eaten. I tell them how I escaped, and the instructor, in normal English, gives me a "well done." We talk about the school, what they're trying to accomplish, and he tells me that very few men will escape, or even try. That really surprises me.

"It's human nature," he says. "Most men are born followers or have been trained to be, and it's only the real individualists who will make the attempt. You wait and see. Almost all of them will just lay back and avoid trouble. If we didn't have a few spec forces men in the classes, we'd rarely see an escape attempt."

Well now, that gives me more food for thought. I had no more thought about vegetating than I had shooting myself in the foot, but what he said made a lot of sense. It wasn't a matter of leadership, it was more a matter of initiative.

We both shot a few sea stories, and then it was time for me to go back inside.

"If you don't mind," he says, "I'd like to work you a bit inside, use you as an example for the others."

I'm flattered, and I say, "Sure. Be glad to." Boy, I am some dummy.

After my rest time expires, we head to the gate. He smiles and says, "You ready for this?" I nod. Ready for what?

We enter the gate, and holy shit, a tornado hits me. The instructor is calling me every name in the book, slinging me around, and slapping the shit out of me. We quickly draw everyone's attention, and he plays to his audience. Man, I'm up, I'm down, my asshole is shaking loose. I'm a "filthy American pig," a "killer of women and children," and a "woman raper." This goes on for a while, until he catches me with a solid slap across the face. Whatever he saw in my eyes made him back right off. He continues to scream, but he don't come close. After a minute I get back under control and he sees it.

"You okay?" he says in an undertone.

I blink, and he says, "We're almost done."

He grabs me, slings me down to the ground, and gives me a few kicks. Then he stands me in the center of the whole camp, stuffs some dirt in my mouth, and orders me to stand there at attention—I am to watch for "imperialist war planes," and shout a warning if I see any. Sure, pal, I think. Don't hold your breath. I am good and mad, and it takes me a few minutes to calm down.

Well, you should have seen those prisoners! They were scared to death, not a one of them wanted to get a beating like I'd just gotten. When I looked around, their eyes dropped away from mine, they just couldn't get involved. Except Sonny, he grins and gives me the finger.

Hey man, I think, it's only a school, but these instructors are experts, and as they work the crowd, I can see the changes in the prisoners. They've forgotten that this is not the real thing. After a few hours the instructors let me leave my plane watch, and by then I have a new plan. I talk to Sonny, and we agree to separate to keep from drawing attention.

I grab a reasonable-looking Marine and tell him, "If you help me, I'll help you." I give him my plan, and he slides casually over close to the gate, me not far behind. I take a few running steps and jam my foot in his cupped hands. He lifts, I jump and reach, and roll right over the top of the gate, landing with a bone-jarring thump on the other side. In continuous motion, I'm up, running, and gone, to call in another successful escape. I left an uproar behind me, I could hear them yelling.

I get my second sandwich and well done, and that sandwich sure tastes fine—must be the adrenaline. Again I shoot the breeze with the same instructor, but this time they sneak me back through the gate quietly—they're making real progress on the prisoners' mental condition, and they don't want to advertise my success.

He tells me, "Things are going pretty well for us, and I'm telling you, you're not going to believe what's gonna happen."

I ask him, but he just smiles. "Wait and see."

That night in the dirt caves is pretty miserable. The desert is cold at night, and nobody gets much sleep. The rest of the prisoners are in a bad way, and I'm not all that thrilled myself. This is turning out to be a real bitch. Well, I grit my teeth and last out the night, and at 0700 they call me out for interrogation. Jeez, I guess I'm special, because I've got four guards all to myself.

They put me through a questioning period and I handle it—name, rank, and serial number only. Then they take me to a cell where there is a black Army corporal. He looks pretty ragged, and they lay into him again, telling him all the while that I'm not getting any abuse because I'm a sergeant and white. Pretty tricky, but very effective. The dude soon loses his temper and starts talking up a storm, and I know that it's all over for him. Then it's my turn. The instructor hands me a bundle of papers and tells me it's the Geneva convention rules for POWs. I look them over and he's not lying, they are the real thing.

"Read this man his rights," he tells me, and I do.

There is a flash of light, and the instructor says, "Gotcha!"

He looks at me and says, "I just took your picture reading your confession of war crimes to another prisoner, and you've cooperated with the enemy."

I am stunned, and I hang my head, I am that ashamed. How could I have been so fucking stupid?

The interrogator tells me, "Don't take it too hard. We get everybody with that one."

But it doesn't make me feel any better. I am disgusted with myself.

He continues, "We also tape the questioning period, and if we can get any kind of conversation going, we can edit it to say whatever we want. That's why you say nothing except for name, rank, and serial number. You don't pose, you don't show, you don't read." Goddamn it! I absolutely hate failing, but this POW stuff is tricky. Well, we go through it again, and this time I get it right. Finally the instructor calls my guard.

"This dog is not cooperating. Take him next door and see if you can't change his mind."

Uh-oh. This don't sound so good. And it isn't. We go into the next room and there are several wooden boxes in there and nothing else. The boxes are really small, and when the guard lifts a lid on one and tells me to get in it, I just gape. But he's serious, and he slaps and kicks me into it. Lordy lordy, it's so small I have to tuck my knees under my stomach, cross my arms, and jam my chin against my chest. The guard forces the lid down against my back, compressing my body even more, and snaps the latch.

Oh my God. I panic, my heart is racing, I can't even draw a good breath, and I start to struggle. But I'm completely immobilized, it's no use. Finally, using every ounce of willpower I possess, I get myself under control, but panic is still hovering right there, ready to pounce if I relax even a second. What am I gonna do now? My breathing finally slows, and I realize I'm not going to suffocate, because there are air holes drilled in the box. Thank God for small favors. I have to keep my breathing very shallow though because I'm too squeezed in to draw a deep breath, and the air hog is in real trouble.

Boom! Boom! Boom! The guard whacks my box with a piece of wood, and I almost lose it again. That motherfucker! Suddenly I am good and mad. I hear him mocking me, and I grit my teeth. Wait till I get out of here. I'll stuff that goddamn club up his ass sideways and give it a good twist. Suddenly the box top opens and a bucket of water splashes down on me, and the box lid slams shut again before I can twitch. Son of a bitch! I struggle heroically, but they have me absolutely helpless. I'm gonna kill. Through my rage I hear the guard tell me to respond, or I'll get more of the same, so I holler, and the pounding stops. Then every few minutes it's *Whack! Whack!* and I have to holler. I think this is their method to make sure I am still alive in the box, but I am as stubborn as a mule, and after a while it gets longer and longer between whacks, and I can hear him going at some guys in the other boxes.

Well, I must have been tired from the previous night, because eventually I fell asleep. Suddenly I wake up, the lid is up on my box, and as it tips over, the guard is pulling me out on the floor. He must think I've passed out. All I know is a world of pain. As my cramped muscles try to relax, it really hurts bad. I open one eye in time to see my guard go streaking out the door to get help. Aha!

I am dead, but I force myself to crawl toward the door. I make it to my hands and knees, then my feet, and I stagger out, turn right, and I'm gone again. Jesus! I could barely walk, so I waited for a while before I called in, and the guard's voice on the other end didn't sound too thrilled. I guess I won't get a pat on the back this time. But I play the game and go back to the office, my joints still kind of creaky.

Well, that's all for me. The head instructor, while I'm eating my sandwich (it melts in my mouth), tells me I've done very well, and he wants me to cease fire.

"I'd like you to spend the rest of class helping others to escape," he said. "See if you can't raise their morale a little bit."

And that's what I did, although I didn't get anybody out. I find that morale has hit rock bottom in the camp, but it really takes a nosedive at final roll call that evening. The "commandant" announced that seventy-five of us had come to their senses and joined the People's Army.

"They are cooperating fully," he said.

And sure as shit, there they were, dressed in communist uniforms. Unbelievable! My first thought upon seeing them was disgust, but that immediately changed. I felt really sorry for them, and very, very uncomfortable to be associated with them. They had just wiped out their military careers, and can you imagine the mental burden they'd carry the rest of their lives? Jesus! I wouldn't be in their shoes for a million dollars. Personally, I think the instructors went too far, that sort of display wasn't necessary. But you know what we talked about the rest of the night.

Next morning early we are lined up for roll call, and when it's done, without warning, the commandant drops his accent and says, "This camp has now been liberated."

As he points to the flagpole, the bugle plays "Colors" and the American flag rises up the pole, and I'm not ashamed to say it, I got chills up my back and a big old lump in my throat. I saw other dudes with tears in their eyes, and this was only a school! Some school. I ain't likely to ever forget it.

We get trucked back and debriefed, and my attitude takes a beating. Only six guys made successful escapes, and some quiet guy from Texas made five on his own. (Quiet? From Texas?) Shit! I wasn't the best. But at least I hadn't broken, and there was never a moment when I would have "cooperated." My reward? My face was all puffed out and I had bruises all over me.

The students who had broken would, of course, never be allowed to get near sensitive jobs or information, and would definitely never get clearances. It seemed awfully harsh to me.

Chapter
Twenty-nine

SEAL TRAINING CONTINUES, and we start making extended trips to the desert in Niland, California, and the Chocolate Mountains. Niland is small-unit tactics, patrolling, chopper ops, and weapons. I've earned a promotion to pay grade E5, second class petty officer, and that's as high as I can go in my first hitch. Now I must also assume some extra command duties. It's not too awful bad, though my friends bust my ass occasionally when I have to display some authority. I tell Rocky to shine my boots, clean my weapon, then go buy me a pizza posthaste, and he tells me what I can do with both weapon and boots. Then he says I should buy him the pizza 'cause I'm so damn ugly!

Choppers are great, and I love 'em! They are noisy as hell, which kind of violates our secret and quiet mode of operation, but we learn that they will land us at one spot, and we will move away from that spot to regain our quiet mode. That sounds okay to me, especially when I think about them flying me away from hot action and saving my ass. But I also find out that you have to watch your shit if the chopper unloads you without actually touching down.

That could happen on a combat or "hot" drop, where we suspect or expect that we will draw fire on the landing zone, or if we have a "cold" LZ, but Charlie is close around. The chopper will swoop down, flare out close to the ground, and you jump. Since speed is the goal in both cases, on a hot LZ, we get down and get firing as quickly as possible, on a cold LZ we can maybe fool Charlie into believing that no troops had been landed. Also, we might have to land in water, or there might be booby traps on the LZ, and in either case the chopper can't touch down.

One day we are practicing a hot drop. I am the last one to step off, and just as I do, I look down, and holy shit, six feet has turned into twenty feet! It's too late for me, however, I am already airborne, and as my feet drill into the LZ, all I can do is a clumsy PLF, my radio gear pulling me flat on my ass and knocking the breath clean out of me. Ron Hahn told me I raised a cloud of dust when I hit. Lucky the ground wasn't concrete, so all I did was strain a tendon in my leg. What had happened was, the pilot didn't adjust his level as the guys jumped off, and as each man's weight left the bird, it raised higher and higher into the air. We all learned a valuable lesson at my expense.

Training is conducted on all the weapons we will be using in Vietnam, and the type that we will end up using depends on two requirements: knockdown power and effective fire versus noise and numbers. As warriors we will want to shoot Charlie, knock him clean off his feet, and kill him dead instantly, no matter how numerous he is. We just don't want any return fire to endanger us. Huh! On my part, if I shoot Charlie, I don't want to see anything left except his empty sandals and unfired weapon.

Opposed to that is convincing the unseen enemy in the area that we are a larger force than just seven or eight men: You better run like hell and not attempt to assault us. Maybe I can say it a better way: If I see Charlie, I want to kill him dead, so give me a powerful weapon and a heavy round, such as an M-60 machine gun with its 7.62mm bullet. But for those enemy that I don't see, that are potentially dangerous to me, give me a weapon with a high rate of fire, noisy, and with a million tracers that will light up the sky and convince the enemy that I am nobody to mess with. A Stoner fits that need.

We are introduced to the Stoner Weapons System, which is a light machine-gun using the M-16 .556mm (.223 caliber) round. The Army had rejected it, but we SEALs loved it. Just goes to show you who is smarter. The ammo is used in 150-round linked belts, which feed from a round metal drum under the barrel. SEALs usually remove the shoulder stock, which leaves the Stoner with just a pistol grip, although a few guys kept the shoulder stock out of personal preference. A short barrel is installed, and a shoulder sling is mounted on the weapon that allows it to be carried hanging horizontally in a ready-to-fire position. Lightweight, mechanically reliable, and with a firing rate of 700 to 900 rounds per minute, it will lay down a huge volume of fire, perfect for a small squad pretending to be much more numerous than it really is. All of us really like the Stoner and it will be our first choice for usage in Vietnam.

One M-60 machine gun (fires the M-14 round in linked belts) will be carried by every squad, that is, two per platoon. It is our "heavy weapon," designed to kick the enemy's ass and quickly convince him we are nobody to mess with. The M-60 was really designed to be used as a fixed or emplaced crew-served weapon, and we think it is way too heavy for our use so we modify it to make it easier to carry. Using a hacksaw, we cut the end of the barrel and the bipod off to the same length as the gas tube. Then we remove the shoulder stock and replace it with a small aluminum cap. Install a canvas ammunition pouch holding a 150-round belt, a shoulder strap that hangs the gun in the ready-to-fire position, and you've made an excellent SEAL weapon that can easily be carried with a significant amount of ammo. The only problem we ever had with ours was that the unrestricted muzzle flash ruined our night vision. On the other hand, it also lit up the area and scared the crap out of Charlie, so we bought off on it.

We learn the Swedish-K 9mm light machine gun, with and without silencer. We're supposed to use it to take out sentries, but with a long magazine that's sure to snag on stuff, and low firepower, it's kind of like a toy, and we don't like it much.

A far better weapon is the 40mm M-79 grenade launcher. We get to learn four kinds and, as radioman, I will use one of them. The M-79 fires high-explosive (HE) rounds, illumination (flare) rounds, white phosphorous (willy peter) rounds, CS gas (tear gas) rounds, and flechette (darts) rounds. These rounds are of different lengths, different colors, and different weights.

The first kind of M-79 is the basic break-open single shot called a "thumper." Reliable and easily carried, it is much like the civilian shotgun I am familiar with. There is also a pump-action version of that weapon, but with the magazine loaded, it's awfully heavy in my hands, since I can't carry it on a sling. I had a few jams when pumping in rounds, and couldn't mix different rounds, because they were of different lengths, so I became soured on the weapon, and didn't use it later. Then there is the XM-148, a light aluminum tube which is mounted under the barrel of an M-16, making a combination over-and-under weapon. This might be just the ticket for me, and I resolve to use it. Finally we fire the Honeywell, which is a grenade launcher machine gun, firing belted rounds at 500 rpm. It isn't a field-carried weapon, so we just play with it for fun. In Vietnam our riverboats carried them, and they were pretty neat.

Another weapon we liked was the twelve-gauge duck-billed shotgun. The duckbill on the end of the barrel would guide the buckshot into a nice controlled fan. It fired conventional 00 buckshot rounds, and also a neat little flechette round. The flechette, instead of lead buckshot, was loaded with several aluminum darts that looked just like tiny V-2 rockets. Supposedly they had super penetration through meat and cartilage, and would do a real number on a human body. I looked forward to using M-79 and shotgun flechette rounds for close-quarter action.

Naturally we all fired the M-16 and our Smith & Wesson 9mm pistols, but few of us expected to carry them much in country. We were provided with the AR-15 model with chrome bolts, which supposedly didn't jam like the M-16, but because of the weapon's poor reputation, we didn't trust it. We also considered the M-16 a toy, with little knockdown power and tiny effective-fire use. We figured they were good to shoot rats, maybe, but not the two-legged kind. Several of us had our own pistols, .357 Mags, .44 Mags, and Browning fourteen-shot 9mms. Again, it was a matter of personal preference.

We fired the US .50 caliber machine gun, and what a thrill that was for me! I felt just like God behind that heavy weapon, especially when I saw how much damage the rounds did, although I still got to figure out how John Wayne picked one up and fired it from the hip. If I had been able, I wouldn't have minded carrying one with my radio.

We train on the LAAW (light antiarmor weapon), which is a fiberglass tube firing a rocket. It is a nasty mother, but you got to watch that backblast so you don't fry your own people, and that would present problems in circular formations. We'll carry one with each patrol, but expect that it will be for special use only, for bunkers and such.

We also throw a shitload of hand grenades the same day, but I'm not real comfortable with hand grenades—seems like they're just as dangerous to the throwers as they are to the throwees, and as it turns out later, most of the shrapnel I picked up in the Nam was from our own grenades.

We spent quite a bit of time with the claymore antipersonnel mine, and it is some fine weapon. I just can't say enough good things about it. For its size and weight (small and light), it will be our most potent firepower. I just love to blow shit up anyway, and when I saw what the claymore did in its blast zone, I became an all-time fan. I called it the Equalizer. Bring on your platoons, companies, and your battalions, give me some claymores and I'll wipe 'em right out! Plus, the claymore pouch, with its shoulder strap, has a dozen different uses to carry stuff.

To this day, I still have two claymore pouches, and I use them occasionally for deer hunting.

Finally we learned and fired the 57mm recoilless rifle (this thing's a cannon) and mortars. I'm kind of partial to the big weapons, but I ain't carrying that shit around in the bush. I breathe a big sigh of relief when I find out we won't have to.

Weapons training is great stuff, and I'm eating it up. Meanwhile, we patrol, patrol, patrol, making the procedures second nature, and we're starting to get good. Turns out the most difficult thing about patrolling was learning to use your weapon with both hands. Because of our small size, we must cover every inch of the terrain around us while we are moving, to disperse our fields of fire in case we walk into the enemy or get ambushed. Therefore, every other man must be carrying his weapon pointing in a different direction. For example, if the man in front of me has his weapon covering right, I must cover left, and the man behind me covers right, and so on down the line. Although I'm left-handed, I am also ambidextrous, so I don't have the problems that the other guys do, but I just can't feel comfortable using my right, and the other guys, who are mostly right-handed, have real problems trying to be lefties. It took a lot of practice to get it right.

Then we go to the Chocolate Mountains for the pop-up range, pinpoint small-arms fire, and also to patrol in a different type of terrain. I find out quickly that I ain't worth a shit shooting at fixed targets. Tom McDonald tells me I don't have a natural "eye." Thanks, Tom, I really needed to hear that. Why don't you step out there aways, and give me some target practice. But he's right. While the other guys are zinging them into the black, I'm only adequate. Give me a moving target, though, and I nail ten of ten. On the pop-up range, there are no friendlies, so you shoot what you see, by instinct, and I do well. We're taught to use three-round bursts, and I kill every target, even the voice box. See, one of the instructors had taken a voice box from a doll and hung it in a tree, activated by a trip wire. It was supposed to be VC voices, so I shot it. The instructor was pretty pissed, but I wasn't. I am one deadly motherfucker.

We also practice instant response, enough to make sure it

really is. This is where you are patrolling along, bump into the enemy, and immediately lay down a strong base of fire, killing all the enemy in sight. Boy, do I love this shit.

Last, but not least, we do small-boat training and rappelling. At this point in the game, we expect that we'll do a lot of our ops using boats, so we learn to insert and extract from them. One thing I quickly learn is that when jumping off the boat into the water, I'd better keep one hand on the boat, otherwise I might disappear. The weight of my radio gear will take me right under the water or stick me in the mud like a spear. The other guys are already on shore and I'm standing there like a fool, completely exposed and unable to move. The guys have to come back and pull me out, which don't make me any friends. Rocky says I should tie a rope around my neck and he'll carry the other end, that way they can pull me ashore easier if I get stuck. I say "Kiss my ass," and tell him he can stick his rope up where the sun don't shine.

Rappelling is great fun, except I like to go too fast, and I keep getting a red-hot braking glove. We also learn the Mcguire rig, which is a harness that you can attach to your body so the chopper will fly away with you dangling below it on a rope. I'm not certain I like the idea of being dragged through the trees on this thing, but I suppose if the action is hot enough, I'll take any rescue I can get, even the one where you put on a straitjacket, send up a balloon, and a fixed-wing plane snags the line and jerks you into the air at high speed. This is the rig they used in the movie *Green Berets*, and I want nothing to do with it. But it does seem to work.

They also teach us various kinds of personal defense, hand-to-hand, karate, judo, that sort of thing. I learn it well to be a stud dog, and for conditioning, but I'm not the greatest student, because I ain't planning on getting that close to the enemy. I will stand off and blast them to confetti, that's more my style.

I'm enjoying all the training and I make a good showing, but I especially enjoy parachute jumping. I just can't seem to get enough jumps. We do water jumps, which are fun, night jumps, which are scary, and equipment jumps, which are usually painful. (300 pounds of SEAL lands a lot harder than 200 pounds.) We also do some "just for fun" jumps, and I don't miss a single one. We jump out of C117s, C123s, C130s, and the UH-46 helicopter, and it's a major milestone when I make my tenth jump and am able to pin on my gold jump wings. We jump modified T10 chutes, and I can't wait until I can learn free fall, and jump a paracommander chute, but I won't have time before my next Nam tour. Soon as I get back, though, it's HALO for me, mister!

Chapter Thirty

I AM ASSIGNED to do my third tour of Vietnam, this one down and dirty, and I'm making my final preparations. My last school is enemy recognition and psychwar, and I pay strict attention; this is the real deal. I have spent most of 1968 learning to be a SEAL, and I am fully confident that I can do my job, but I know that I am still as green as grass. The only reservation I have now is about how I will react under fire, and I won't know about that until it happens. Otherwise I am ready to meet Mr. Charlie, kick some ass, and take some names.

Then I get terrible news. My good friend Ron Hahn is rejected from SEAL team because he cannot obtain a Top Secret clearance. Some relative in Chicago, where Ron was from, had once worked with Al Capone, or some such stupid shit. Ron has come all this way, he is an outstanding SEAL, and they won't have him. Goddamn stinking military mentality! Ron, I hope it worked out for you down the line.

In preparation for leaving, we've been experimenting with our weapons and gear to try and get the best results, or in some cases, satisfy personal preference. SEALs never cease that experimentation because we're always looking for a better way.

One thing I do is question any of the old pros who will give me a minute about what it's like in the Nam. I want to know as much as possible, and I make myself a real pest. Over beers at the Tradewinds one night, I question an East Coast SEAL from Team 2, he's visiting us on his way to the Nam. His name was Hardy, or Handy, something like that.

He considered it for a moment, sipping his beer. "Oh, sure," he said. "You'll find things different over there."

Ah, this was more like it. He goes on to fill me in. I find out that Charlie is ten feet tall and impervious to bullets and explosives, that he will sneak right up behind me and cut off my balls. The NVA? Shit, if you run into them, you might as well pack it in, because you're dead meat. I hear that water buffalo will gore me at the slightest excuse, leeches are as big as cigars and will head immediately for my prime young body, there to find a home. A hundred different kinds of snakes will bite me any chance they get. I hope he's joking, but I ain't certain, and I'm hanging on every word.

"And mosquitoes? Man, you ain't seen mosquitoes until you've been to the Nam. Jeez, when they drill in and fire up their pumps, you can feel the blood rushing to them, and if enough of them hit you, you'll pass out from loss of blood.

"I tell you, one night I was up north near Hue, something whacked me in the leg, I thought it was a round, until I felt the drill go in. I gave it a good slap and hurt my hand."

He paused for another drink of beer, and like a dummy, I bit. "What was it?"

He gave me a grin. "Son of a bitch was wearin' a flak jacket and helmet."

Shit. I cringed while everyone around me laughed. I'd been had. Goddamn East Coast SEALs. See, us West Coast dudes, SEAL 1, we were laid back and cool, I mean, sun and fun, surf's up, all that kind of stuff. But those East Coast guys, SEAL 2, they were brain-damaged. I don't know why, maybe because of the colder water and being near to Washington, maybe because East Coast women didn't compare to ours, who knows? We all knew they weren't quite right in the head, and would do some strange shit. But Hardy, he had a saving grace, he was a dog man.

He had him a great big old German shepherd that he was taking to the Nam to operate with. That was the most dangerous-looking dog I ever saw, and by far the hardest one to approach.

See, me and dogs, we'd always had a certain understanding. At home I'd always had one, every size and shape and breed, so I knew them inside out, and I'd never been bitten or threatened. Whenever I would meet a strange dog, I'd go slow, give him a chance to get my scent, never pin his eyes with mine, and I could always get up to him and make a friend. Yowda! This one was different. I saw him chained out back of our area, and I didn't know who he belonged to or where he came from, but hell, a dog is a dog. I'm telling you, it took me almost half an hour of my most persuasive talking to get close to him before he finally relaxed and accepted me. I was just about to reach out and let him sniff my hand when old Hardy comes buzzin' right out, mad as could be. Some of the guys and the bosun followed him.

Oh, Hardy was cool, he kept his voice level so his dog wouldn't attack me, but he sure was pissed.

"What the fuck are you doing?" was his first question. I didn't like his tone at all, and made myself mentally ready to take him on.

I say, "Hey, just trying to make friends with the dog is all."

Hardy starts going off with all kinds of bullshit about how this one is his, a one-man dog, and he'll tear my throat out, get my ass out of there before he does so, and so on and so forth. I ain't backing up, but then Bosun Campbell tells me I should go, and from him I accept it. That story went the rounds, and everyone was amazed that I had been able to get so close to a K-9 without being eaten. I couldn't figure out all the fuss—like I said, me and dogs understood one another. I went on about getting ready to leave.

I like jungle boots because they protect my feet, but they're noisy walking. They squelch and suck in the mud and they snap twigs whenever I step on any. Coral shoes are much more quiet and comfortable, and they drain water faster, but they'd give me zero protection against punjis. Finally I pack two pair of boots and two pair of corals, we'll see what happens.

Our camo pants are fine, but I like them loose and baggy for easy movement and so my dick can breathe. I don't like our camo shirts at all. Because of my combat/radio rig I can't use the pockets, and they chafe my body under the rig, so I buy several long-sleeve T-shirts, light and comfortable. Why long-sleeve? To cover my lily-white arms so I wouldn't have to paint them with camo. And most of us are not completely happy with the color of our cammies, they're too bright a green, and are easily seen in light cover. Anything with a sharp-lined pattern, like the camo splotches, is easily picked up by the human eye. But the eye just slides right past a smudgy pattern.

Our solution is to dye everything black, and that does the trick. Black and green come out as dark gray, which seems to blend with every background, and the sharp lines of our camo splotches disappear in the gray nicely. Another big plus, the gray is invisible at night. Black we can plainly see as a silhouette, especially against a light background, but dark gray we cannot. It fades into any background. We used the Coronado Laundromat washers to do our dyeing, and I pity the next person to use them, especially if they washed a load of whites.

Hats? Man, there were every kind, size, and shape. Some wore our camo beret. Some wore hillbilly hats or boonie hats. Dee even tried the wool navy watch cap, but it was way too hot, so that idea died. The problem with any kind of hat is the silhouette. A round head or the sharp outline of a hat stood out plainly against the night sky, and in fact that was how we could "see" other SEALs during night ops. Since gooks were generally a lot shorter than we were, they'd see that silhouette even better than we could. It was one problem we never did solve, so we ended up wearing whatever we favored. I liked a hat to keep rain out of my eyes, but since I sweated easily and copiously, the hat was useless in keeping sweat out of my eyes. A headband, which I liked the most, was excellent for the sweat problem, but useless in rain. Doggone it! What to do? I took both with me.

We all use an H-harness. This is made up of green canvas suspenders hooked to a web belt, with claymore bags sewn on the belts with nylon thread. Most guys also attach the small knapsack in the rear, positioned so it hangs between the shoulder blades, but to accommodate my radio rig, mine has to be dropped down to my ass. We put collapsible plastic quart canteens in the claymore pouch, hang grenades, knives, and other gear from the harness, and use the knapsack for medical supplies, food, flares, shitpaper, and whatever else. This setup makes a nice one-piece rig. When you put on your H-harness, you put on your entire combat outfit, and it is just as easily removed. I find I can do the same. I put on my H-harness, then put on my radio harness over it. This allows the weight of our combat gear to hang on our shoulders, which makes for less fatigue and easier movement. A few of the guys take along the combat "vest" which is kind of a shirt with several pockets and straps, but it appears too bulky and hot and will probably not fit our needs. With the radio, I can't use it.

Now, I've never liked knives, and the idea of getting up close and personal with someone and sticking them with a knife makes me ill. I have to think awhile, but I come up with a good solution. I take a military hatchet, cut off all but six inches of the handle, and drill it for a wrist thong. Then I sharpen that sucker up, giving it a razor edge, and have the canvas carrying case sewn to my web belt. It's Velcro quick-release, it's sharp, it's perfect. I figure I can stand off from someone and give them a good chop in the neck or the head, and drop them in their tracks. No muss, no fuss. If I wanted to, I could even throw it, and no matter how it hit, unlike a knife, it would do some damage. I adopt it, and the "war axe" starts earning me some major verbal abuse, but I just ignore that.

Our issue handgun, the S&W 9mm, is not one of my favorite weapons. In training I had shot a magazineload into a log, and when I walked up to the log, there lay my slugs on the ground. I decide that ain't gonna work. I was good with a handgun, and definitely would carry one, but when I shot the enemy, I wanted to kill him, not piss him off, so I went out and bought my own .44 Magnum revolver. It came with a western quickdraw rig, but I also obtained a belly holster for it. The belly rig is just like a shoulder holster, but the gun lies across your belly instead of hanging under your arm. I didn't much like the idea of my gun pointing at my groin, but again, because of my radio rig, I didn't have a whole lot of choice. I figure if I am ever down to using a handgun, I want to kill with it, rather than make a lot of noise, so the multishot pistols didn't turn me on. I believe I can get it done with six rounds of .44 Magnum, one per gook.*

As radioman, I expected that I'd carry an M-16 with the grenade launcher under the barrel, but again, I wasn't thrilled with that weapon. I wanted to carry at least a .50 cal, but they told me the other patrol members would be doing most of the firefighting with machine guns, and I would only have to do illumination and radio work. Hey, if I feel Froggy, I can always lob out a few HE, so I guess I have to accept it.

I closed out my personal life too. I didn't want to leave any women behind me to mourn if I got killed, and I definitely didn't like the thought of Jody fucking my woman while I was in the Nam, so I dumped my steady in L.A.—it was a lot harder than I thought it would be. I was a fool, I should have hung on and married her, but after what happened later, she wouldn't have had me anyway.

I sold my trusty old Ford, and bought a mint '63 Chevy convertible from Jim Richards. It was a Texas car, and it was fucking beautiful! Someone had stolen the transmission out of it, so I got it cheap. Then I arranged with a local GM dealer to store it and make some changes while I was gone. The '63 was a 300-horse 327 factory optioned, and I wanted a new Muncie transmission, Hurst shifter, and 4:11 rear gears installed, plus a custom paint job. That way, when I came back (if I came back), I would have like a brand-new car waiting for me.

Last of all, I notified my landlord of my leave date. I was ready to go.

---

*What a dummy I was. For pure knockdown power, there is no better handgun than the good old .45 military pistol. With its big and slow slug, you might outrun it, but if it hits you, it will flatten the biggest human or maybe tear off an arm or leg, and he won't be going anywhere at all. Sometimes the old ways are the best ways, as I was to learn later.

Chapter
Thirty-one

FEBRUARY 23, 1969, we arrive in Saigon, and then load onto a couple of six-bys to truck from Saigon to Vinh Long, and then Sa Dec. I draw in a super-heated breath of good old Vietnam air, and smell the unique odors that bring the memories flooding back. It's almost like a homecoming, but not quite. I am no longer a tourist. It's into the bush for me.

I'm wearing my .44 mag quickdraw rig (John Wayne has arrived!) because our long weapons are packed away, and it's fully loaded with six rounds. As we're careening down the road, standing to ease the bumps, *bang!* goes my .44, and it flips out of the holster and lands in the bed of the truck. The .44 slug goes down through the outer rim of my boot heel, through the bed of the truck, and blows out one of the truck tires. As the truck screeches to a halt, everybody's ducking and hollering, my heart is racing, and I feel the complete fool. After a few minutes of discussion, everything gets sorted out. Jim Richards nails me.

"Miller, you dumb motherfucker! You never carry a single-action revolver with a round under the hammer!" (Hey, nobody ever told me . . .)

He swears that as my gun flipped out of its holster, he was looking right down the barrel.

We're quartered on a base on the Sa Dec River, and we don't dick around very long. Our first mission is to get us personal transportation, so we head for the PX in Saigon, and liberate a new jeep. It's got a general's flag on the fender, but we throw that away. It's also got a .45 cal grease gun in the front seat (an M-3, a WW II–era submachine gun), and we keep that; we'll

Class 40 at UDT training in the mud flats, January 1967. The young woman was not part of our class.

"Hit the bay!" Class 40 in February 1967. Ollivera has his back to the camera.

UDT-11, Vung Tau harbor, RVN. That's me going in. Mike Bennett is the dropmaster, and Bob Anderson is prone behind him.

UDT-11, Det Bravo, preparing for a recon at Con Sohn Islands.

SEAL training, March 1968. Me rappelling 100 feet down Otay Dam in California.

Me, in ambush position, during SEAL training at Niland, California, April 1968.

First Squad, Echo Platoon, SEAL Team One, in Sa Dec, RVN, March 1969: (standing, left to right) Tom McDonald, me, D'Angelo, Emerson, and Cochlin; (kneeling) Arch Woodard, Gieng, and McIntosh.

Gil Espinoza and Nguyen Van Toung (LDNN), Sa Dec, March 1969.

Tich and McDonald checking a VC sampan near Sa Dec, March 1969.

Me, Tich, and Jim Richards extracting near Sa Dec, March 1969.

A captured VC (left), me, and Bill Noyce after an op near Sa Dec, March 1969.

First Squad extracting near Sa Dec, April 1969.

Dee, the barely visible Lt. Marsh behind Hyatt, and me. That's 110 pounds on my little body.

Left to right: Slim Wilkins, Lou Hyatt, John Marsh, and Doc Cantalupi at Moc Hoa, May 1969.

Roger Cochlin at the office and prepared to work, Moc Hoa, June 1969.

C'mon VC! Me on an ambush near Tuyen Nhon, July 1969.

Four-day ops? Love 'em! Daytime laager near Tuyen Nhon, July 1969.

Me holding our sawed-off M-60 on an LCPL while we're towing an LSSC (Light SEAL Support Craft) near Vin, August 1969.

August '69 in Cat Lo: (standing, left to right) Larry D'Angelo, Doc Cantalupi, Bill Noyce, and me; (kneeling) Louie McIntosh and Le.

trade it for something good. We alter the jeep's serial number, and presto! Our own wheels.

As soon as we arrived, I got appointed as communications man by Mr. Woodard. I would be typing out patrol reports and other documents and sending them through the communications net. I couldn't have been happier, because now I would be completely in the know.

Our first op is scheduled the second day we are there, is wisely placed in a pacified area, and is led by Lieutenant JG Bliss, whose platoon, Alpha, we are replacing. It's pure orientation, and goes well, although we are all nervous. We patrol a klick or two, search a small ville, and "capture" a woman and two kids for questioning. Then we set a night ambush, and at 2200 we release the prisoners and extract by boat. We learn what a pain in the ass terrified prisoners are, especially noisy women and kids, and also that Mr. Bliss has been there too long—he's overconfident. During our ambush he wanders off then comes strolling back to our line. He was damn lucky we didn't fill him full of lead. With green troops on their first op, wandering around's just asking to get your ass shot off. Second squad went out with Barry Enoch on the same kind of op, and you can bet he didn't make the same mistake. In fact, four or five of us were able to corner Barry and got the real skinny about how to operate. The one thing I remember him telling us was that our biggest enemy would be confusion. Know your job, do it well, and back up your buddies. If you get confused out in the bush, you'll certainly die or, worse yet, get someone else killed. That info was incredibly helpful, because it was the real thing, not out of some book. Barry was a well-known primo operator. He'd given us some of our early SEAL training.

Next we do a platoon-size patrol and ambush. That thing just didn't work at all. None of us liked it, because it was just too many guys getting in each other's way. We were fourteen of Echo platoon, three LDNN (Vietnamese SEALs) scouts, Mr. Bliss, and Enoch. It was awkward, noisy, and patrol communication was lousy. Good thing it was an orientation and we didn't run into any action, because some of us would certainly have shot each other. I know one thing, it sure convinced us that squad-size ops were the only way to go.

March 1, 1969, First Squad (mine) is going on our first real operation. We're going to accompany an ARVN (Army of the Republic of Vietnam) company while they sweep an area so we can observe how regular Vietnamese troops do their thing.

What a joke that turns out to be! We reach the ARVN base at 0730, and just before they move out, ARVN fires a mortar round. Holy jumpin' Jesus! As we climb out of the holes we have instantaneously burrowed in the ground, we are appalled to find out that this is coexistence in South Vietnam: the ARVN *warn* the VC with a mortar round when they're coming out on patrol so that the VC can clear out for the day, and that way everybody's happy. Except us.

Well, we may be green, but we're not fools—we let the ARVNs move out and we follow in their rear. And we shake our heads in disbelief. Marvin the ARVN, when he's on patrol, strolls along, rifle on his shoulder, spitting, coughing, laughing, and talking a mile a minute. It's literally like a Sunday walk with guns, and we can hardly bear it; it's a complete waste of time. I mean, we're green as grass, and we're following the methods we've been taught religiously, and here are these clowns acting like they're in downtown Saigon. We lose all respect for them immediately, and no way in the world are we tempted to follow their example. Naturally we don't see anything, but it's a learning experience—ARVN is useless.

Then on March 4, 1969, First Squad gets a mission warning. A mission warning is simply this: the squad is notified that they will be going out on an op and is given a time to meet for a mission briefing.

At 1300, we all meet for the mission briefing, and this is what we hear: We will accompany ARVN on another daylight sweep (yow!) but this time, when ARVN leaves we'll stay behind and hide to set up a night recon/ambush, and hopefully catch Charlie filtering back into the area. The Iron Triangle, where we'll be going, is a VC haven, so if we get lucky we should see some action.

Our patrol will be made up of seven SEALs and one LDNN

scout. LDNN scouts are South Vietnamese noncoms, the equivalent of UDT. They are also damn nice guys and good operators as we find out later while working with them. They're not anything like ARVN.

1. Jim Richards is our point scout. He will carry a Stoner with 150-round drum, two 150-round bandoliers, handcuffs, two hand grenades, one pop-up flare, and in case we find tunnels (none of us wants to play tunnel rat, and thank God I am too big for it), one gas grenade.
2. LDNN Gieng will follow Richards. He will carry an M-16 with 100 rounds of ammo, two hand grenades, one CS gas grenade, and one claymore.
3. Following Gieng, Mr. Woodard is patrol leader. He will carry an M-16, 100 rounds of ammo, two grenades, two pop flares, map, compass, and Starlight scope (night sight).
4. I follow the patrol leader as radioman. I carry the PRC 77 radio, M-16 with XM-148 grenade launcher, seventy-five rounds of M-16 ammo and fifteen launcher grenades—three flechette rounds, six high-explosive rounds, four illumination rounds, one CS round, and one willy peter round. I also carry a hooded strobe light with blue lens, and two hand grenades.
5. Then comes Dee (Larry D'Angelo). He carries the M-60 with 150-round pouch, two 150-round bandoliers, and two grenades.
6. Louie McIntosh is next, carrying a Stoner with 150-round drum, two 150-round bandoliers, two grenades, one LAAW, and one claymore.
7. Number seven is Lou Hyatt. He's carrying a Stoner with 450 rounds, four grenades, and one claymore.
8. Rear guard is Roger Cochlin. He carries a Stoner with 450 rounds, four grenades, and one claymore.

Our mission will be to patrol with ARVN, drop off and recon patrol to a likely site, and set up a night recon/ambush. If there is no enemy contact, we break ambush the next morning, patrol back to the extraction point, and extract, using PBRs (Patrol

Boat, River). Fire support is Marine artillery—call sign Tiger 87, and two Cobra helicopter gunships, call sign Red Dog 5. Our call sign is Threadbare One, home base is Whirltop. Then we are given general compass headings in and out with alternatives for escape and evasion (E & E), and rally points. We also hear a terrain description and a description of potential danger points. After all the questions are answered, the briefing concludes.

Now we'll do our individual preparation. We lay out clothing, weapons, ammo, and supplies. Everything is packed or loaded on our carrying rigs and checked for noise, then weapons and other items are loaded and checked for proper function. I load a fresh radio battery and do a communications check. Each man lays or hangs his equipment and weapons next to his rack in preparation, and no one else may touch them for any reason. We are now ready to go.

Next morning we awake, dress, eat breakfast, apply camo face paint, and don our patrol gear. The patrol leader makes a final visual check to make sure everyone's prepared, and then we load onto our boats. At 0800 we arrive at the ARVN base, 0900 ARVN fires his mortar round, and 0905 we move out, safeties off, SEALs to the rear.

The day's sweep is uneventful until around noon, when we hear a burst of fire from the front, and the ARVN column stops and drops. Mr. Woodard and I (the radioman is always the patrol leader's shadow) walk up to the front of the column to see what's going on. Suddenly I hear *snap! snap!* right by my head, and I drop and play Mr. Woodchuck, burrowing about three feet down in about as many seconds. I may be green, but I ain't no dummy, and I know bullets when I hear them. I also know that when you can hear the snap of the slugs, they are too goddamn close! I won't ever again forget that I am carrying a big bull's-eye on my body—the radio and its antenna.

Well, I'm ready to cancel, but I get up anyway, shake the shit out of my pantslegs, and follow Mr. Woodard to the head of the column, where the ARVN's Green Beret adviser fills us in as sporadic firing continues. Seems ARVN has accidentally walked up on some stray VC, the VC have killed the two point scouts, taken their weapons, and forted up across a stream. For some reason, the VC have set up and refuse to move, which he says is unusual. They must not have gotten the word, and he figures they might be protecting someone or something ahead of us.

Well, I'm listening, but I'm also eyeing the two ARVN bodies lying there. A third ARVN is sitting nearby getting treated for a round in the leg. It's my first combat dead person, and I'm feeling very strange. I want to appear cool, but a macabre fascination keeps drawing my eyes to the bodies. The dead guys' eyes are open, but there's no life in them, and that throws me. I'm too used to neat and clean TV and movie deaths, I guess.

At Mr. Woodard's direction, I get on the horn and call in artillery on the VC, and walk it around and across their position. Amazingly, it works, and I don't blow us up. Hah! As soon as the artillery stops, the VC resume firing. Arty don't even seem to bother them. The Cobra gunships are in the air, so I direct them on a firing run. The gunships have a LOH with them (light observation helicopter, pronounced *loach;* it looks like a big dragonfly) and he reports that six armed women have run into the tree-line and disappeared. Women? Are you shitting me? I tell Mr. Woodard.

The Green Beret speaks up. "That explains it. Dumbass women don't realize that Charlie is supposed to hit and run. They're too stupid to know any better."

Well now. I already knew that we didn't want to run into any NVA, but I hadn't considered women dangerous. In fact I hadn't considered them at all, except for the usual purpose. I quickly added women to the dangerous list, but it would take some getting used to, after being raised so many years to protect them. It will probably be okay, though, as long as I don't recognize them while I am aiming.

The Green Beret continued, "They're good fighters. And they don't know how to back up." Hmm . . . Makes you think, doesn't it?

I cast a quick look at the other guys' faces, and they're stark and strained, fully concentrating. They are just as wired as I am.

Things get even more tense for us when we start finding trip traps. They are all around us, four on one side, two on the other, and Rich on point is leading us in doglegs, zeeing back and forth in between them. I see Mr. Woodard halt and point down, and I either step around or carefully over the brown trip wires, then I do the same for Dee, and he shows the next guy. I catch myself bobbing my head like a cork, trying to scan my surroundings and at the same time watch my path cautiously for trip wires and punji pits. I've got to figure we're coming up on something important for certain, and Charlie's got it well protected. I drop to one knee during a pause while Rich is searching a way through the belt of booby traps, and when I scan around me, I almost shit. First, I see the almost invisible trip wire, then I follow it to its source four feet away, and it is a mortar round. It looks to be an 82mm Russian, and it's wired a foot off the ground to a stake and partially covered with grass fronds. *Yowza!* Mr. Patrol Leader, I think we should go right back the way we came; I ain't Flak Body. But Mr. Woodard moves out, so I follow.

The heart was out of the ARVN, and a couple hours later they packed it in and headed back. We SEALs get our shit together, form up, get our intervals, and start doing some serious recon patrolling. Time to earn our pay. There's fresh VC sign all over, well-beaten trails and the like, and we stay very alert. I keep the big scan going; I'm as nervous as a first-time father. I expect any second that I will see Charlie jump up and sight on the middle of my chest, but my imagination is running wild and I'm really afraid that I won't see him, I will only feel his bullet hit me. My mouth is dry, my palms are sweaty, and my breath is coming short. Jesus, I hate feeling like this. As I wipe my wet hands on my pants, I realize I'm waiting for something to happen, anything at all, to end the intense suspense.

The terrain is tiny grass fields and low swampy spots bordered with treelines. It's probably an old French plantation. There are many well-defined trails, and we find two empty base camps, small ones. Then we come in sight of a real oddity, a small one-story concrete hootch sitting in the U of a tiny stream. VC sign is heavy and fresh, so we decide to set up here, a ways from the hootch, and see what happens. It's only 1630, but the sign is so heavy and the site so good that we decide it would be foolish to pass it up.

We set up a U-shaped ambush conforming to the stream, but once we get down on the ground in position, we find out that visibility is not good, because there's an awful lot of heavy underbrush. The stuff is easy to hide in, but it's thick to the point where we can't see what we're doing. Our lines of sight are limited to spaces and corridors through the brush. Worse, most patrol members are out of sight of each other, especially the flanks and rear guard. I can only see Dee on my right and Lou on my left, and the fuckers have forced me to sit in a wet spot, in about ten inches of water. I grit my teeth and cuss silently as Lou grins at me. Although the rest of the patrol members are no more than ten or twelve feet away from me, I can't see them, and I'm not real comfortable with that.

Because I'm new at this, I simply sit down with all my gear on and freeze in position. Immediately I discover all kinds of bumps, lumps, and sharp corners digging into my body. We'd prechecked our rigs for noise and function, but none of us had thought to check for comfort. Another lesson learned. With nothing to lean back against, the weight of my gear is pulling me over backward, and it sure feels weird to be sitting in water to my belt line. I suffer it in silence, because it's too late now to move around.

We aren't there and set up more than twenty minutes before there's a short Stoner burst from the right flank of our ambush, where Richards and Mr. Woodard are. Instantly our adrenaline and weapons are up and we're looking hard, wired because we don't know what's happening. Then the word comes whispering from man to man. Two armed VC walked right up on the right flank, and Richards had no choice but to drop them. We're to stay put and stay quiet. Stay quiet? You bet your ass! I shrink down in my puddle wishing it was three feet deeper.

About thirty minutes later word comes around that we're to move. We'll cross the stream and set up near the concrete hootch. The stream is only eight feet wide and neck-deep, but heavy as I am I have some struggle to get across. Dee said all he could see was the radio antenna and bubbles moving across the stream. Sure. Laugh if you will, but already I am completely soaked and muddy. I'm not looking forward to the next several hours.

We set up a line ambush on the right side of the hootch, and Cochlin and I are the left flank. I'm butted against the hootch wall, but at least I'm on dry ground. I remove my radio rig and lie on my stomach, because I've got no cover to hide behind.

We soon realize we've hit the jackpot, because Roger and I spot a VC walking a trail right toward us; he's obviously heading for the hootch. The guy is carrying a U.S. M-1 .30 cal carbine, has a small field pack, and is wearing blue shorts and shirt. He's real skinny, and brown as a nut, with a mop of straight black hair. So that's Charlie. Say your prayers, asshole.

The dude appears to be totally unconcerned, but I'm not. My pulse is racing, my mouth is bone-dry, and my intensity is so high that my hands are trembling and I'm breathing like a race-horse. This is the real thing, and that's the real enemy! From my low vantage point on my belly, he looks like a giant.

Roger is Mr. Pro, so he lets the VC walk right up close (Jesus H. Christ, I'm thinking, Rocky, will you shoot already!) before he gives him a Stoner burst in the chest. The VC drops right in his tracks, but then I get even more nervous, because we can no longer see him, and that I don't like at all. While I stay ready for the VC to jump up and kill me, Roger passes word of the contact to the rest of the patrol.

The seconds stretch out, and after about five minutes to let things cool down, Roger and I ease carefully out toward the VC to check him. Yup. There he is, deader than a mackerel, with five bullet holes in his chest. But those fucking M-16 rounds! The dude has not only crawled about twelve feet from where he dropped, and left blood smeared all over the ground, but he's also somehow hidden his weapon and gear. There's nothing on him at all. Shit. How can that be? We search around quick, but can't find a thing, so we *di di mau* back to our ambush positions, cursing all the way. Goddamn it, I had wanted that carbine, and was prepared to go hand to hand with Rocky for it.

I keep the big scan going, nobody is gonna walk up close to

me, and soon I notice a danger point. There is a ditch on the far side of the hootch, and it makes me nervous. Charlie could come sneaking up it, get behind me, and shoot me right in the ass. I can't have that, so when I can't stand it anymore, I tell Roger about it. He says, "So what?" So what? Is he nuts? "I'm gonna set up inside the hootch, and cover that ditch," I tell him.

"Okay," he says. I go through the open doorway.

Excellent. It's clean, empty, and dry inside, with only the one door opening, plus an empty opening overlooking the ditch. The hootch has a firepit in the center of the dirt floor, cool to my searching fingers. The other two walls are solid. The hootch has good cover and observation, and it's just what the doctor ordered. I look out the "window" to see that the ditch is about four feet deep, and I can see about forty feet of it before it bends, looks like an old streambed. I drop to one knee and set up to wait and watch. I put a hand grenade and an extra M-16 mag on the windowsill, my launcher is loaded with a flechette round, my radio rig is parked next to my feet, and by God, I'm ready! I think. I wipe my wet palms on my thighs, and suddenly I've got to take a ferocious shit. I do my best to ignore it.

Thank you, God! I spot movement in the ditch. Three VC are sneaking down it, their weapons are up, they're alert, and they're looking and listening. They also look confident. I ain't ready for this, and the sweat is pouring off me, my pits and crotch are soaked. Jesus! I want to tell somebody, anybody, but I don't dare take my eyes off the VC for one second. I ease to my feet and bring my M-16 up, but I've got no confidence in it against three of them, so I lean it against the sill, grab my grenade, pull the pin, and lob that sucker through the window opening toward the VC. Take that, motherfuckers!

Except the grenade hits a tree and bounces back against the wall of the hootch. Oh shit. I quickly turn my back and open my mouth wide, and *baroom!* The son of a bitch goes off so close I can feel the concussion, and shrapnel peppers my back. (Or maybe concrete chips?) I grab my M-16 and aim out the window, but all I see is one back disappearing as the VC beat feet out of there. I'm so excited I yank the trigger, but all I get is three rounds and a *click.* Shit. A misfire. But I am one deadly motherfucker, and I see the VC go down and kick around like a chicken with his head cut off. Oh boy, I got him.

Damn it! He's still dangerous! I eject and try again, *click*— misfire. Fuck me! The VC has stopped moving though, so I pause, and only then do I remember my flechette round in the tube. I am ready to let him have it when I hear the low calls, "What's happening? What the hell is going on?" I slide out the door right into the muzzle of Roger's Stoner. I push it aside and give him the word, and he passes it on. I go back inside to clean out my pants and keep an eye on the supposedly dead VC. I told Rocky I don't dare go near him, because I figure the other two are sitting there aiming, waiting for me to do just that.

We wait a while, eventually it's dusk, and I reluctantly exchange my flechette round for an illumination. Just about then I hear a grenade blow, along with a quick burst of fire. Immediately after, we get the word, we're moving out to extract. I breathe a sigh of relief, because I've really been sweating it. As we patrol to the extraction point, we are monitored by the VC—we can occasionally spot them quite a distance away, paralleling our line of march, and that makes us nervous. We're all carrying the same thought, let's get the fuck out of here and live to fight another day!

When we get close, I call in the boats, and we extract without incident. We're all pretty high, since we're blooded now, and still alive. We talk our asses off all the way back to the barge, because the adrenaline is still flowing. When we arrive, we immediately go to debrief, and each of us relates his piece of the action, and we find out just how much we didn't know about what had happened. Here's the complete story.

1. Shortly after we set up ambush, Richards and Woodard observed two armed VC approaching the right flank, walking right toward them, so Richards had to drop both with his Stoner. One crawled away, leaving a heavy blood trail, but he didn't go very far. Rich recovered two M-1 carbines and a field pack. Result: two VC KIA.

2. A short time later, voices were heard quite a distance from the ambush, and since we were no longer in recon mode,

the patrol leader decided to move the formation toward them, so we crossed the stream and reset the ambush.

3. Miller and Cochlin on left flank observe one armed VC approach, and Cochlin drops him. Result: one VC KIA.

4. (And I hadn't known anything about this!) Voices are heard out in front, and objects are thrown at our formation to draw fire.

5. Miller observes three armed VC approach rear of the hootch, takes under fire, but weapon jams. Result: one VC KIA.

6. Four armed VC approach front, ambush initiates fire, weapons jam, results unknown.

7. Decision made by patrol leader to extract.

7a. Miller kicks his own ass for stupidity in action. I didn't reveal the fact that my own grenade had bounced back on me through carelessness because I felt that I had made a poor showing and hadn't done my job. John Wayne was frowning on me.

Well, we were damn lucky. We'd made many mistakes yet none of us had been injured. We'd have to improve, and improve immediately. We spent a good portion of the debrief discussing our mistakes and changes we would make to prevent them from happening again.

Dropping off a daylight sweep and setting up the ambush—that worked real well, no problem there. At our first ambush site, though, we'd been out of sight of each other and out of communication. That was totally unacceptable, and in future, conditions permitting, we wouldn't allow that to happen again.

Another problem was the radio placement. All agreed that the radio should be centered in the ambush, not on the flank as I had been. The radio was our only link to outside help, and should not be exposed. (I agree, I agree!) And ditto the placement of the patrol leader. Most of us felt he should also be centered, to maintain control, although the point was made that as well trained as we were, anyone could step up in times of emergency. But who wanted to?

Independent movement after the ambush was set up (Emerson to me: "Miller, you dumb fuck!") was out from now on.

Turns out nobody knew I had moved into the hootch except Roger. My reasons for doing so were accepted, but the word should have been passed to the rest of the patrol members. It was a valid point—my own SEALs could have shot me.

Finally, our biggest fuckup—claymores. For a variety of reasons, none acceptable, only one claymore had been set up, and it hadn't even been fired. I especially had had the perfect use for one (I should have used Rocky's) in the ditch behind the hootch. Ambush center and rear guard had not set theirs up because the terrain was flat, they were afraid of the backblast. The right flank had set up their claymore, but it was angled wrong and did not cover their eventual contact, so it wasn't fired. It was a very poor showing for us.

Well, we talked it to death, but finally the debrief ended, and we headed for the showers. (The line to clean pants out forms to the right.) In the showers, minus our weapons, we step under the spray, wash, and strip off our gear, then our wears. Finally we wash our bodies, go get a good meal, and then sleep, sleep, sleep. Physically the op had been an easy one, but we were all amazed at how much the mental strain took out of us. We slept like dead men.

Next day we cleaned and oiled our weapons, and I got to check out my M-16. Damn. A broken firing pin. What a piece of shit. Well, as far as I'm concerned, that's all she wrote. I pack the useless weapon in the back of the weapons locker, never to be used again. I replace it with a thumper (M-79). I want a real weapon from now on.

Meanwhile, I am doing some heavy contemplating about my first combat. My first feeling was one of incredible relief and pride. I hadn't frozen up or disgraced myself in front of the guys, I hadn't peed my pants. I can't tell you how good that made me feel. But my next feeling was one of disappointment. If only I had been more on the ball. I should have gotten all three VC in the ditch. If only I hadn't been so excited and flustered. I wasn't proud of that. Finally, I went through all the "what ifs." What if I hadn't gone into the hootch? What if I had opened up with the M-16 or the flechette round instead of the grenade? What if the VC hadn't run, but had opened up on me? What if I had had to dodge enemy grenades? What if my own grenade had blown me up? What if I had cowarded out? Yow! I had to cut off the what ifs. But one thing is certain. I've learned from the experience, and I'm gonna do it differently next time.

So, you've done a mission with us, what's your opinion? I don't really wanna hear it! This one's over except for the follow-up. It was later determined that we'd stumbled on a VC rallying point, the concrete hootch. Our mission info was a very important addition to local intelligence, and was used to mount several ops by conventional forces. The PRUs later had several contacts in there, and ended up killing quite a few VC.

Numbers? Not so good. Three VC KIA by body count, and one VC KIA probable, but we should have gotten them all. No friendly casualties though, and that was always excellent news. (I can too add! The VC I'd shot in the ditch had to be reported as a "Probable," because I hadn't checked him. You never know, he might have been playing possum.)

Chapter
Thirty-two

WE'D BEEN BLOODED, and gained valuable experience at no cost to us (except to our pride) and now we settled in to do our job. We ran fourteen ops in March, one every other night, and provided a good amount of intell about our area of operations (AO). We refused to conduct any further ops with ARVN, but we did start working with the PRUs (Provincial Reconnaissance Units), and they weren't bad. They were somewhat like us, and if they weren't gung ho like we were, at least they were serious about getting the job done. The main accomplishment that we made during this period was to establish our comfort level, and that's more key than you might imagine. As highly trained but still green troops, we did it all by the numbers, but we were not comfortable yet, so we were at all times really wired and tensed up. That ate up an incredible amount of energy, mentally and physically, and it hurt us. Once we gained some OJT, we became far more comfortable and relaxed in the bush; I mean, we still did it all, but we were loose and confident. We didn't use all our energy so we had plenty of reserve at all times, in case the shit hit the fan. Our effectiveness and potential had increased hugely.

March 8, 1969, found First Squad with a different kind of mission, going after a specific target. A VC sapper squad, approximately seven in number, was based at Rach Vam Hang village, near the river, and was operating against nearby U.S. installations, rocketing and mortaring and sniping. Our mission: go in after them and take them out. We would be operating under Giao Duc PRU intell, which was usually excellent.

The briefing held no surprises for us, but as always, we listened attentively. The terrain, details picked up during a chopper flyover by Mr. Woodard, was familiar, swampy low ground and mangrove swamp with heavy brush cover and the occasional small clearing, broken by many shitditches, canals, and streams. Contact here with Charlie would be very close range, usually one to ten meters, and the action would be fast and furious. As always, our basic mission would apply: sneak in undetected, do our thing, then get back out.

We were supplied with every scrap of information that PRU had about the enemy, and basically what we wanted to do was insert off the river south of the ville, patrol inland in an arc about a klick, and come up on the ville from behind. Our aircover, two Navy Seawolf choppers, were call sign Seawolf 52 and 56, PBR was Blue Mike, Marine support artillery was Thunder 17, First Squad was Threadbare One, and home plate was Whirltop. I memorized Thunder 17, but the others were as familiar to me as my own name. Then we were assigned our minimum equipment load, which most of us would add to, according to our personal preference, especially ammunition. Lou Hyatt had been working with Second Squad lately, and wouldn't be going out with us, so we were six SEALs and one VN scout, Tich.

At 1500 we were geared up and ready to go, applying face paint and being inspected by the patrol leader, Mr. Woodard, for final readiness. At 1510 we loaded on the PBR for the forty-minute trip to insertion, sucking down our cigarettes on the way, because we knew they would be our last until tomorrow morning. At 1550 we stubbed out the last butts, loaded and shifted in our gear for one last check for comfort, popped a Dexamil pill to help stay awake later, then lined up along the front of the PBR. The steady roar of the PBR engines dropped as it came off plane to maneuvering speed, then dropped again to idle as the boat cut a hard right turn and nosed into the bank. We hit with a mushy thump, and instantly we were over the side, moving quickly to the riverbank. As usual, I had speared into water and mud to my chin, but because I had held on to the boat with one hand, I was able to pull myself forward until I could grab some bushes on the bank, and pull myself up and on. Vaguely aware of the PBR backing away behind me, I quickly formed up with the others, and as Rich and Tich moved out, I followed the patrol leader, giving a silent sigh of relief. Insertion always scared me the most.

The patrol was a nightmare for me. We crossed several shit-ditches and small streams, and every one was a struggle because of the weight I was carrying. The mud and the water quickly sucked the strength from my body, and I had to call on my reserves to keep up. Finally, after almost a klick of silent patrolling without contact of any kind, we approached the target ville in the gathering darkness. After crossing a final particularly nasty shitditch, I lay on the "dry" ground blowing like a whale while Rich checked out the area. Rocky is grinning at me, enjoying my discomfort. In the dim light I can see white teeth against his dark face paint, so I recover as quickly as I can, knowing I'm gonna hear all about it tomorrow. The guys all get a big kick out of my struggles to carry my gear, and I'm always getting a lot of flak, but I sure don't see no hands raised to help carry some of my stuff. You'd think my radio was a rattlesnake, the way they avoided going anywhere near the idea of carrying it. According to them I am the expert, and it would be wasteful for anyone else to give me the occasional relief. Sure. I believe 'em. I sit up to look around, and exchange my flechette round for a flare.

Rich came back and had a whispered conversation with Mr. Woodard, and we moved closer to the ville, maybe fifty meters out. We're just off a hardbeaten trail which leads from the ville, about five meters away, and at Mr. Woodard's sign, we move to ambush positions. Because we are so close to the ville and may have to pick up and run fast, I leave all my gear on. I clear an observation path through the small bushes in front of me, kick up some of the loose wet dirt into a mound, then carefully sit, resting my radio on the mound. Not quite right, and I roll over and add material to the pile. This time when I sit back, the radio rests comfortably on the mound, relieving the weight on my shoulders that had been pulling me over backward. I suck a deep draft from my canteen, lay out a flechette round and another flare round, squirm in my gear until I am comfortable, check my thumper barrel for mud and obstructions, then lay it across my legs and freeze in position. I know that Rich and Rocky are setting claymores out on each end of the linear ambush line, and I rouse momentarily to receive the signal line from Mr. Woodard and pass the loose end on to Dee, then I go still again. Now, with all senses on the alert, I become aware of movement in the ville. I can see the silhouettes of people passing in front of the hootch lights, and I am close enough to hear Vietnamese being spoken. I can't see clearly everything that's going on, but that's not a problem, it's not my job. There's some activity at the river's edge, and I can't quite make it out, but in the vague blackness I can see Mr. Woodard using the Starlight scope. He'll know what's happening, and record it in his brain to feed back to PRU at the debrief.

We've been set up maybe a couple of hours, and I've been hearing voices all around us, especially in or near the ville, when all of a sudden I hear voices close by, and the signal line jerks once, hard. I'm thinking it sounds like women to me when a body momentarily blots out the light in front of me, and then another and another, scaring the crap right out of me. My adrenaline fires and my thumper comes up to firing position, but Mr. Woodard doesn't initiate, and I hang there stuck in tense mode while the voices fade. I don't like this at all, but I remain motionless and then come down a bit as the seconds pass. Why hadn't we blasted them? I won't know what's going on until tomorrow, and that really grits my teeth.

Several hours go by and the ville has long since quieted down. So have I, although I plan to bitch at tomorrow's debrief. I am just about to ease a slow look at my Rolex when in the stillness I hear a scuffle and a couple of thumps. What is going on? That's the worst thing about night ops. Unless you're told, you have no idea what's happening around you, and you just sit there dreaming up your own scenarios, and believe me, they are never rosy. Silence descends again, and then the signal line from Mr. Woodard jerks four distinct times. Now this is more like it. I give Dee four jerks, then position my thumper between my legs pointed almost straight up. My mouth has gone dry, my heart is racing with intensity, and I've got to pee. Here we go. All at the same instant a body crosses silently in front of me, a second, and then Mr. Woodard's M-16 chatters, followed by the sustained roar of machine guns. I have pulled my trigger and the flare goes skyward. In one continuous practiced motion, I immediately break the thumper, load in a flechette round, close and fire it low in my kill zone, then load and fire a second flare.

Night has turned to day, and as my eyes partially adjust, I can see a body out on the trail in front of me, and it ain't moving. I've already loaded a third flare round, but I wait nervously up on one knee, as I sense more than see Rich and Rocky checking out the bodies on the trail, then as pure blackness comes back to my blinded eyes, Mr. Woodard grabs my arm and we are up and moving quickly away. I make sure Dee is following. I hear shots behind us, but they are already distant. We are long gone.

The patrol back was no easier on me, but now I am fueled by "going-home" juices. I stay up close to Mr. Woodard's back until my night vision comes back to me, then I open my interval. Eventually, sooner than I expected, I almost climb up that back as it halts, and Dee walks up on my heels. Mr. Woodard turns and grabs my arm, then whispers in my ear, "Boats." I get on the horn.

"Whirltop, Whirltop, Threadbare One. Over," I say low into the mouthpiece, cupping my other hand around my mouth.

The reply is instantaneous. "Threadbare One, Whirltop. Over."

"Whirltop, Threadbare, contact. Extract scramble three. Over."

"Threadbare, Whirltop. Understand extract scramble three. Over."

"Roger. Threadbare out."

What I had told Whirltop was that we'd had contact with Charlie, had completed our mission, and the "scramble three" alerted them that we were away clean and not under fire. That meant come get us at normal speed, we were ready to come out. The Seawolves would remain on the ground unless called for. Scramble four would have signified a target of opportunity for the Seawolves, PBR to follow and pull us. Scramble two would have told them we were under fire or about to be, but holding our own. Speed it up and bring the Seawolves for air cover. Scramble one meant come get us immediately, we were in desperate straits, and needed them badly if we were to survive. Drop what you're doing and hit it immediately if not sooner. It was an agreed-upon method of using boat and air support efficiently.

We arrived at the extraction point and waited only a few minutes in circular security formation until we heard the welcome roar of the PBR. I was on the edge of the riverbank and had the handset pressed to my ear.

"Threadbare One, this is Blue Mike. Say status. Over."

"Blue Mike, Threadbare. Clean and quiet. Over."

"Roger. Stand by."

I clicked on my blue strobe light and pointed it at the noise of the boat, and when it nosed into the bank, we quickly scrambled on board. Somebody grabbed my gear and pulled me up and in even as the boat was backing out, then I rolled helplessly and banged into somebody's legs as the PBR reversed and jumped out at full throttle.

"Fuck you, man," I reply drolly to Rich's "Watch it, Miller, you clumsy oaf!"

Within seconds we were planing out of there at high speed.

We stripped off our harnesses with relief and lit the first of several cigarettes during the trip home. We talked it up while the adrenaline subsided and we slipped back into normal mode. I find out that Rich has captured a prisoner, a dude. Good going, Rich. It had been a good op, clean and smooth.

Once back at the base, first we laughed loud and long at Rich's prisoner. It was a kid, about ten years old, and we asked Rich if he'd had much trouble subduing him, then we abused Rich for molesting him. Dee accuses Rich of not capturing a woman, because she would have kicked his ass. Rich replies to us, and the air turns blue. All this while we are unloading our weapons before we walk into the showers to wash our gear, our wears, and then our bodies. But we waste no time, and soon we are slumbering like babies in our racks.

Later that day is the debrief, and it's short and sweet, the kind we like. The op had gone like clockwork, except that we'd killed only four VC, and by the gear they were carrying, they were all regular foot soldiers. We'd recovered one M-16 and three M-1 carbines, along with three field packs. Were they the sappers? Doubtful, but we'd probably never know. It really didn't matter. We'd served notice on Charlie that he was no longer safe to operate out of that ville. And as I'd suspected, the women who had walked through our ambush had been a complete surprise. They appeared out of nowhere, and since none were armed and one was carrying a baby, Mr. Woodard had made an immediate decision not to open up on them. Good thing, because none of us liked the idea of shooting up women, much less a baby.

Men? Hell, we'd shoot them front, rear, or sideways, but most preferably, right in the back. Are you grimacing and saying, "That's not fair?" If you are, I've got to tell you, "fair" doesn't exist in war. No way in the world we're going to meet Charlie at high noon in the middle of the street for a "fair draw." Nope. A dead Charlie was a nondangerous Charlie, one who could no longer put a hole in you. That's the only kind we wanted to see. We may give women mercy if they aren't warriors, but no way we're gonna shoot kids, all of us agreed on that. (It's interesting that on this particular op, the kid that

Richards captured was running point element for the VC we'd ambushed. The kid [willing or not] was lucky that Rich "John Wayne'd" him, otherwise we would have mowed him down like any other VC.)

A week later we got further word from PRU intell. Nope. We hadn't been lucky enough to zap the sappers, we'd greased some of their security forces. Regardless, Charlie was gone from the ville. No way he wanted to face an enemy with the kind of skill and firepower we had displayed.

IV Corps turned out to be ideally suited for SEAL ops. It was 90 percent water and mud, which was home territory to us. The enemy population was scattered, with very few major concentrations of enemy troops. Our foe would be contacted in groups of one to twenty-five, all VC, with an occasional NVA adviser or political officer, and we firmly believed that we could easily handle that many. The enemy moved or rallied only at night to avoid being spotted by our aircraft, and to exploit that movement, so did we.

We'd insert and move to our objective just before dark, and if we didn't have any contact, we'd move out and extract at first light the next morning. Occasionally we'd run a two- or three-day op, and during the daylight hours we'd laager (lay up) in thick cover. It all worked very well for us because of the terrain.

The area was made up of small fields or paddies, broken or bordered by treelines and areas of heavy brush cover. All of this was crisscrossed by a million small streams, canals and ditches. And let me be very clear on waterways, from shitditches to streams. SEAL patrols, especially at night, moved on a direct compass course. That meant that you had to traverse the terrain in a straight line, taking whatever came your way, unless you ran into a booby-trapped area that you had to work around or through. And if you ran into a ditch with three feet of mud in it covered by two inches of nasty water, or a stream that was seven feet deep and filled with man-eating manachitas, that was tough. You couldn't stop and search for a fording spot or any kind of bridge. You crossed where you hit it, and it was, "Get your dumb ass in gear and get across that sucker." Oh, very, very rarely, we'd run into a monkey bridge, which was simply a bamboo log laid from bank to bank, but they were built for 90-pound Viets, not 200-pound "running imperialist dogs," and I couldn't use them. Richards and some of the others could, and that pissed me right off as I struggled through the muck.

But back to terrain: It was flat and wet, with many, many bomb craters filled with water. But it was not quite pure swamp; there were lots of villes and hootches. All travel was done by trails and waterways, which provided perfect setups for our recon/ambushes. Unfortunately, since we almost never walked trails (to avoid leaving signs of our passage and to avoid booby traps and ambushes), we became intimately acquainted with mud. It got to the point where if I didn't have mud all over me, I didn't feel right. I weighed 180 pounds, my combat gear was another 100, and I usually had another twenty pounds of mud glued to me. Eventually, when I'd start out on patrol clean and dry, I'd jump in the first mudhole and wallow around a bit, just to get it over with. Then I'd feel normal.

And where the other guys could cross a ditch without problem, I would immediately sink waist- or chest-deep. More times than I like to think about, I became completely mired, and had to be hauled out by the others, who still wouldn't volunteer to relieve me of any of the gear that I carried or give me the three or four extra inches of leg length that I needed to make up the difference. I needed four-wheel drive, or maybe just water-wings.

Crossing streams was also a problem for me. If the water was waist-deep to the others, it would lap my chin. If chest-deep to the others, I was under, fighting to keep from drowning. I had to carry our collapsible life vest at all times, and since I couldn't wear it on my chest and blow it up under my radio/combat harness, I kept it folded in my claymore pouch. At a deep water crossing, I'd blow it up and hold it in one hand before I stepped into the water. I'd take a deep breath, and as the water closed over my head, I'd lean forward and walk as many steps as I could on the stream bottom before I ran out of air. Then, by pulling down on the life vest and lunging upward, I could break surface with my face and grab another big gulp of air before I sank back to the bottom to start walking again. Very tricky at times, but I'm here to tell you that it worked. They didn't call me Submarine Dude for nothing. Now that I think about it, maybe I should have tried a snorkel.

The area intelligence net feeding us was pretty good, and of course we contributed a lot to it. We ran squad ops every other night, and used our boats for insertion and extraction. We used PBRs mostly, because our LSSC (Light SEAL Support Craft) didn't fulfill its promise. The LSSC was a small, very low-silhouette boat, designed specifically for SEAL use. With water-jet propulsion instead of an exposed propeller, and only about ten inches of draft, that baby could go up the shallowest stream, as long as we remembered to allow enough room to turn it around. The official rated speed was thirty knots, but when we brought that sucker up on plane, it went a whole lot faster than that. The radar dome was the highest spot on the boat, and that was only four feet above water level. It had four fixed M-60s for firepower, and the boat was driven by two silenced Ford 406 cube V8 engines. But that was the problem, as far as I was concerned—Ford. Those engines rarely ran, the damn things would die at the most inappropriate times, and we'd have to be towed. Now if they had been Chevys . . .

In fact, in my mind, our most dangerous times were on the boats. The VC loved to ambush boats on the waterways, and in a boat (especially dead ones) we were sitting ducks. The worst time was the moment of insertion.

I'd be sitting or lying on the deck, all geared up and face painted, weapon off safe and scared to death. The boat is idled back and slowly and quietly gliding in to the bank, and we are at our most vulnerable. I just know there's a grinning VC sitting there with his sights centered on the middle of my chest. Each time after we slide quietly off the boat into the water and ease to the bank where we crawl ashore and rally, I breathe a big sigh of relief—I've made it one more time. And if the water was too shallow and we had to wade any distance to the shore, that was much worse, because we were exposed longer. I sure wished I was Jesus, so I could walk or run on the water and get quickly ashore, but since I wasn't, I would have to move slowly through the water and then the mud as quietly as possible, forcing myself not to go as fast as I could, and then gratefully crawl up on the bank. Echo platoon was lucky, I guess, because that grinning VC never shot me.

Our missions were fairly straightforward. It was always a recon setup, but if the enemy walked up on us, discovered us, or if a target appeared to be do-able, we'd open up and wipe 'em out, otherwise we'd stay hidden and quiet. If the target was doubtful, we'd let it pass, or we might capture some prisoners for questioning, and depending on who they appeared to be, bring them back to intelligence for more detailed interrogation.

One fact became immediately apparent. Although our basic mission was recon, what we all really wanted to do was ambush. See, it wasn't that we were "trained and eager killers," interested in racking up a big body count (hmm . . . maybe I'm not so certain of that), it just turned out to be incredibly frustrating to let Charlie go by without wasting him. It's sort of like dangling the carrot in front of us, we wanted to grab that carrot and obtain some tangible results of our hard work. And we can't forget, an armed live enemy is dangerous. At any time he could turn and put holes in us. It was especially difficult for me later when I was patrol leader. My first tendency was always to shoot Charlie. I always asked the same question when they talked recon only: "Whattaya mean, I can't kill 'em? Why the hell not?"

When assigned a snatch or specific kill, SOP controlled the op—locate the target, do our thing, and get back out. This kind of op was rare for us, since specific targets in the huge civilian population that lived in the Mekong area were hard for intelligence to pin down.

If the op was pure reconnaissance, however, based on what we ran into, we would simply sneak and peek, looking, listening, and recording info. The object was not to let the enemy know we were there, or had been there. We liked to take prisoners if we thought we could do it without being detected. One of our most effective psychwar tactics was to sneak into an area or ville, take a prisoner or prisoners, and then sneak back out. The enemy would be confused and terrified whenever one of their people just disappeared during the night. All kinds of "ghost soldiers" stories got to circulating among the VC, and that was definitely to our advantage. Occasionally one of our prisoners would return to his people, and the horror stories he or she told about being snatched by monsters of the night (that's us!) just destroyed Charlie's morale. It was very very effective. We heard later that Charlie got to calling us "the men with green faces." But while taking advantage, we all thought we looked pretty cool. Fu Manchu mustaches, goatees, sweat-streaked face paint in every shade and pattern, Slim Wilkins's cowboy hat, Bill Noyce's conquistador hat, various kinds of headbands, our dog-crap gray uniforms, bandoliers of machine gun ammo, bristling with weapons and covered with mud and dirt, we were quite stylish, or so we thought. Hey, we knew we stunk to high heaven, but we couldn't help that. Right Guard didn't quite make it in the bush.

On ops, our criteria for identifying the enemy were pretty simple: If you're carrying a weapon or military supplies, you were in the wrong place at the wrong time, or you looked a little hinky, you were a VC and we were gonna blast you. Otherwise, we'd give you the benefit of the doubt. Maybe.

Sometimes we had to operate in heavily populated areas and do ID checks. This type of op was a real snorer and was usually done just to see who was moving around, and to display ourselves. If we spotted anyone who wasn't an obvious VC, we'd stop them to check their ID, eyeball them carefully, and question them.

General appearance would tell us a lot about what kind of person the Viets were. Your regular Vietnamese noncombatant worked his or her ass off just to put food on the table, and their appearance showed it. Their clothing, what we called PJs, consisted of loose, thin pajama-like pants (or shorts for men) and a collarless pajama-like shirt. They were usually black, although I also saw blue, brown, and green. The women wore the same thing, but never shorts, because rural Orientals are a very modest people where their women are concerned. In the villes, however, the women also commonly wore an *ao dai,* which is a white shirt that is ankle-length, but split on the sides to the waist, so that they could easily squat on their haunches when needed.

The working Viet's clothes were worn and shabby, because even a replacement garment only stayed "new" a few days in the humid climate. The Viet's physical appearance could also be very informative. Gnarled hands, calluses, and broken or worn finger and toenails made their occupations obvious. So, if you were clean, groomed, or well-dressed, we'd nab you. Save your protests for interrogation.

Our interrogation techniques we had learned in training, but in the real world of the Nam, we soon refined them. As you might guess, our biggest problem was that none of us was fluent in Vietnamese. Oh, sure, that's what we had LDNNs for, but I did not like to rely on someone else's interpretation. I had gone to school, but I could barely make myself understood, and there was no way could I understand a Viet talking at full speed. (The best way to learn any language is to shack up with a native speaker, and I could really go for that, but who had the time or the opportunity?) The only thing I could do was watch the suspect like a hawk, trying to interpret his body language and eyes, but that was not very effective. Basically all we could do was put ourselves in a "scare" mode and let the LDNN do his job. Another big problem with our style of interrogation was that we were never quite certain of the reliability of the info we obtained. Is that dude lying? Is this woman exaggerating? Who knows?

But as I mentioned earlier, Orientals placed a high value on "face," and this turned out to be the key to successful interrogation. We must violate their "face," scare the shit out of them, and only then might we hear the truth. It wasn't hard at all, and we soon got it down.

Get up close and personal. That was the way it was done. You would (looking as ferocious as you possibly could) get right up in their face and keep your hands on them. Grab their arms and hang on, or put your hands on their shoulders. The best trick, however, was a head hold. Grab a handful of hair, an ear, or just keep your hand on their head or neck, and it would rattle them like you can't believe. And as they try to back away from you, stay right with them, maintaining contact.

The head, we found out, is sacred territory to the Vietnamese, and it is taboo to touch it without the person's express permission. In fact, many Americans were puzzled and dismayed when, after they had patted a child on the head, the Vietnamese would vamoose, or the child would run away.

So if you threatened or violated the head area, you could always count on a response from the Vietnamese. When they started smiling, you were getting to them, and when they started laughing nervously, you had won. And the "war axe," oh my. They were absolutely terrified of my hatchet. All I had to do was take it out and let them get a good look at the sharpened and shiny edge, and they were ready to talk. I liked to lay the edge against their cheek, and it was guaranteed to make the most hardened Vietnamese start spouting his guts. I stopped getting flak about my war axe from the guys.

Using these techniques, we detained a large number of suspected VC, and quite a few were later confirmed. I won't easily forget, though, one that got away. We were checking IDs on a riverbank next to a ville, and stopped a woman with two male companions. Besides being good-looking, she was immaculate. She wore a clean white *ao dai* with white pants, her hair was long, clean, and neat, and her hands were soft, with clean and manicured nails. The big thing to me was that her toes were not all spread out. Rural Vietnamese walk all their lives barefoot or with sandals, and their toes naturally get spread out from that. Hers weren't and I was absolutely certain that she was VC cadre, a big shot in the infrastructure, but no one else agreed with me. Their papers were correct so we let them go. A major mistake, I still believe, although it's possible she could have been some big shot's mistress, and therefore probably non-VC.

March 11, 1969, we moaned and griped when we received a mission warning at 0900. We were griping because we had been operating without letup for three straight weeks. Don't get me wrong, it wasn't the physical that was the problem, because UDT and SEAL training had built our bodies into indestructible machines, or so we believed. It was the mental stress that created cumulative fatigue, dulling our sharpness, and that could get to be damned dangerous if allowed to continue, both for the individual and the group. The required high level of alertness and continual awareness that each op called for, the dragging darkness hours sitting waiting for instant and furious action, then the adrenaline rush that resulted, plus the strain of getting out and away without getting your ass shot off, those were the culprits. We were quite concerned.

The problem was, we lived and died on intelligence. Informative, hot intelligence was hard to come by, and had to be acted on immediately. Here in Sa Dec Province, we had been getting excellent intell feed from the PRUs, NILO (Naval Intelligence Liaison Officer), and Phoenix, and believe me, when you got good intell, you grabbed it and ran with it. We had no choice but to continue.

We shuffle into the mission briefing at 1100, joking and grab-assing, but that all stopped as soon as the briefing started. This was our trade, some serious business, and we paid our usual strict attention to the information we were given.

We were to hit Rach Ca Sao village, located on the Rach Ca Sao stream, and capture a VC big shot, a district chief. Phoenix intell had received word that he was using the ville as one of his four mobile bases, arranging troop movements and supplies, and generally being a pain in the ass. Phoenix wanted him out of there, and we were to go in and get him. Bosun Campbell was leading, and he filled us in. We would depart home plate at 1540, patrol approximately three klicks in, and arrive at the ville between 1800 and 1900. We would recon the ville, try to spot the VC we were after, and then take him. We would then patrol out to extraction, maybe a klick or so south of the ville, or wherever it was feasible. We got the usual compass headings and terrain detail, along with E & E routes in case we had to scatter like quail. Once again Bosun went over our scramble calls, just in case "Miller got his dumb ass wounded or killed." What? You talkin' 'bout me? I immediately questioned the bosun.

"Say Bosun, I want to try some other positions so that I can be an all-around SEAL. How 'bout me carrying a Stoner this time, and letting somebody else get some experience on the radio? You know, just in case?"

That got me immediate catcalls and boos.

Rocky took it right up. He plays serious and puts on his most sincere look.

"Damn it, Miller, stop bullshitting around. You know you're the best there is on the radio, and none of us could do as good a job. We need you right where you are."

Hah! It got a good laugh, but he just wanted to bust my balls. And avoid carrying the radio.

He continued, "Quit your whining and hold up your end. Plus, I don't want you anywhere around me with a Stoner, you'd be more dangerous than Charlie."

I started to plead my case, but the bosun shot me down.

"No, Rocky's right. This one could get hairy, and I want the pro." I glowered a bit, but then he snubbed that. He grinned and said, "I tell you what, you can be Super-SEAL next op." More laughs.

Huh. I knew that would be a cold day in hell, but what could I do? When you're built like a pack mule, they'll load you up every time. I resigned myself.

Finally the bosun gave us our basic equipment load. There were few questions. We knew the score. When the bosun had finished, Captain Mix of Phoenix took over, and gave us his intell on the target. Surprise, surprise, he was going in with us! And that was not a pleasant surprise, because we SEALs knew and relied on each other, and we did not like unknown quantities such as a non-SEAL conventional forces officer. We'd have to keep a close eye on this bird.

Immediately after the briefing we scattered to prepare our equipment. Dee went out to fire off a belt on the M-60, because he'd had a jam the previous op, and wanted to be certain it had been a bad link in his belt, rather than the weapon itself. We socked down a heavy lunch, because we knew we'd miss supper, except for a few goodies we might carry on patrol.

At 1430, we were painting our faces and shrugging into our combat gear. I'd been having skin problems because of the constant application of face paint thinned with mosquito repellent and the filth I picked up on patrol, so I just did a charcoal job—I coated my face with a light layer of black. Once again I looked at Tom McDonald with envy and gave him a few comments. Tom was a black man, and all he ever had to do was dust his face to cover any shiny surfaces. Unlike me, he never had to worry about any skin problems. I can't really give him the abuse, though, because it was now Chief Tom McDonald, plus he was a pro, a primo operator. I liked working with him and trusted him implicitly. (And that goes for the rest of my mates. I could trust my back to any of these guys without a care in the world; they'd see it remained unpunctured.)

I was wearing coral shoes, black PJ pants, and a long-sleeved black T-shirt this trip. We were also trying something new from China Lakes, individual small radios. They consisted of a small lightweight receiver and transmitter which you carried in your pocket, with a cord that went to a clip-on earpiece. The idea was to have full inter-squad communications with these things, but they would mostly be used to just monitor, so that everyone would know what was going on at all times. They were very short range, so they couldn't be used for station-to-station com, and you know what that meant. Yup. Even though I had received, set up, and tested these new radios, I was still carrying my good old PRC 77. I gotta find a way to get rid of that thing sometimes.

At 1500 we loaded onto the PBR and left home plate. I lit up the first of several cigarettes and sprawled back to enjoy the ease of just riding empty-minded. Soon I'd have to click on full alert mode, and I knew from experience that would take it out of me. I'd need every bit I had so that I wouldn't let the guys down.

Here we go. Bosun signals we're getting close, and I stub out my last butt and move forward to the front of the boat, lining up with the others for landing. As always, this is the part I hate most, insertion. I know one thing, I sure got to pee. I'll let go as soon as I am safely on shore so I don't piss off the boat captain. My bowels clamor that I've got to take a shit, even though I had made sure to go before I left. I mentally cross my fingers and get ready to move. It's all regular stuff, and by now I'm used to it.

The PBR turns into the bank and I drop off into the water and hold on until my feet touch bottom. I let go and go under momentarily, but then I come up and follow the bosun. I have to halt for a second as the guys in front of me pull themselves up on the bank, and I use the occasion to pee. Captain Mix pulls Bosun up on the bank, and then Bosun gives me a hand. I turn and grab Dee's hand and pull. Then we move forward a few yards and huddle in a circular security formation on one knee until all of us are on the bank. Rocky, as rear guard, gives Bosun a thumbs-up and Rich immediately moves out on point. It's Rich, then Toung, then Captain Mix, followed by Bosun, me, Dee, Lou Hyatt, and Rocky. We set up at intervals of about ten feet and begin patrolling to our objective.

It's not bad at all to begin with and we make good time, only having to cross four ditches and one stream. I am lucky for once; the stream water only comes up to my nose. So by standing on my toes I am able to make it across without going under again. Excellent. At least my hair stayed dry. Then, in the gathering dusk, we come to a real bastard. It's a ditch, a big deep one, about twelve feet wide and just as deep. There is a monkey bridge across it, a bamboo log, and the guys negotiate it successfully, although Captain Mix does some fancy arm-waving trying to keep his balance. Me? Forget it. With all my weight and the globs of mud glued to my legs and feet, ain't no way I'm gonna make it across that log, and I don't even try. I'd had monkey bridges collapse under me before, and it was always noisy and painful. Down I slide into the waist-deep odorous mud, and Dee follows me down—he's also heavy, and smarter than he looks. What a struggle! I think I'm gonna die, then I wish I would, because with nothing to grab on to, I have to use every ounce of physical effort to get across. It took a combination of crawling and swimming and "walking." I get to the far bank and I'm completely wasted. I can't climb up and I'm really wired, because I'm holding up the whole patrol. Finally three of them grab me and haul me up and out, then Dee. You never heard such grunting and groaning in your life. And aw . . . they got their hands muddy. Poor babies. I stand up on wobbling legs and I got mud three inches thick all over me, and it's then I notice that I am missing a coral shoe. It's buried somewhere in the muck behind me. I hobble after Bosun as he moves out.

My chicken legs are hollering "uncle" and it is amazing how much a quarter-inch of missing rubber sole throws my stride off. It's not painful, but it sure is awkward. I'm not liking the idea of bare feet in this country of wrigglers and crawlers, but I ain't got much choice. The next time we halt while Rich is negotiating a shallow stream, I take off my remaining coral shoe and tie it to my harness, where naturally it swings and sways and bumps, constantly getting in my way. Eventually I lose patience, and at the next shitditch I stick the shoe in the mud and step on it, pushing it well under. Now I'm cookin'.

Man, that was some long patrol. My tender feet are soon cut and bruised, making me limp like Chester on *Gunsmoke,* and my crotch, lubricated by the mud and gunk that I crawled through, turns raw. But when we finally reached the target ville, by God, I was ready. I was ready for Charlie to pay up for my misery, that's how I had been able to keep myself going, thinking about what I'd like to do to Charlie. Look out, mother, 'cause by now I am one nasty son of a bitch.

Charlie gave me no opportunity, however. We move up close to the ville and I squat on one knee gratefully while the guys in front of me give the ville the big scan, Bosun using the Starlight. As I recover my breath, I give it my own scan. There were the usual oil lamps in the hootches, visible since these particular hootches had no walls, or at best half walls. There were seven hootches that I could see, instead of the four we'd expected. They were tucked neatly into the banana grove, which I couldn't see but knew was there from the briefing.

And I want to take a moment to talk about these hootches, because they were pretty amazing. These hootches, or "grass" houses, had evolved in this tropical climate to perfectly satisfy the Vietnamese housing needs. They were usually fairly small, maybe ten feet by twelve feet, although I've seen them much larger, and generally one room. They contained no furniture, except maybe a bamboo bed rack, but more usually sleeping mats. No table or chairs, because the Viets squatted on their built-in chairs, their haunches. If not on high and dry ground, they would be built on stilts to raise them above the waterline. The "grass" was actually a bamboo framework thatched with cane leaves, and these flimsy huts were not only dry and cool, they were strong enough to withstand the severe weather of the monsoon seasons. And they were naturally camouflaged. The dun color of a hootch set against trees or brush would blend amazingly well into the green background, and if they were hard to see on the ground, they were just about invisible from the air. It was an excellent situation for the South Viets because if the Army couldn't see the hootches, they couldn't indiscriminately bomb or shoot them up, and of course the enemy just loved their invisibility. If the Viet hootches had a single disadvantage, it was fire; hootches would ignite like gasoline and could be set on fire with a simple Zippo lighter, as many a Marine or dog will tell you. Otherwise, these things were really the perfect housing for the country, and they lasted many years once built. Pretty doggone impressive. Okay, now back to the patrol.

Overall visibility was real good because of the almost full moon above us, and we had almost no cover. The place was open, way too open for my comfort. As always, I depend on Rich and the patrol leader to do the right thing by me. The group in front of me splits apart, and we move closer to the ville. Then, about twenty meters out, as we'd planned, we form into a U-shaped line, and point on a large hootch that I assume contains the target.

All of a sudden I have cardiac arrest. I hear a loud snort and a water buffalo runs from us, scaring the crap right out of me. I almost yanked my trigger. A dog barked, joined immediately by others, and the ville came alive. Out of the corner of my eye I see Rich, Toung, and Captain Mix hit the hootch in front of us, yelling "Chieu hoi! Chieu hoi!" and there is a short flurry of arms and legs. I had my thumper pointed skyward, ready to illuminate, but the struggle was over almost as soon as it had started, and they hustled four males right past me into the center of our "U." We walked backward, keeping the ville under our guns. It had become noisy with yells and kids crying. Suddenly we turned and ran. Jumpin' Jesus! That run was hard on my bare feet, but ain't no way I'm getting left behind. I *di di mau*ed at full speed. The run was short, though, and we stopped and took the time to cuff our prisoners' hands, and also to cuff their heads a few times to establish and ensure their silence. One of them had a cool hat on, a shapeless felt fedora, and I immediately "captured" that. I needed a good hat. Wasting no more time, we moved out at speed. Toung had two prisoners, and Captain Mix had two, and they were hustling them right along. Suddenly, from the right side, another small body catapulted into Captain Mix, hitting with a thud and grunts, almost knocking him down. Bosun joined the struggle, and next thing I know here he comes, prisoner in tow, and whispers in my ear.

"A woman. Pass her back to Hyatt."

A woman? Oh boy! Shit, I can handle a mere woman. She's a handful, though, struggling and grunting against the hand I've got plastered over her mouth, and trying to bite my ass. Bosun ties her wrists and then, working together, we get a piece of duct tape over her mouth to stifle her attempted yells of protest. She don't want to go in front of me, and I have to half push, half knee her into moving out. Once she realizes I mean business, she eventually gets going, and we smoke out of there. There is no noise that we can hear from the ville behind us, and that could be good or bad. At least Charlie ain't laying down a base of fire or signaling his brothers, but he may be on the move behind us, trying to catch up and do an ambush. We don't wait to find out, but after twenty minutes or so of fast walking along the stream bank, we halt and circle up. I push the woman down and she automatically squats on her haunches, and I stay tight up against her for control. Bosun tells me to call extraction, and I already have the handset ready.

"Whirltop, Whirltop. Threadbare One. Over." I feel the woman jump at my low-voiced American.

"Threadbare One, this is Whirltop. Over."

Things were quiet, so I took a chance. I could always update if necessary.

"Whirltop, this is Threadbare. Contact. Ready to extract. Scramble three. One klick below target on water, over."

"Threadbare, Whirltop. Understand extract. Scramble three, one klick, on water. Over."

"Roger, Whirltop. Threadbare out."

I waited, listening.

Then, "Threadbare, Threadbare, Blue Mike. Over."

"Blue Mike, Threadbare. Go."

"Threadbare, Blue Mike. ETA ten mikes. Over."

"Roger."

That told me that Lieutenant Johanssen had anticipated us and moved his boat up the stream from our insertion point while he waited for our call, to save us precious minutes before pickup. My kind of guy. I got out my hooded strobe light and tested it momentarily against my cupped hand. Yup, blue light. Then I put it back and gave my prisoner a body search to make sure she wasn't carrying anything concealed. I ignored all the noises coming out from under the duct tape on her mouth; I'm certain I didn't want to hear it. I bet it would have blistered my ears. I get my light ready and hold my handset to my ear. Right on time the handset speaks to me.

"Threadbare One, Blue Mike. ETA four mikes. Say status. Over." I can barely hear a faint drone. He's farther away than he thinks.

"Blue Mike, Threadbare. Clean and quiet. I can just hear you, over."

"Rog. Stand by."

It's more like six or seven minutes, while the roar of his engines at full throttle increases, and I point my strobe downstream over the water and click it on, holding steady on his noise. The woman stirs against me, and I lean on her to still her.

"Threadbare, I see true blue. Stand by to load."

"Roger." We're ready.

The boat noses in and we climb aboard, and I have a struggle, controlling my prisoner with one hand. She don't want to be climbing on no boat, and tries to kick me in the nuts. Bosun gives me a hand, and we get it done, but I've got a few new bruises. I want to give her a good slug, but I can't be hitting no woman.

On the way back she's one giant pain in the ass, and I wish I had given her to one of the other guys. Instead of powering down from the op and relaxing, I got to pay attention to this dumbass woman. I got a hand clamped around her neck, and every time I try to move, like lighting a much-needed cigarette, she struggles. Rocky comes over "to help me out," and he speaks nice and loud so that everyone will hear.

"Hey Miller, awful lot of gruntin' and cussin' going on over here. What you doing to that poor defenseless girl?" And as you can imagine, the comments start flying.

Huh! Defenseless girl my ass. I am tempted to give her to Rocky, but I am Dutch stubborn. Ain't no mere woman gonna get me down. I give her neck a good squeeze, and she settles down somewhat while I fend off the comments coming my way. I tell you one thing though, I was damn glad to get rid of her when we tied up at home plate, especially after she stomped all over the tops of my poor feet while I was blindfolding her. Hers were callused, and they felt just like boots stomping me, only lighter. I propelled her onto the dock and was thrilled to death to give her to Captain Mix. Just for some payback I ripped the duct tape off her mouth, but she didn't do no crying, instead she started burning my ears up with her gabble. Toung was cracking up, giving me the big laugh, but he wouldn't tell me what she was saying. In this case I guess I didn't need an interpreter. I headed for the peaceful haven of the showers, and when Rocky pointed to my limping feet and asked did the woman steal my shoes, I just grunted. I knew I'd never hear the end of it.

Follow-up? We'd missed the district chief, but had gotten his aides. That wasn't so bad. And I had captured a fine hat. It turned out to be dark green, and after I ripped out the lining and stretched the hat a bit, it fit pretty good. Oh, and according to Captain Mix, the woman was a nobody, who just happened to have had the bad luck to run head-on into our patrol. I wasn't certain I agreed with him. I figure she was one of the aides' girlfriend or wife, or maybe a special agitator that Charlie had sent just to make my life miserable.

Our op area was not a free-fire zone, and although there was a dusk-to-dawn curfew, the Vietnamese pretty much ignored it if they wanted to eat. The waterways at night would be crowded with sampans out fishing, and the fishers would hang a lantern on their boat so they could net the fish that swam to the pool of light. This was their livelihood, but it made it damn difficult for us. The VC loved it though, because those motherfuckers blended right in with the civilian populace.

We stopped and searched a million of these sampans with minimal results—how the devil can you tell a VC from a fisherman, unless you can find a weapon? After a while, with poor results, we didn't even bother. We concentrated on "land" ops and intelligence-driven ops.

As an example of our difficulties, one op that we ran was a stream ambush. Intelligence had gotten wind of a VC supply crossing, and we planned to exploit it. It's darker than pitch, we're sitting on the canal bank, and a dozen sampans go up and down, they're all lighted, and none appear suspicious. Which ones are VC? Who the hell knows? But finally, in the wee hours of the morning, two unlighted sampans come down the canal. Through the Starlight scope we can see three people in each boat. Ah, this was more like it. Our LDNN hails them, but they don't respond, oh boy, so we open up. I initiate with an illumination round, and as soon as it pops, the guns start roaring, and tracers are arcing into the sampans.

Immediately after I fire illumination, and I get deafened by Dee's M-60 roaring right in my ear, I pop in an HE round and let fly at the second sampan. In the burst of light I see one of the occupants cartwheel out, and both sampans overturn. After I put out a second illumination round and we cease fire, we see a couple of heads in the water, and one of them yells out. Our LDNN directs the two suspects to swim to us, and they do, one towing the other. I get on the horn and call in our boats. When we get the two suspects on the bank, one is unwounded but terrified—chattering and crying up a storm. The other is a mess. He's got a couple of bullet holes, multiple shrap wounds, and his lower jaw is gone. What a sickening sight. One of us has hit it, and we suspect my HE round did the damage. Man, I don't want the credit. I can't even look at the guy. My stomach is churning and I feel lousy. I try to blame Dee's M-60, but nobody's paying me any attention. Doc Mahner bandages him up and we extract, and we're hitting it at high RPMs rushing this guy to medical help. Earlier, we'd done our best to kill him, but since he had survived, we were now rushing to save him. I shake my head. I'm very confused. This is some fucked-up war—we should have just finished him. Well, to close this out, we never did find out if these people were actually VC, or just dumb fishermen. They screwed up and we shot 'em. Go figure.

March 17, 1969, it's catastrophe, and we lose Bosun Campbell to wounds. It hits us hard, 'cause we all like and respect him. Besides, he'd been a balance for Mr. Woodard. Although Arch Woodard was an excellent officer, he was academy-trained, and he wanted us to attack battalions and stuff. Bosun was a warrant officer, up from the ranks, and he didn't believe in attacking battalions with a SEAL squad. We like that kind of thinking.

What happened is that on patrol, Second Squad searched a hootch with two men and three women inside and questioned them. These people assured the SEALs that there was no VC activity in the area, but if they would follow a certain trail, there was another hootch on it, and they might be VC.

So (oh foolish ones) the patrol took the trail, and the third man in line, the bosun, stepped on a mine. He was lucky(?)—the blast and shrapnel went up the back of his legs and ass. Although tore up pretty good, he wasn't crippled or dead. Emerson had taken three good chunks of shrapnel in the ass cheek (sorry Mike, I couldn't resist) and Gong, the LDNN, also got hit with shrap. As the squad moved out to extraction, they heard a shot from the hootch they'd searched, so the SEALs poured fire into it as they moved by. Hey, this is war: *Xin loi*, assholes!

Bosun and Gong got dustoff (medevac chopper), but Emerson came back on the boat, hanging his ass over the side. He was hanging tough. It was the least painful way he could sit, but after they arrived, Doc took a look and sent Mike on medevac also. We got Emerson back, but lost the bosun and Gong to wounds.

Chapter
Thirty-three

DURING THE MONTH of April 1969, we worked our asses off, conducting twenty-five ops in thirty days. I guess you could say we were hungry, especially after the first op of the month.

April 1, 1969, Second Squad had a lively one. Tom McDonald led four other SEALs and some Giao Duc PRUs into a ville on hot intelligence to kill a big shot VC. Because the ville was huge, the guys decided to go in by sampan. The choice was a smart one, and as they paddled in just before dawn, they were able to get almost to the center of the ville before the first alarm was raised. The hoi chan with them pointed out the target hootch, quickly obvious to the SEALs because dinks were vacating it like lemmings. The action was brisk, and when the smoke cleared, Second Squad had killed seven VC and captured four. The SEALs started taking small arms fire from the surrounding treelines, so they scampered out of there. Nice going, Second Squad, especially understrength, but I sure wish I could have watched those great big guys attempting to maneuver in those dinky little sampans. That must have been an interesting sight.

Holy shit! I just got a letter from my former L.A. girl, and she tells me I gave her VD! I am diseased, man, it's the Creeping Congoloid Crud! Her letter is terse, but the name of the disease is not, it's about twenty letters long and scares the crap out of me. What am I gonna do now? I just know that they will kick me out of SEAL team when they find out, and that's only if I don't die from whatever it is I've got. I grab Doc Mahner and swear him to secrecy, then show him the letter. He don't know what it is either, so we beat feet to the base doctor and ask him to look it up. He goes through one of his medical books, and then breaks out laughing. I don't.

"Which one of you has got this terrible disease?" he asks.

Without thinking, I blurt, "I do." Then I cuss myself. I also got a big mouth.

He grins at me. "How do you know? You got any symptoms?"

Well, the jig is up, so I tell him the truth and show him the letter. He laughs again, which I ain't appreciating, and says, "I now pronounce you cured."

Man oh man, what the hell is going on? Is this guy on drugs, or what? I want to drop the sucker, but he's a lieutenant commander, and I can't. Then he starts asking me weird questions. How long ago did I have sex with this woman? What were the circumstances? Did she display any pain? And so on and so forth. I answer truthfully, but I sure am confused. Finally he clears it all up.

Still laughing, he says, "What you got is nothing. Zero. What she's got, or had, was an exaggerated yeast infection."

Whew! That's good news for me, but I still have no idea what he's talking about. I say so.

He continues. "What happened was, you went to school for a month, got all horny, and when you came back and had hot sex with this girl, you were too rough and gave her a small tear inside. That tear got infected, and gave her the same symptoms as venereal disease. Obviously, her doctor only told her the disease name, not what actually caused it. I recommend you send her a letter and ease her mind."

Man was I relieved! I didn't have the Black Death or the Creeping Crud. I quickly wrote a letter in reply, but I don't think she believed me, because I never heard from her again. What can you do? I shrugged my shoulders and went on about my business.

* * *

First Squad temporarily moved to Duc Than, a short distance away, and we ran a few ops. On April 11 we ran one in which we saw a military supply column on the move, but as sometimes happens, we were unable to do anything about it other than observe and report. We're set up, it's misty, quiet, and dark, it's really creepy, and movement is spotted. I'm telling you, it was ghostly. Out in front of us about twenty meters, slanting across our right flank, we saw several gooks walking along in file carrying huge loads on their shoulders and heads, and they moved in absolute silence. It's like they were floating over the ground. I had to pinch myself to make sure I was awake, but I was. I counted fourteen before Mr. Woodard had me get on the horn to call in the Seawolves, and when I was able to look again, they were still coming. They were moving at just the right angle so we couldn't open up on them, so we figured we could get them with supporting fire as a target of opportunity. No dice. Our Seawolves had been diverted to help some Marines and weren't readily available. By the time they were, the gooks were long gone, so we sat it out and cussed the Marine Corps. Well, it was excellent intelligence, but I sure would like to have seen what was in those bundles they were carrying. At the debrief, the total number of VC "pack mules" counted had been thirty-eight. What a wasted opportunity!

And this is the time I want to lodge an official complaint with somebody. That goddamn Charlie was tricky, and he didn't play by the rules. See, the way it's supposed to work is that Charlie always gives us plenty of warning he's coming, approaches us directly in our kill zone lined up like ducks in a shooting gallery, meekly submits to getting shot or blown up to red mist, and never, ever, fires a shot at us in anger. But like I said, you couldn't trust Charlie to do the right thing. If we sat up on a stream, he might come down it, but then he might also walk right up on our backside, screwing up our plans. And I might be sitting there highly alert and vigilant, you know, God and Country, that sort of thing, constantly visually scanning my own piece of the kill zone. I'd sweep left to right and see nothing, and all of a sudden, when I looked back, there stands Charlie, come out of nowhere, already on top of me and looking directly at me, so I was scared to raise my weapon. It just wasn't fair. Charlie would come strolling up to us from any direction, at any time, and the son of a bitch wouldn't just stand there and submit or surrender. At the first sound he was gone at a dead run, ruining my fun, and then he had the unmitigated gall to stop in cover and shoot back at me. Somebody somewhere should sit him down and give him some counseling. I mean, I was a SEAL. I had a job to do. So why wouldn't he cooperate?

Lt. JG John Marsh has joined us to replace Bosun Campbell. Mr. Marsh is OCS, and appears to be one of the good ones. He plays a nice Gibson guitar which he brought with him, and that's all the credentials he needs with me. He accompanied us on a couple of patrols to gain experience, and then led his first one, taking Second Squad out on PRU intell. The guys tell me afterward that he did very well. They used a slick (Huey) to insert, and had no sooner started patrolling than they heard warning shots and spotted several VC moving along out in front of them. Mr. Marsh did not make the new guy's mistake of following or chasing the VC, instead he did the smart thing and cut the patrol at a hard right angle, to set up on a large stream nearby. The squad saw movement during the night, but nothing close to them, and they extracted the next morning without firing a shot. No VC body count, but by the same token, no wounded or dead SEALs. That's excellent.

Mr. Marsh received our final SEAL of approval on April 16. He'd led four ops by then, and on this one, he guided Second Squad into Tuyen Nhon hamlet on a rare body-snatch op. PRU had generated the intell that a high-ranking VCI was visiting the ville, and Mr. Marsh did it all right. Second Squad not only captured the VCI, but also two of his staff. They were in and out and gone, all without firing a shot or risking a SEAL. Way to go, Mr. Marsh!

Then it was our turn. Tom McDonald led us on a routine stream ambush, and we got set up about four in the afternoon on a stream offshooting the river. We were sitting in hip-deep water (chest-deep on me) leaning comfortably back against the stream bank so that we could be close enough to the stream to get a good field of observation, when we spotted a sampan with two males in it and, lordy lordy, an AK-47 sticking up in plain sight. Oh boy! We were patient, and the dummies paddled right up into the kill zone and landed the sampan. Perfect. We took advantage of the situation, let them get on shore, and blasted the shit out of them. I shot a flechette round right into the middle of the lead dude, who was already jumping from Stoner rounds hitting him. Our concentrated fire, short though it was, tore those poor bastards all to pieces, and we didn't even let off a claymore. Didn't have to. Me, I couldn't wait to see what kind of damage my flechette round had done. We get to our feet to go check out what was left of the bodies, and the whole world erupts.

Jesus, we were taking heavy fire from the right flank, sounded like a .51 caliber machine gun, and the tracers and bullets were pouring in. We ran for our lives down a dike, and I'm telling you, the rounds went right through our formation as we were running. I don't know to this day why none of us got hit. I do know for certain that I saw a tracer flash right in front of my chest. Man, that wasn't no AK round!

We ran a short way and then went to ground, prepared to defend ourselves. The enemy fire continued but didn't follow us, and shortly afterward it stopped, so we were certain Charlie had lost sight of us. Yowza! That was a close one. I get on the horn and call in our boats, and while we wait, Rocky and Rich check out the sampan, which is right full of gear.

There were mags and ammo for the AKs, some field packs, a big jar full of rice, six Chicom grenades, a B-40 rocket launcher, a pouch of documents, a bundle of medicines, and assorted clothing. Hey, this was big-time stuff. Our boats came up on the net for instructions, so I gave them the okay to come in, and we extracted.

Once we get on the boats, we finally get it all sorted out. The fire we received was friendly fire! What happened was, when we opened up on the VC, some of our tracers had kicked out onto the river, and an ASPB out there was violating our op area. They'd spotted the tracers, thought they were under attack, and had opened up on us with .50 cal and 20mm. Holy shit! All that big stuff had to do was touch you, and you lost an arm, or a leg, or maybe your whole chest area. Man, had we been lucky. Louie McIntosh claimed it was skill, not luck, because he was "Flak Body" and the rounds would have bounced right off. Sure. I believe him. I'll just put him in front of me from now on.

The PRUs went back in the next day and confirmed our kills. Better yet, they ID'd them as the VC district chief and his aide, and part of the gear we had captured from the sampan was propaganda material and organizational documents. Intelligence was very pleased. Seems this guy had been a fox.

Early April, Doc Mahner leaves us to go with another platoon, and he is replaced by Doc Cantalupi, who seems to be a nice guy. Poor Doc Mahner. We heard later that he was killed when one of the SEALs in our sister platoon, Ron Pace, tried to disarm a Chicom mortar round in the barracks and the thing went off, wiping out several sailors. It was kept very low-key at the time, so I'm not certain I remember the facts correctly. If I got it wrong and you're still alive out there, Doc, more power to you.

For some time now, John Wayne has been whispering in my ear telling me to go for it, so on April 17, I volunteer to lead my first op as patrol leader. As my reward for being so brave and honest and courageous and worthy, I get assigned to take a patrol into the Fishhook area, sometimes called the Parrot's Beak, which is a VC stronghold. Uh-oh. Although that news made me extremely nervous and I am shitting bricks, I hid my fears and played the role. I had to do it, and was determined to do it well. God, please don't let me get anybody killed.

NILO (Navy intelligence) has heard of a potential troop movement out in the Fishhook, and they want us to check it out. But I must plan a totally different op than we are used to, because the Fishhook area is very open, fairly dry grassland, and has occasional clumps of brush, usually along the waterways. Long trails lead to and from these brush clumps, and the VC move company-size combat units and supply columns along these trails. Their usual formation is two or three point scouts moving about 100 meters ahead of the main body to provide an early warning system.

I plan to run this op differently because of the high visibility problem we will now face. We'll night-insert two klicks away from the objective, patrol to the site, laager and relax during the day, then set our recon/ambush at dusk from the same location. The less we move around, the better, because we'll be a long way from home, easy to spot, and we're going out short—six SEALs only. Our LDNNs are on home leave.

We inserted by chopper at 0320 and, following my compass course while counting my steps to estimate distance (with my fingers, toes, and nuts crossed for luck) we patrolled in. Naturally I'd done a previous flyover, but at 2,000 feet, you don't always spot all the terrain detail, and now I discovered a million small streams and ditches that weren't on the map and that I hadn't planned for, so it turned out to be no easy stroll. We are up and down, in and out of the mud and water, and I can sense the patrol members aren't very happy, because I'd promised them dry ground. I am stepping out lightly, though, because for once I'm not loaded down with the radio. I'd given that privilege to Flak Body McIntosh. Instead, I was carrying a Stoner and felt like I had wings on my feet.

Incredibly, at first light I am close enough to the objective to spot it visually, and we quickly move in so I can give the site a quick scan. It's a good one, a pocket of thick brush, maybe thirty feet long and ten feet wide, bordering a decent-sized stream. On the other side of the brush was a beaten trail. No fresh signs of use, but since the trail was dry, it was hard to tell. Out from the trail was waist-high dry grass, as far as you could see. The site appeared to have potential, and that was good enough for me.

After mentally placing our squad to get the best results out of this particular site, I moved cautiously into position, parting the brush carefully to check for trip wires, and trying to leave no sign of my passage. As patrol leader I am ambush center, so when I am satisfied, I raise my arm, and the other members of the patrol move into their positions on each side of me as carefully as I had.

Once each man had selected his position "nest," he cleaned it of obstructions. The claymores, under my unneeded supervision, were placed on each end of the linear ambush formation, aimed to cross in the kill zones, both in the middle of the stream and in the middle of the trail. Then we cleared firing lanes and removed and positioned our gear. Finally we sat down in our nests and hid ourselves as well as we could, assumed a comfortable body position, and prepared to wait out the day. But we sure didn't get much chance to relax. By 0900 there are Vietnamese all around us, some fishing in the stream, and others cutting grass and making it up into bundles, all of them without a care in the world. They are women, children, and a few old men, two of whom were missing an arm. (Missing two arms? One each? One between them? Hey, you know what I mean.)

And here I want to digress a bit. All my life I have been greatly entertained by observing the behavior of people around me. It was always more fun to watch and listen, as opposed to participating and being the center of attention. I learned early that people have two sets of behavior, one for public display, and another (usually quite different) for private use. All of us seem to play the role and perform for our public. In private we are more low-key, and certainly much more relaxed. The private person is the real person, and was the one I always wanted to know, so that I could form valid opinions of them as human beings. The private person is rarely seen, though, except in the most intimate relationships, that were limited to things like spouses and best friends. Since most people never displayed their private selves, I was forced to judge people by their public personas. That led me to receive several nasty shocks in my life, however, when someone behaved differently from what I had expected of them, and I hadn't liked that at all.

Vietnam gave me my first real opportunity to observe people going about their lives in a normal manner, unaware that I was watching them. Be they enemy or not, it turned out to be spooky, but also a real kick. Actually, it was usually quite entertaining, and sometimes I'd have to keep from cracking up at their antics. I am sure that I would be just as funny to someone else if they were observing me act naturally. (Nah—that's not true, I am at all times Mr. Cool.)

Nevertheless, several times in Vietnam I got this opportunity, and it was always interesting. If you ever get the chance, watch someone scratch their crotch, adjust the hang of their dick, pick their nose, whatever, and I guarantee you'll be rolling on the ground in no time. The fact that these were foreigners made it even more entertaining. Oddly, I usually felt a strange sense of power over these people. If they had any idea I was here . . . I mean, if I suddenly stood up and hollered, they'd shit their pants. But I have to admit it, knowing I had that power to terrorize made me feel superior to them. Weird, huh? I'll tell you one thing. I always regretted that I never had a good opportunity to do just that, jump up and scream like a Comanche. Can you imagine what fun that would be? Oh man, I have daydreamed about it. Course, with my luck, some clown wouldn't appreciate the joke, and would whip out a gun and shoot my nuts off.

Well, back to business. Instead of setting a light watch for security and the rest of us sleeping, we must stay alert in case anyone stumbles on us. See, it's a guy thing, men like to pee against a bush whenever possible, and here we were sitting in the only bushes in the area, so we expected the worst. We also did some heavy praying that no aircraft would appear. First we'd get trampled by the Viets running for cover, then we'd get shot up by the aircraft, who wouldn't discriminate between us.

It's the old story: you do something for the best of reasons, but occasionally it backfires, and some fool wants to make you suffer. I'm talking about our "uniforms." Except for our weapons and bandoliered ammo belts, we looked nothing like any kind of U.S. troops, nor did we look like enemy troops. Well, maybe we resembled a band of Pancho Villa's guys, but other than that . . .

Our appearance was based on several factors: camouflage was number one. Forget all about those movie dudes in their new, starched and pressed camo greens with brass insignia and group patches. Real life for us was off-black, dark grays, or browns that blended with plain old dirt, and you know what color muddy, wet dirt is, don't you?

Green? Forget it. We're not gonna roost in trees, so we're not gonna dress like Robin Hood. We spend our ops wading through or crawling and lying in mud, so that's what we want to look like. Our wears had never seen starch or pressing, had been faded by countless wettings and rolling in mud, and contained no insignia, patches, or markings of any kind, if you didn't count whitened creases and stains caused by sweat salt.

Appearance factor number two was comfort—whatever did the job best with the most comfort for the wearer. I'll cite myself as an example. A quick, one-night ambush? I might wear a hat. If it was a longer op, where I would be sweating my ass off, a headband was a must, both to keep sweat out of my eyes and to keep my "makeup" from running. I couldn't wear regular shirts because of my radio rig—I would roast in them and the slightest wrinkle would quickly chafe to a huge blister. I wore T-shirts, long- and short-sleeved. And no way in the world could I wear tight or regular-fitting pants. The first time I squatted, or struggled out of a nasty shitditch, I would split my crotch wide open. Ain't no way I'm gonna be sittin' out in the bush with my groin exposed to the creepers and crawlers. *Wear underwear shorts, you dummy!* is what you're thinking. Uh-uh. Half an hour of water, mud, and sweat and my crotch would be raw meat. Think again. What worked for me were camo pants three sizes too large. I looked like Charlie Chaplin, but they worked perfectly. Jungle boots? Certainly, 90 percent of the time, except if you had holes in your feet from infected blisters. Then you must wear the softer coral shoes. Remember, you can't slow down or endanger the patrol just because your feet hurt.

Factor number three and the last one I'm going to gabble on about is personal preference. You may be an Academy officer, concerned about your appearance, so you will wear issue camo greens, a camo beret or boonie hat, and jungle boots. Or you might be an OCS officer and wear the ugliest hillbilly hat I ever saw in my life. You might be a long, lanky Texan, like Slim Wilkins, and wear high-riser green fatigue pants and a camo cowboy hat. You might want to look different, like Bill Noyce, and wear a hat that looks just like a conquistador helmet. You might want to be a pro like Tom McDonald and wear tiger-stripe camos. And finally, you might want to be a point scout like Jim Richards, who wore black PJ pants, tiger-stripe shirt, bare feet, and the tiniest boonie hat I ever saw.

So, after all that, what I'm saying, basically, is that anyone who saw us in the bush did not know what we were. We confused Charlie, we confused U.S. troops, hell, we even confused ourselves. But the kicker is that gung ho conventional forces, especially hotshot aircraft people, couldn't recognize us as friendlies and would shoot us without hesitation. It was a chance that we took.

Finally, around noon, the Viets all packed up and left the area, and we let out a big sigh of relief, certain we hadn't been discovered. They had at all times been completely relaxed, spitting, laughing, and coughing, and gabbling up a storm. It was strange, the Vietnamese I ran into seemed to have bad lungs—the climate, maybe?

But we'd no sooner relaxed a bit than we heard choppers coming. Oh shit, this is real trouble. We all know that "friendly fire" is the most deadly fire in Vietnam. Sure enough, we soon spot two LOHs flying low, scouting all the cover and trying to draw fire. We also know that high up, there'd be two or more Cobra gunships ready to pounce. Well what could we do? We hid and prayed. The fact that these bastards were violating our op area was meaningless, we'd be just as dead. They're on an unknown radio frequency, so we can't even contact them, and quite simply, if they saw us, they'd kill us, because conventional forces lived for body count, and they wouldn't hesitate. ("Whattaya mean I can't kill 'em? They're there, aren't they?")

But God (and maybe Buddha and Muhammad) must have heard six fervent prayers that day. The LOHs didn't spot us, and eventually moved on out of sight and hearing. Me, I'd been lying on my back, ready to return fire. Fuck the rules, if you shoot at me, I'm gonna shoot back, I'll be goddamned if I'm gonna go out passively. I had looked right into the eyes of one of the LOH pilots, but he didn't see me. Man, I never was so scared. After cleaning out our pants, I reset a light watch and waited. Another close call for me.

At dusk we were prepared, set up in a staggered double line. One line would cover the stream, and the other, facing opposite, would cover the trail. As a contingency, if only one or two enemy came along, or if the point scouts got close enough, we might try to do a John Wayne and capture them, then ambush the main body. Ah, the best-laid plans . . .

Shortly after full dark, two VC walk right up on me. As I shift my Stoner to cover them, the links in the ammo drum rattle, and without hesitation, the VC run. I opened upon them, and down they went. Did I get them? I don't know, but as the thumper's illumination flare is drifting down, no one's stirring out in front of me. I sit tight, not certain of what I want to do, when suddenly the grass in front of us catches fire from the illum round, and the flames spread quickly. Shit. We never thought of that happening. As the whole area goes up in flames, we're compromised, so we might as well *di di*. I cuss Flak Body out for being a firebug, then tell him to call the choppers, when all of a sudden we start taking long-range fire from the north. That's the moment when I realize we're kind of stuck here between the stream and the fire. I may have made a bad choice of location.

Hmm . . . what to do? Should we go for a swim and cross the stream? Or should we move toward the VC and then dogleg? C'mon, Miller, shit or get off the pot. But the enemy fire slackened and then stopped, so I decided to stay put but stay alert, in case the main body decides to investigate us. I put out a fifth claymore to cover for that.

Uh-oh. When the choppers arrive, they draw fire from the main body, and it gets quite heavy. The Seawolves come down to suppress it, while the slick swoops in to get us, but even so, long-range tracers are arcing into us while we're loading. As patrol leader, I am last on board, and we pick up and fly out of there. It was a totally fucked-up op, but I'd learned something—grass burns. I'd also learned something else. Having the responsibility for my friends' lives in my hands was too much for me to handle, and I didn't feel up to it. I just wasn't good enough. I figured my fellow patrol members wanted to go on living, so I wouldn't volunteer to lead any more ops for a while.

When we get back, Mr. Marsh didn't buy that, however, and he gave me a pep talk. So on April 25, I agree to take out another op, but this one is going to be easy, a fire mission for our Seawolves.

Tuyen Nhon PF (Popular Forces) intell has located (so they claim) a supply cache with a permanent guard of five to ten VC. The problem is, it's located right out in the open, dug into a hump of raised ground, so we can't realistically approach it with a patrol unless we have a death wish. It's not an important enough target to bomb, so we won't use fast movers (jets). Instead we figure to give our Seawolves a chance to get some firing runs under their belts, and then we SEALs will land and check results. The Seawolf dudes are all excited at the prospect of some action, so I grab Jim Richards and Louie McIntosh, and at the last moment Mr. Woodard wants to come along, so we let him.

We load on the slick and fly out to watch the fun. It's pretty neat. The Seawolves make three firing runs, tearing the place up, then the slick drops us, and the slick door gunner asks can he come along. Since there has been no enemy fire, we say sure, come on along, there's nothing happening here.

Uh-huh . . . That's true. We search the area, and find we're a little bit too late. No fresh sign at all, and no Charlie. There are some deserted bunkers, a hole that might once have been a cache, and a single pair of shot-up rubber tire sandals. There were also five sampans upside-down on racks, but that's not unusual, because that's the way they are stored until needed, whether it's a week or a year.

I quickly capture the Ho Chi Minh sandals. They'll make excellent trading material to the REMFs. Then we set up a couple of claymores to blow the "cache," and prepare to destroy the sampans with hand grenades. When the claymores explode, they send up a big shower of dirt and a satisfying boom, and we can tell the door gunner is eating this shit up. When we get grenades ready to blow the sampans, the door gunner asks can he throw one, and I say sure, why not. Man, I should have known better. We chuck the grenades under the sampans, run a few steps, and drop to the ground. Except for the door gunner—he's dumb and keeps on running. The grenades go bang, the gunner hollers, and down he goes. He's whining up a storm, so we check him out, and find he's only got a few small shrap chunks in the ass. I'd also gotten some small pieces in my shoulder, but man, it wasn't anything to get excited about. The door gunner, though, you'd think he was on death's doorstep, the way he was hollerin'. I think he wanted dustoff, but we shamed him into climbing on the slick; we figured they could take him to medical help after they'd dropped us off. You know, that dude got a Purple Heart for that wound? I wonder what story he told his friends and relatives in later years? I bet it's a good one, full of blood and guts and glory, and you can bet nothing will be said about being wounded in the ass by friendly fire. Am I being too cynical? Maybe.

I became cynical about medals because of what I saw in Vietnam. Like every young kid, at various times I had dreamed of becoming a hero and winning a chestful of medals. Reality in Vietnam quickly disillusioned me. The real heroes did heroic things as a matter of getting the job done, and were rarely recognized for their heroic deeds. Instead, it always seemed that men were awarded medals for stupid things, things that usually had nothing to do with being brave. I saw "Hearts" awarded to a guy who had fallen down drunk and broken his wrist, and another who'd broken his finger falling out of his bunk. I saw Silver and Bronze Stars awarded to officers who did nothing more than fly in a chopper 2,000 feet over the action on the ground. Or awarded Stars "for showing outstanding leadership" on such and such a date. Wasn't that their job?

Generally it turned out to be this way: if you were Enlisted, you had to have a Padre, a person who would write you up on paper for every action. Dudes who received a lot of medals usually had these Padres, or were sucking up to their officers, and those that didn't got no medals. I saw and heard of many men performing heroic acts who not only didn't have a Padre, they were too modest to push their own claim. Uh-huh. They went unrewarded.

And please, please don't give me the line about career soldiers deserving medals to help their careers. That's pure bullshit. Oh, meritorious service, stuff like that, I have no problem with. But medals for valor or bravery should be given only to those who earn them, and all of those who earn them.

In Vietnam, conventional forces staff officers who won medals of valor for combat were almost without exception undeserving. They never participated in actual combat, so how could they earn combat medals? I will except the low-rankers, the officers who actually led their men on the ground, and also pilots. But the "old boy network" of the military in Vietnam awarded each other medals regularly to further their careers, and they tarnished the importance and integrity of those awards.

Years later I started to write a song about it after hearing the line somewhere about only young men dying in war, and although I knew damn well it would never be a million-seller, I think it says it all.

Old men begin wars, young men fight them.
Old men safely direct wars, and young men die in them.
Old men retire rich and "just fade away."
Young men adorn the Black Wall the hard way.
And old men modestly bask in history; others will recount
     their deeds.
But young men live on only in the memories of those who
     loved and lost them.

I know. Pretty harsh stuff. You're reading, and you're saying, this guy is really bitter. You're right. Do I think I should have gotten some medals? Nope. I was never a hero. Besides, SEAL team was real good about awarding medals. Do I dislike officers? You bet I do, except for a certain few who could and would do their job of leading their men. You see, I was very privileged to work with some of the best officers in the military, SEAL and UDT officers. They were *leaders*, in every sense of that word.

I'm told it was a completely different story in WW II. Maybe, but in Vietnam, I considered most officers more dangerous to their own men than the enemy, and that makes them the enemy. If you doubt me, watch the movie called *The Boys in Company C* some time. That Marine company commander was typical of the conventional forces officers in Vietnam, men with their heads up their ass. Enough said.

Next day, April 26, I take out another one. Might as well, since I can't dance. Well, it turns out to be a screwed-up mess. Seems like every once in a while you get one of those, at least that's what Mr. Marsh tells me later to make me feel better. (So how come I always seem to get them?)

A hoi chan (aka *chieu hoi*) swears that he knows about a day-time VC supply crossing on a canal, and can lead us right to it. The moment I see this guy, I don't like the look of him. He's hinky, and I certainly don't buy this daylight crossing bit, because that's not like Charlie.

But hey, I want the experience under my belt, so I agree to go. I never said I was smart, just handsome. I grab four "volunteers," Mr. Woodard, D'Angelo, Richards, Flak Body McIntosh, and add two LDNNs, Gieng and Toung. We insert at 0230 by Boston Whalers, and start following this fool hoi chan around.

Man, we go north, we go south, we go west, but it was when we headed east that I checked the dude to see if he was smoking the funny stuff. It's already daylight when I tell Gieng to give the guy a talking to, and get him straightened out. Shit! What a mistake that was. Off they go into a hot burst of Vietnamese, waving hands and stomping feet, getting louder and louder. I quickly call a halt to that nonsense, we've wasted way too much time, and I give Gieng the final word.

"Tell that motherfucker that if he don't take us to the location right now, I'm gonna give him a chop with the war axe!"

I ease it out of its holster and let him see the sun flash off the edge, and quicker than you can believe, he's Mr. Cooperative, and steps right out. Now this is more like it, and I feel better when he leads us to the Song Vam Cotay River, and points out a crossing. Well, the location ain't great, but it ain't all that bad, so we set up.

Jesus! We just aren't used to the daylight. There is absolutely no cover, and we're sitting right out in the sun. It isn't long before we overheat, and Richards and Flak Body are showing signs of heat stroke. Nothing's happening, and no one wants to be there, so I say the hell with it, and call for extraction. Mr.

Woodard isn't very happy about leaving, but since the rest of us are, with or without him, he decides to tag along. I set a course back to where we inserted, and it only takes us half an hour. That *dien cai dau* (crazy) hoi chan had led us in circles!

Ten minutes pass, then twenty, then thirty, and where the hell are the boats? I get on the horn, and they swear they're on location, waiting for us. Well, I just can't believe it. Something's fucked up. We argue back and forth for five minutes, and finally I am disgusted. I tell them, "I'll pop a flare, see if you can spot it."

I kick out a hand-held, and they come back immediately. "We see a red flare south of us. Proceeding to it."

About three minutes later we hear them, guide them in, and climb on board, and then the shit starts flying.

"You're wrong!" "Nope, you're wrong!" Back and forth, back and forth.

Finally I tell everybody to shut the hell up, it don't matter who's wrong, just get me back to a cool beer. We never did resolve that argument, and it caused some hard feelings between us and our boat guys for a while. Naturally I wasn't wrong.

We ran several more ops before April ended, and only one of them was kind of interesting. See, a lot of our ops would be conducted without any sort of contact, and those were the really tough ones as far as we were concerned, because our fiercest enemy then was boredom. Imagine, if you will, sitting down and remaining motionless for eight to ten hours, without a single thing around you to capture and hold your attention. It's dark, so there's no visual or audible stimulus at all, and all you can do is use your mind.

On many an op, in my mind, I slept with every girl I'd ever known (and all the ones I hadn't slept with but wanted to) in a hundred different ways. I built my dream house stick by stick, I built my dream car bolt by bolt, I built my fortune dollar by dollar, and I did a shitload of philosophizing. I relived many episodes in my life, interesting or not. But unfortunately, many times I just existed, mind blanked out. You click a switch: 10 percent alert, 90 percent flyaway. A noncontact op was a pain in the ass, and might be described as follows:

Well, here we are, sitting on a stream bank in ambush. It's hot, dark, and quiet. I'm all alone. I can't hear anyone around me, I can't see anyone around me, and only occasionally can I smell another SEAL, but my inner senses tell me they are there.

We've been motionless for hours, and even though we've taken our Dexamil to stay awake, we're still sleepy, and have to make a conscious effort to stay alert. I'm trying to ignore the splash in the stream that I heard a few minutes ago. It must have been a fish or a frog . . . I hope.

I've got to pee awfully bad, so I let go in my pants, and the acid urine burns the sensitive chafed skin of my groin, and mixes with the muddy wetness of the last stream crossing. The odor rises to my nostrils.

I want a cigarette in the worst way, and that tickle in my throat is bound and determined to make me cough. I rub my throat gently with a finger to suppress it.

My asshole is burning, but we've got to stay vigilant for the slightest sound or motion. Our aching eyes must remain on full strain to monitor the outlines around us in the darkness, because almost certainly our first warning will be movement.

My eyes keep flicking to the branch that is sticking out right in my line of fire, and although it's really distracting, it's too late now to remove it. Plus I've got to keep checking that clump of brush that looks exactly like a VC with an AK-47, to make sure it hasn't moved since I last looked. If I stare at it hard enough, I can make it move.

Our uniforms are wet and muddy, our armpits and crotches stink, and we've got to take an urgent shit. Our face paint, mixed with mosquito repellent and sweat, is making our eyes burn, and tastes horrible on our lips.

There's an itch between my shoulder blades that I am unable to scratch, and kamikaze mosquitoes are conducting guerrilla warfare on our heads, necks, and hands.

Then I scrunch my shoulders and in super slow motion begin to ease out my poncho liner. It's starting to rain, and I get ready to shiver with cold. I focus my eyes on the luminous dial of my Rolex. Hell, it's only 2200, six hours to go.

And that's the way most of them went when nothing was happening. Sometimes, heaven forbid, you might feel some hard object that one of the guys had thrown thump off your ribs, and you'd have to hang your head, 'cause you knew you'd been snoring. It happened to the best of us. What was really embarrassing was looking around at first light and seeing several bullets lying around and on you. Prepare to take some major verbal flak, 'cause you're gonna get it.

Anyway, this one op, we were set up on the Kinh Ngang canal one night, in a full ambush, and nothing was happening. After several noncontact ops I am wired, and I can hardly keep my finger off the trigger of my Stoner. While I finger the signal string that is running to the men on either side of me, I dream of convoys of VC passing helplessly in front of my position, and imagine the pleasure of wiping them out single-handedly in huge numbers, thereby becoming the Audie Murphy of Vietnam.

But nothing is stirring except my imagination. I mean, it is Dead City, until we all hear that "fish" splash in the water, and shortly thereafter, feel tugs on the signal string to alert us all. Lo and behold, the Starlight scope shows it's a single male, swimming and pushing a little raft across the canal. Man, that dude must really be desperate if he can't find a boat.

Who cares? Rich dude, poor dude, let's shoot that sucker! Finally Tich hails him in Vietnamese.

"Hey, motherfucker! Just where in the hell do you think you're going?"

The dude don't reply, so we let him have it. I put out a whole belt in one continuous burst, blinding myself from the muzzle flash. But it appears our aim is bad. He deserts his raft and makes it across the canal, crawls up on the bank, and beats feet at high speed, although he was limping. Well, kiss my ass! That is one tough gook. We get his raft though, and it has an M-16, six magazines, six Chicom grenades, a few clothes, and a meager supply of food and medicine. We kind of felt sorry for the guy, taking what little he had, but we never did figure out who he was or where he was coming from.

Chapter
Thirty-four

IN MAY 1969, we slowed down a bit, running only nineteen ops. On the seventh, we tried a claymore ambush, which we found out doesn't work well on the water, apparently because the distances involved are too extreme. We had been briefed by the PRUs about a large stream that was getting a lot of boat traffic at night, and we wanted to try initiating with claymores only, and then, instead of leaving, stay set up and see if the traffic continued. We hoped that the VC might think the first group had just set off a booby trap, and would come to investigate, that way we'd get two chances at them. So we all carried extra claymores, set up on a normal stream ambush, and waited, forever, it seemed like. At 2210, two unlighted sampans come by. We hail them, they don't respond, and we fire off two claymores, one set up on each end of the line ambush, their patterns aimed to cross in the kill zone. The claymores go boom, the gooks holler, the sampans stop, and we direct them in to us. Hell, it was just three women, and only one of them was slightly wounded. Most of the ball bearings in the claymores had missed the boats completely, but the boom of the explosion had scared the crap out of them. Good thing, as it later turned out that these were only fisherwomen violating the curfew. I volunteered to guard them while we were waiting, and I gave them a body search to see if they had any weapons, then I handcuffed them. We wait and wait, but no other traffic shows, and at daylight we extract, the released women giving me a glare of outrage. Hey, lady, I was just doing my job.

On the ninth, Mr. Woodard takes one out, and this one drove us, or should I say me, crazy in the end, because we performed poorly. Problem is you can't bitch much to an officer.

Ciao Lahn Police ("Cops? Are you shitting me?") have a hoi chan who will locate a VC supply depot for us, and we'll recon it for possible later action by the Green Beret–advised CIDG (Civilian Irregular Defense Group, local militia) troops. We are not that eager, never having worked with VN Police before, and we'd all heard some nasty stories about the White Mice in the cities.

But these guys were different, as we quickly found out. You'd think we'd learn. You just can't lump groups together in the Nam, because they can sometimes surprise you, and this time we definitely got surprised. The cops were good patrollers, and did a fine job of controlling the hoi chan. They were far better than any ARVNs we'd met before.

We insert at 0330, follow this hoi chan to a ville of about ten hootches, and set up both observation security and ambush, figuring we'll have some fun watching the villagers go about their business, but we don't expect any action.

I set up in a nice little hole that is just the right size for me and the radio, and I've got my long antenna pointing up through the branches of a convenient tree. I get a good radio check, I am settled back chewing on some fruit cake as first light rolls in, and suddenly, along with the rest of our guys, I go on full combat alert and put my shit away.

There are people moving in the ville, and each one seems to have a weapon. As I watch I count up twelve of them, and we can hear others that we can't see. I smell a heavy odor of incense over the normal odors of the ville, somebody in there must be religious. But that don't matter, because we seem to have set up on a definite VC ville, and this is some serious shit. Fuck CIDG. If I had my druthers, I'd open up on them right now, but I'm not leading this op, so I wait for Mr. Woodard's cue.

It don't happen. We sit, we watch, and I get increasingly restive as I watch the VC going about their routine. Why the hell aren't we blasting them? One woman is cooking something over a fire, and there's a guy squatting on the stoop of a hootch cleaning his weapon. Five more men are squatted in a circle shooting the shit, one woman is giving another a headache rub, and two more guys are playing with a couple of kids, laughing up a storm. The remaining VC keeps walking in and out of the main hootch, carrying small stuff. All these people are keeping their weapons with them at all times, and they handle them with an easy familiarity, so I figure them to be pros. I've got my thumper lined on the group of five, they're a perfect target for an HE round, and I am fully prepared to wipe them out.

Then I notice several more kids on the left flank doing something in the small stream, and I can't make out if they are playing or what, until I see one of them stand up with a river rat hanging in each hand. Aha, they're just collecting the contents of their rat traps, probably that night's supper for Charlie. Yeeck! Rats! Makes my stomach roll, but the Viets love 'em.

Then I became alert when I saw a kid run into the ville; he came out of nowhere. He jabbered to the group of five, and without warning, Charlie scrambles. One second all is cool, and the next second Charlie yells and is gone, I mean it happened just that fast. Damn, that's the end of that.

Out of the blue, Mr. Woodard initiated, catching us all by surprise. We joined in tardily, but we've got no targets. I lob an HE into the main hootch, 'cause it's all the target I've got, but I know damn well I'm wasting my time. We continued to fire up the hootches, and we're not receiving any return, so we soon slack off and cease fire. I, for one, was reluctant to hit any of those kids, but I needn't have worried, they were long gone, had vanished like smoke.

We do a cautious approach, and conduct a thorough hootch search, but we don't find shit. We know there's got to be stuff hidden in the ville, but we just aren't skillful (or lucky) enough to find anything except one wounded VC, and he ain't hurt that bad, but the son of a bitch has made sure to ditch his weapon.

I am incredibly disappointed, and I know the other guys are too, because we've blown this one. What an excellent target! It would have given us the greatest satisfaction in the world to best an obviously professional Charlie on his own home ground.

If it had remained pure recon, the intell would have been excellent for a future CIDG or SEAL op, but since we opened up on him, Charlie's warned and gone, and we know from experience that he won't be back. If it was ambush, we had extremely poor results. No bodies, no weapons, no gear. As professionals, we are thoroughly embarrassed, so we don't pass on the full details in our patrol report, and we can't face the police dudes, because we expect they're disgusted with our performance, and they are. The worst thing is, you can bet they aren't going to give us any future business, and that hurts, because this had been a primo target.

Debrief tells us all that the kids had sprung the op by walking up on and spotting one of the SEALs. That's no comfort to us. Charlie had been alert, professional, and in our minds, had shown us up. It's the old story: you get complacent, you get burned. I suppose it could have been worse, if Charlie had counterattacked, and that's what pros usually do. But way down south, here, that's pretty rare. It's certainly not a matter of courage, just that Charlie is a pure guerrilla, and he likes to run and fight another day.

May 12 we had an eerie one, one that still bothers me because I can't figure it out. Second Squad had run an ambush the previous night, and had seen troop movement, but the people were too far away to make out details, and they hadn't come into the kill zone. First Squad, four of us, went out on the twelfth and set up to observe the area where Second had seen the troops. Sure enough, at 0321 we spot a guy, and through the Starlight scope he appears to be a Caucasian! He's big and tall, around six feet, wearing web gear and carrying what appears to be an AK-47, and he keeps moving around in front of us, never getting too close. I broke radio silence and called up Tuyen Nhon to see if there are any friendlies in the area, and they say no. Who is this guy? Is he a renegade American who has gone over, or is he a monster-size North Vietnamese? And what should we have done if he'd gotten closer? I think about shooting a possible American, and I don't care who he is, that thought bothers me to no end. That's a decision I don't want to face.

We don't know the answers to these questions, and we never

find out. It's very, very frustrating, and sets us to speculating after the op. We wonder how many MIAs are really men who have gone over to the enemy.

We know that some MIAs are obviously men who have been blown to red mist by bombs and rockets and mines and such, or have gone down in thick shit and their bodies never found, and we also know that some MIAs are men who have left the country and gone on to places like Cambodia, Thailand, New Zealand, and even Europe, to get out of combat. But how many actually deserted to join the enemy? We hope the number is small, but we know there are some, and these guys can never come back home.

Higher-higher puts out the word that most MIAs are men that have been taken prisoner, and we know right away that's mostly a lie. Charlie don't take many prisoners in South Vietnam, unless they are high-ranking officers, and how many of those are missing? How could they be when, except for pilots, most of them made sure that they never got close to combat? We puzzle it over, everyone seems to have a different opinion, and we never do get it settled.*

May 14 to 16, we had our most productive op. Typically, it started out as routine. (And by this time it was routine, we were the best goddamned warriors on the planet!) On general intelligence from Cai Cai NILO, we insert by UH-1D slick near the Cambodian border. We will recon patrol around during the day looking for a good ambush site. You know, just standard, everyday stuff. The terrain here is open, flat grassland with no cover, and we're really just going through the motions, not expecting any action, because the area is deserted. I mean, there

---

*Just recently I was asked if I thought there were any POWs left in Vietnam. I immediately replied no. Then I thought more about it and qualified my answer. "In 1967, no question, yes there were POWs. In 1970, definitely yes, but by 1980, no. Any POWs that weren't released at the end of the war would have died of wounds or privation by 1980. If there are any Americans left in Vietnam, they would be deserters who are too afraid to return, or turncoats who don't want to return. That's my belief." But the kicker is whether there are any POWs left in Russia. There were several rumors floating around that some POWs had been taken to Russia by the Russian advisers to the NVA. Man, I just don't know. I sure don't want to think so.

can't be anybody within a hundred miles. There's nothing to
see, but that's not it. It's hard to describe correctly, we just don't
"feel" Charlie is anywhere around. I wouldn't call it a sixth
sense, but after you've become a pro, you get a feeling, maybe
created by unobvious signs: disturbed grass, a broken branch,
the animal life, hell, I don't know what causes it, but anyhow,
it's there. But on this op, it's not there. Charlie's not home
today.

Sure enough, we insert at 1630, recon around until dark, then
set up an ambush on an old trail just because it's handy. Because
of the lack of any kind of cover, and because of unlimited visibility, we use the partial ambush procedure. This is where three
guys are awake and watching as security. The rest of us sleep,
and we alternate during the night. If anything should happen,
there will be plenty of time to wake everyone and get them on
line, and out in the open like this, we would look for most
enemy movement to be at last light and first light. But as we
expect, nothing is happening, and the night passes uneventfully.

Next day we wander around lackadaisically. We can see for a
hundred miles, it's hotter than a motherfucker, and there's not a
smidgen of sign. Fortunately, in the afternoon we find a nice
swimming hole, a bomb crater, and everyone strips down and
jumps in for needed relief. Ah, that's much better. After our
swim we keep wandering, angling very close to the Cambodian
border, if not over it, until we stumble on a pile of belts of linked
.30 caliber ammo. What in the world? None of us can figure out
how it had gotten there, and who might use it. Does Charlie
have an old .30 caliber? We don't know.

It's a real puzzler, but the belts lay close to a faint trail, so we
decide to set up on it. Might as well, since we can't dance and
it's too wet to plow. We select our ambush sites in the six-inch
grass, settle into them, and break out some rations.

Some guys had K-rats, but I preferred Cs. By now we'd tried
all the different kinds of rations. K-rat prepared dry meals, survival rations, and C-rations. K-rats were popular because they
were light, so you could carry a bunch of them. Heat some
water with a chunk of C4 explosive, pour it into your food
pouch, and you had a decent meal, or so the other guys said.

Survival rats, or "chalk rats" as we called them, were dried, concentrated food pellets, and though also very light, they were disgusting, looking like dog food and tasting like chalk. Sure, you could mix them with water, but all you'd get would be a gooey, nasty mess. We were all big chowhounds and would eat most anything, but nobody liked chalk rats.

I could tolerate K-rats, absolutely refused to eat chalk rats, but I really enjoyed C-rats, even ham and motherfuckers (lima beans). Hell, if you ate the grease layer of beef and potatoes first, and got it stuck to the roof of your mouth, you could enjoy the taste of your meal for hours after you had eaten it. I liked the cigarette packs, I liked the gum, I liked the fruit, and I even liked the fruit cake. The other guys called me an oddball (along with other unmentionable things), but with a mouthful of pound cake, I didn't bother to reply. Amazingly, we had once been supplied with a couple of cases of Cs dated 1945, and I had eaten them right up. They were fine. If there was any problem with Cs, it was the fact that they were heavy. But so what? I was Hercules, and could carry as much as I wanted.

And it's the same story with hand grenades. As part of our "field-testing" role with China Lakes Experimental Station in California, we had been issued apple grenades; they were the size of a baseball, round, smooth, and powerful, and you could pretend to be Ty Cobb. We had also been given cherry grenades, they were small, and you could throw them a mile, but they were mostly harassment toys. For pure noise and damage, though, give me the WW II pineapples every time. So, call me square and old-fashioned. Fuck you.

China Lakes would design new war goodies, SEALs would field-test them and give their opinion. It was a perfect marriage. As far as I know, the grenades were one of the very few items that didn't pan out, at least they didn't for me. Oh, and don't forget those nasty chalk rations.

Anyhow (I digressed again, forgive me), we're lined up in circular ambush, we're set up and relaxed, and there ain't nothing happening except the stars in the sky. I do an early watch, so about midnight I go to sleep. Around 0400, I'm lying on my back cutting some fine Zs, when a thumper round goes out of the tube and awakens me. Damn. Before I can even twitch I got M-60 tracers going right across my chest, and I'm pinned down and helpless, nailed to the ground. Yowda yowda! I'm lying right in the kill zone, and I can't move or grab my weapon.

When the flare dies and the firing stops, I yell out and do one hell of a caterpillar crawl to my radio and weapon, which I'd carelessly left with the guy on watch. I mean, my trail was smoking, I was dumb, dumb, dumb! I ask for the word, and it's my usual luck. The guys on watch had heard many voices walking up to them, and with no time to prepare, had illumi-nated and initiated on ten to twelve people. The guys were sure of some hits, but there was nothing moving out in front of us, and no noise. I call the choppers and tell them to come get us at daylight, but meanwhile, we wait. You can bet I didn't do any more sleeping.

As first light slowly filters in, we see at least two bodies. When we're sure that nothing is stirring, we hold our breaths, and cautiously ease out to check them. One male, one female (she's a cutie), both with head shots, had dropped right in their tracks. There were five blood trails, and at the end of one of them was another dead male. The 60 had chewed him up pretty bad in the hip and groin area, a perfect burst. (Most troops tended to shoot high, and it had been drummed into us again and again, shoot for the hips to nail your target. Here was the proof.)

But the first male was somebody special, we could tell that just by looking at him. He was clean and well-groomed, and his fingernails were in good shape. He was obviously no farmer. Also, he was wearing a pistol belt and holster, and carrying a leather document pouch. Some honcho, you can bet. We searched the area carefully, took all the gear from the bodies, and booby-trapped them. It was too bad about the woman, she was a looker, and had probably been the honcho's girlfriend, or maybe his aide. We all felt bad about her for about two minutes.

Not only did I not get to fire a shot, I had the distinction (?) of being mentioned in the patrol report under lessons learned— "All personnel should sleep with their weapons beside them, ready to fire." Hmm . . . seems like every time I get a little careless, something happens to bring me back to earth. If I don't get my shit together, one of these days it's gonna cost me.

A week later, after intelligence had been able to peruse all the documents we'd captured, we get the word. Gadzooks! The honcho we'd killed was in fact a high-ranker in the Viet Cong infrastructure. He was in charge of the anti–*chieu hoi* program in the Mekong Delta—had been, that is.

Intelligence was delighted, and a few weeks later, our overall commander, Admiral Zumwalt, came out to visit us for congratulations. We were very flattered, but I found it hard to talk to the man. I was eating chow, and this guy with all kinds of gold on him sits down across from me and asks me what I think about my little piece of the war, did I have any complaints. Are you shitting me? I mumbled and fumbled out a lame answer.

"No sir, things are okay sir, I've got everything I need sir, I'm doing just fine sir."

I flushed with embarrassment, thinking what a jerk I was for being so awed, but he was a nice guy, and his friendly and attentive manner soon got us talking.

Admiral Elmo Zumwalt was the SEALs' friend. Although he was Commander of Naval Forces in Vietnam (COMNAV-FORV), he liked and respected SEALs, and firmly believed in their mission capabilities. He seemed to be the only high-ranking conventional forces officer who did, and thank God for us, he happened to be the boss. If SEALs needed something bad enough, or got into serious trouble, a call to his office in Saigon would usually resolve the problem. Naturally we wouldn't take advantage of our clout.

Like hell we wouldn't! He saved my young ass once, and I ain't likely to forget it. I was looking to add an AK-47 to my weapons collection, for possible use in the bush. I figured that the green AK tracers might fool the enemy, and I sure wanted to give it a try.

One night in a bar, I met a CID (or so he claimed) guy, and he told me he knew where he could get his hands on a couple of AKs for next to nothing. Seems he knew of a ARVN outpost that had several. Aha, that's music to my ears, and when Slim

Wilkins decides he wants one too, the three of us climb in a jeep and go careening around the dark countryside, heading for this outpost. Well, we arrive, everything's fine, but when we walk up toward the outpost wall, ARVN gets scared and opens up on us with M-16s. Jesus H. Christ! Here we are, standing right out in the open, and slugs are cracking around my ears. We hit the deck fast, and the CID guy starts yelling, and the firing finally stops. This is one of the times I wish I'd paid better attention in Vietnamese language school, instead of spending my time admiring the beautiful young instructor, but we are finally able to convince ARVN that we are not the enemy, and we go inside the outpost—the district commander wants to talk to us on the radio. I answer him, and find out that he's some prick Army colonel, and he wants our ass. I tried explaining, but he ain't having any of it, and plans to roast us. We're to stay right where we are, and he'll send someone to arrest us.

Arrest? I hear the word *arrest*, I say fuck you, and away we go at high speed. I know where safety lies, and that's with my fellow SEALs. When we arrive, I wake Mr. Woodard up and tell him the story, and he ain't real thrilled. He knows what must be done though, so he puts in a call to Admiral Zumwalt. Thank you, sir!

Before the shit can hit the fan, and some dumbass dogs get shot by me for attempting arrest, the admiral contacts the colonel, and calms him down. Can you imagine what it would have been like for the jealous dogs to get a couple of poor, defenseless sailors in their hands? We would have been gone geese, but you can bet I never would have surrendered without a fight. Luckily I didn't have to.

But, "be it known to all," somewhere in Army red-tapedom there reposes a written and sworn statement from Rad Miller Jr. and Ray Wilkins, Esquire, etc. etc. as to how the Army CID guy fucked them. End of story.

None of us had forgotten the sighting we'd gotten of the Caucasian (?), and on May 17, Tom McDonald led Second Squad back to the same area, looking for him. It was a poor night for an op, or so they thought, windy and raining. Once Second Squad arrived on site, they discovered visibility was so poor that they wouldn't see anybody moving, so they set up a stream ambush instead. At 0300, the guys saw a sampan coming down the stream with a lighted lantern in the bow, and following it at a slight distance, a second one. Both were heavily loaded and low in the water, and weapons were seen. As usual, Charlie showed us he was no dummy, he was using the poor conditions to operate safely. But he was dealing with SEALs, not ARVN, and Second Squad opened up and wiped him from the face of the earth. Both sampans were sunk. Result: two VC KIA, two VC WIA and captured, four KIA probables. After the action, more lights were seen upstream, and some warning shots were heard, but Charlie knew better than to come down past an unknown enemy who could lay down such ferocious firepower. Later we figured that Second Squad had hit the lead element of a large force, and the guys were really disappointed, but that was the way it went sometimes.

You always ask yourself the same old questions. Should they have let the lead boats pass? But how did they know that the boats they saw were lead elements? It's always a toss of the dice, but personally I thought Tom was right in opening up when he did. You've heard the old saying, "A bird in the hand . . ." etc. etc. If it had been one boat and one man, I might have hesitated, but otherwise, nothing is getting by me. However, there's always plenty more Charlies where those came from—we'll get 'em next time.

Yow! I'm stuck with another pure recon op. PRU intell has picked up increased activity around a small isolated ville off the river, and Mr. Marsh tells me to take out a patrol and check it out. Recon only, unless we get our ass in a sling, because this is a PRU area of operations.

So I set it up, and ask for "volunteers." Rich wants to go, and so does Flak Body McIntosh. Rocky gives in then, and Gieng asks can he go. That's only four SEALs, but what the hell, it's recon only, so that should be plenty. I do my flyover, then I give the briefing, and I tell the guys to carry enough gear to do a two-dayer just in case. I'd seen about eight hootches alongside a large stream, and there was another small stream that ran from the main river and petered out almost at the ville, or vice versa. I plan to insert at the mouth of the small stream, follow it up to the ville, then set up on a dike behind the ville, which should give us a good field of observation. I figured to insert at night, lay up the first day and observe, and depending on what we saw, either extract that night or stick around for another day's observation.

I packed up my gear, and knowing that I'd be spending a lot of time without being able to smoke, I put in quite a few cans of C-rat fruit and some other chewable goodies. I would be both radioman and patrol leader, because the other guys didn't want to carry the radio. They pointed out that I was the expert, why change? Sure. Lazy bastards. Ah, what the hell. My radio was my second skin by then, so I accepted. Whoa! When I picked up my loaded rig, the weight startled me, but then I shrugged it off. I can hack it.

Just before 2200, the PBR we're using for insertion comes down off plane, and I ease into my combat harness, then my radio rig. Jesus! I staggered a bit. I got a lot of weight on me, and something digs into my back muscle, must be a twisted strap or a fold of my shirt. As the PBR, engines dying to a low rumble, glides quietly in toward the bank, I wiggle my shoulders uncomfortably. I'll have to adjust my gear when we get ashore, otherwise I'll get a blister.

The PBR hit the bank with a mushy thump, and I dropped over the side into neck-deep water. Fucking Richards jumps off the prow, he hardly gets wet to the knees, but then he sinks down into the water and enters the stream mouth. I ease in to the bank following Gieng, and then pull myself up into the mouth of the stream we were to follow. Ouch! I get a lightning flash of pain in my back, and it don't go away. But Rich is on the move, and I can't stop. I grit my teeth and follow, twisting in my harness, trying to ease it. I get on the horn and call in to Whirltop that we are on the move. Then my toe catches a root, I almost go flat on my face, and I get a tearing pain in my back which almost makes me holler. Then the pain eases to a dull ache, and it's bearable, so I keep going. The stream is deep enough at this point so the bank is just about at head level to me, and I know the lighter guys can see over the edge. It's only the overloaded pack mule and five foot four Gieng who can't.

We've gone about fifty meters up the stream and it's incredibly hard going. The mud is about thigh-deep under a couple feet or so of stinking water, and it's sucking the strength right out of my body. I figure it's about time to climb out and patrol along the bank, but then in the dim light I see and sense Gieng stop. Then Rich eases back to me. He puts two fingers to his eyes, then his ears, and points right and left, flashing his fingers. I interpret. He's seen and heard movement both to our left and right, eight on one side and ten on the other. Uh-oh. That's not good news. If people are up and about this time of night, they're bound to be Charlie, and that kills my plan of climbing out of the stream; we'll just have to wing it. I nod and point Rich on, then turn and sign to Flak Body to pass on the information.

Man, we're about a third of a klick in and I wish I could die. The weight I'm carrying and the thick mud have sucked all the strength right out of my body. About halfway in, I'm a goner, and wish I would die and get it over with. I am completely numb, my body don't exist except as pain, and I am completely oblivious to sight, sound, and senses. I follow Gieng's back like an automaton, and I have put myself and my patrol members in extreme danger. Not only have I slowed the patrol down because I just can't go any faster, I am now useless as a leader. This is the worst.

Nope. It gets worse when we start running into brush that has grown down into the diminishing stream, and I am literally pulling myself along by grabbing it, and roots when I can find them. I put my hand on one and it wriggles in my hand and then escapes, but I am so exhausted that I pay no attention. My legs are pretty much gone now, and I spend a lot of time on my knees pulling myself along. In occasional flashes of clarity, I can sense that the others are having the same struggle, the going is that bad. Finally I pull myself forward into Gieng's back, and I stop and wait, blowing like a whale. Then I realize that Rich is there, yanking my arm. I come partially alive, and he's signaling that we've reached the end of the stream, he's pointing down to it and making a cutthroat motion, then pointing up and to the left. I have recovered enough to nod to him and motion him on. I don't know how I'm gonna follow. I'm kneeling in mud and water to my chest.

But I got to do it. I see Rich's silhouette above me momentarily as he climbs up on the bank, and then Gieng's, and I wash off me what mud I can with my hands, so that I don't leave too much sign on the bank, then I crawl up behind him. Somehow I force myself to my feet, and it's all I can do not to groan out loud as I stay crouched over. I fumble in my claymore pouch and bring out the compass and take a direction. Rich is watching, and I point him and he moves out at a tangent to the stream we've been following. I'm recovering somewhat, now that the mud is no longer dragging on me, and I follow Gieng, becoming aware of my surroundings. My bird legs are hollering for mercy, even while they're trying to cramp up. I keep going. I hear voices around at some distance from us, and there's the ville, off to my right, where I can see pinpoints of oil lamp lights. There are a lot of them, more than I expected. We all freeze suddenly as we hear a heavy snort out in front of us, and then the sound of a water buffalo moving away. I give a sigh of relief as I recognize it for what it is, and thank my lucky stars it didn't attack us.

We soon hit the dike, and it's pretty big, it's like eight feet high; it's the biggest one I've ever seen. We halt on one knee while Rich checks it out, and then he comes back to report. He whispers directly in my ear, the dike has a footpath on the top, but the side toward the ville is covered with brush, and he figures that's where we should laager. But he wants to move up about twenty meters. I nod agreement, then turn and pass on the info to Flak Body. We wade carefully and quietly through the low brush along the bottom of the dike, until Gieng stops in front of me and moves up the side of the dike. I follow, and then move away from him slightly to get my interval, and I stumble and almost go head over heels into a spider hole. Oh boy. Just what the doctor ordered. I check it out, and it's old, almost filled in. Perfect. I'm home. I shrug off my radio rig and then my combat harness. Wow! That really hurts. Then I kneel down and clean out the hole with my hands and hatchet. Pretty soon I've got a comfortable seat carved out, so that I can sit on one dirt shelf, lean back against the dike with my back, and stretch out my legs on a lower shelf. Then I carve out a niche for my radio on my left, assemble the sections of my whip antenna, and make my radio check in a low voice.

"Whirltop, Threadbare One. Over."

"Threadbare, Whirltop. Over."

"Threadbare on station. Out."

"Roger. Understand Threadbare on station. Whirltop out."

I took my antenna apart at the second joint, but left it assembled and slid it into the brush. I might need it quickly, and this way I could plug the one joint fast in case of emergency. Last thing I did was carve a small shelf for my combat harness and lay out a few items to hand: my M-79 rounds and one of my canteens. I settled back gingerly to wait for first light. Goddamn it, no question I had a blister on my back, I could feel my shirt sticking.

As the gray light filtered in, fog came with it, and I checked out my immediate surroundings. Not bad. Not bad at all. Rich had chosen well. We were in a thick brush clump, one of the few in the immediate area, and we were well hidden. I could see Gieng and Flak Body plainly, about four feet away, but the guys on each flank only vaguely through the brush screen. Gieng was dug in like me, but Flak Body was just sprawled on the surface, his long, lean body weaved into the brush he was lying in, M-60 by his side, ready to rock and roll. I had to laugh to myself, though, because they were muddy from head to toe. It blended nicely with our surroundings, but they sure looked funny. Flak Body grinned back at me, a flash of white teeth, and I realized I looked just as bad, probably worse.

As the light grew, I made a final cleanup of my position to make sure I was as well hidden as possible, put the radio antenna in a handier position, carefully opened and checked my M-79 for mud, and settled back to wait for good visibility. A thought hit me, and I checked first my combat harness, then my radio rig. Uh-huh. There it was. One of the radio straps was hanging loose, and the buckle must have been the culprit that stabbed me in the back. I rebuckled the strap properly.

About 0800 the sun burned the fog off, and as it wisped away, I became more alert as I saw more of my surroundings. Surprise, surprise, this wasn't no small ville. On my flyover I'd figured eight hootches, but now I counted ten more hidden in the banana grove. And there were a shitload of people starting to move around. The trails were hard-packed dirt, which meant heavy use, and they were all over the place. I saw the usual numbers of women of all ages, a multitude of kids running around, and more to the point, combat-aged males, quite a few of them. The males stayed under or close to overhead cover at all times, and that firmed up my growing suspicions. I knew by their actions that if an aircraft appeared, these guys would melt into the cover, remaining unseen. Then I spotted a handmade overhead brush canopy, connecting the two sections of the ville, the obvious one and the hidden one, under which the men were walking, and I was pretty certain. Some if not all of these guys were Charlie. Had to be. By 0900, however, activity had slowed to almost nothing. Some women were out in the paddies, some were dicking around next to the large stream, and the men had disappeared.

I broke out my pad and pen, and made myself a comprehensive map of the area on the first page, including every detail that I could see. I estimated distances and locations and added a couple of compass bearings. Starting on the second page, I wrote a narrative and description, noting every detail. The ville was shaped like a stubby backward L, with the hidden hootches as the bottom of the L, and we were facing them. The obvious, or long side of the L lay on the large stream, and there were eleven sampans in sight tied to posts next to a little landing dock. To the north of the ville, the banana grove tapered into heavy cane or bamboo growth, a real thicket of it. The east was the stream, and the south was six large rice paddies. Our side, the west, was grass and low brush, contained by the dike on which we were hidden. The entire area showed long occupation and cultivation, and I estimated this ville to be maybe seventy-five to a hundred people, probably more, and that was quite large for this area. It took me almost an hour before I was satisfied I had everything down on paper. As I placed the pad and pen back into their plastic carrying bag, I speculated as to whether we should do a sneak into the ville at night, to try and pick up more details. Might be worth a shot.

As the end of the day approached, however, that idea was canceled. There were people everywhere, on the move. We'd had a close call about 1500 when seven or eight women walked the dike trail above us. They came out of nowhere, and the first we knew they were there was when we could hear them gabbling like a flock of geese and giggling at some unknown something as they passed by only three feet away. It was disconcerting, and it was damn scary, because they were to our backs, and all I could do was twist sideways and crane my neck to get a glimpse of muddy legs and feet, literally within reaching distance. It was the old story though. They never in this world expected us to be there, so their eyes, unfocused by lack of concentration or expectation, passed right over our group unseeing. And we had expected that, that's what hiding is all about. If we had a single worry, it was that we would be smelled. I know I stunk to high heaven from the copious sweat generated by last night's run in, and seasoned by the day's fresh sweat under the fierce Vietnam sun. But mixed in, and maybe diluting my body smell, was the ripe aroma of the mud and stagnant water that we had waded through to get in.

A half hour before dark, we saw Charlie. He formed up in the ville into a group, fifteen in number, and then dispersed in every direction. Charlie was black-PJed, he was carrying an assortment of arms, M-16s, carbines, and AKs, and he wasn't dicking around. He was quiet, he was military, and he was obviously posting sentries, spreading out to blanket the area around the ville. I wondered if we had been detected, but that thought fled as I watched the villagers moving around us. They weren't searching, they were just going about their normal business. Nobody, including the sentries, came too near us. As the light disappeared, so did the people, except for the sounds of their voices as they conversed among themselves. I noticed a lot of activity at the edge of the stream, around the sampans. I saw some bundles being loaded, but it might just have been that they were setting up for night fishing. It was hard to tell.

Then a bunch of them, dimly seen, gathered around a large, open-faced hootch in the center of the ville, and a woman started haranguing them in Vietnamese. Well I'll be a son of a bitch! I'm looking at my first ever political rally. I made up my mind at that instant, and turned to McIntosh to pass the word, and then Gieng. We're sticking. I figure that if I can get enough obvious VC troops out in front of me, I'll call in fire support and do a number on them. From what I've seen so far, that's a real possibility. PRU will just have to grin and bear it. Then I assembled my antenna and breathed into the handset.

"Whirltop, Whirltop, Threadbare One. Over."

"Threadbare, this is Whirltop. Over."

"Threadbare. Plan Bravo. Out."

"Threadbare, Whirltop. Understand Plan Bravo. Out."

Plan Bravo, as preagreed with the parties concerned, told Whirltop what we were doing, that is, staying for another night and day. Under Plan Bravo Whirltop would notify our two Seawolf choppers that we weren't extracting tonight; they were to remain on standby until the end of tomorrow night. Then Whirltop would notify our PBR. The PBR, which after inserting us had maintained station in the general area, would be spelled off by another, and would remain on standby until tomorrow night, at which time they would expect to be called to come in and get us. This was all as opposed to Plan A, which would have meant action sometime tonight. It was a time-proven method to allow us to have both transportation and air cover on warm standby at all times we were in the bush.

I opened another fruit can, tasted peaches with pleasure, and settled back. I was disgruntled to be spending another night and day out here, and I shifted my filthy body in discomfort. I bet the other guys were pissed too. But as patrol leader, I had to put my personal feelings aside, there was just too much intell here. I wouldn't be doing my job if I didn't get as much of that intell as possible.

As there had been the previous night, there was a lot going on in and around the ville, a lot of movement, and what else we weren't able to see. A sneak-in flat wouldn't have worked for us, because with all the movement around, there was no way we could have remained undetected. Once again I scanned the immediate area with the Starlight scope, but saw nothing significant. The activity in the ville proper was pretty much a blur; it was just too far away from me.

The next day revealed a couple of things: the sampans were all gone, and so were a lot of the combat-aged males. I didn't see any more than five of them before they went under cover for the day. It appeared to me that they'd shipped out last night, bound who knows where, and that canceled my idea of blasting the ville. Regardless, it all went into my notebook. On each side of me, Gieng and McIntosh were sleeping, and I knew that along with myself, Rich and Rocky were awake and observing. That had been the plan, no more than two of us sleeping at any time. Around 1000, having wakened, Mac signaled my turn, and I lay back with a sigh of pleasure. On this kind of an op, fatigue was cumulative, and today would really drag.

Something was poking me in the belly, and I awoke with the sound of a dog's persistent barking in my ears, and flashed a groggy look at my Rolex. It was 1330. I looked at Flak Body and it was he who was poking me with a stick, and he wasn't smiling. He pointed to our front, and I came fully alert, as he already was. Oh shit. As I'd been afraid of, we'd been smelled out by one of the ville dogs, and he was letting the world know about it; he was tied about forty meters away. My pulse started racing. He hadn't been there before, and I had no idea when he'd been tied there, but it was incredibly lucky that none of the ville people had come out yet to check his upset. And the stupid mutt was bound and determined, he wasn't going to shut his mouth. What in the hell should I do? He was too far away to chunk a stick at, and Charlie was no dummy. I was amazed that he wasn't yet out searching, but I knew it wouldn't be long. I saw some women gathering at the big hootch, obviously concerned about the dog's barking. Then four kids, I don't know, maybe eight or ten years old, headed for the dog. I quickly plugged in my radio antenna and got ready to call up the troops. I had the desperate thought that maybe I could call up the Seawolves for a flyover, which would make the villagers go under cover, but that wouldn't solve the problem of that fucking dog.

Maybe they would shoot him. Fat chance of that. The kids milled around the dog for a few minutes, halfheartedly looked around the area and directly at and through us. Then the oldest boy gave the dog a kick, a good solid thump in the ribs, and the dog yelped and shut his mouth. He untied the dog and dragged him back into the ville, chattering up a storm at the dog; he was calling him every name in the book. I grinned with relief and pleasure, and when I looked at Gieng, he was laughing silently. He gave me a thumbs-up, and lay back, relaxed. Thank God for an impatient youngster. He'd saved somebody's life, probably mine. Thank you, pal.

Darkness was close upon us, and we were getting ready to pull out. As the other guys were doing, I cleaned up my area, pulling a final layer of dirt over the hole in which I'd buried my C-rat cans and trash. Last light I gave one final scan to my area, smoothed out where my feet had gouged, and spotted my P38 can opener laying there where I had dropped it. I picked it up and put it away, then I eased into my combat harness, and then my radio rig. Ouch. My back hurt, but not all that much. I ignored it.

The ville, although still active, was fairly quiet. We were moving out during or shortly after the supper hour, when the ville people would be at their least alert. We got to our feet and silently worked out the kinks in our legs and bodies, then Rich went, then Gieng, and I followed. The first few meters were slow, while we got our leg muscles working smoothly, and then the pace picked up. I knew Rich wanted to reach and get down into the stream as soon as possible. I dreaded the coming muddy going, but I was a lot lighter now that I'd eaten most of my C-rats, and besides, we were going home. That made a world of difference in my attitude.

Suddenly there was a short cry ahead of me, and a quiet scuffle. I froze and Flak Body walked right into me. I waited, weapon up and ready for anything, and after a few moments Gieng came to me and I bent down to let him whisper in my ear. Rich had stumbled over a woman out taking a pee, and falling on top of her, had made her a prisoner. Should we take her with us? He already knew the answer, but he wanted it official from the patrol leader. "Hell yeah, we'll take her," I spoke in Gieng's ear. "If we get in any shit, waste her, but otherwise, bring her along." Gieng gripped my arm in answer, then moved forward, and I followed. I could sense by vague sight and sound that Gieng had her, just as he was supposed to, and was propelling her along. She made noises of crying and fear, but they were hardly audible, muffled by the duct tape I knew they had applied across her mouth. I also knew she'd be handcuffed. It was SOP.

In no time we arrived at and slid down into the stream, and we breathed a big sigh of relief. Now we were hidden while we were moving, and had a clear path ahead of us, we hoped. We'd have to stay alert, though, just in case Charlie had seen our sign and set up an ambush to catch us coming out. It was six of one and a half dozen of the other. To prevent that sort of thing happening, we rarely used the same path in and out, but in this unique case, two things had helped me make my decision. One, Charlie would have expected us to come out last night, not tonight. Two, because of the high numbers of personnel moving around the area, this was the only way that we could remain undetected. There was also a third reason—experience. Muddy streams were commonplace in this section of the country, and generally wouldn't excite Charlie's interest. It was only if we'd left an obvious sign identifying us, such as bootprints, that Charlie would be alerted. Since we'd stayed in the center of the stream, and because the damn mud was so deep, and finally because we'd been careful to crawl out of the stream at the ville, rather than walking out, there should be no identifiable sign. Only time would tell, but the problem was, if I was wrong, the price could be high. I'd made the commitment, so I kept walking. It was still tough going, but nowhere near as bad as coming in fully loaded. Gieng was towing the prisoner by her handcuffed wrists, and he kept her humping in front of me. Going-home juices fueled my tired muscles, and I was able to match the pace.

But I was surprised and very pleased when Rich halted us and came back to me. We were closing on the extraction point, about two-thirds out, and since he had detected no signs of the enemy, Rich wanted to get up on the stream bank for the final distance. Even though we were all dog-tired, I reluctantly vetoed him; we'd come in and done our thing and were almost out, all undetected, and I wasn't taking any chance of blowing that. I could tell he wasn't really happy with my answer, but away he went. I checked my Rolex, and we'd been on the move slightly over three hours. We'd been hustling.

Well, I'm here to tell you, that last third stretched on forever. I regretted my decision a hundred times before it was finally over. But then it was, and I climbed up on the bank and got on the horn as Gieng blindfolded the prisoner.

"Whirltop, Whirltop, Threadbare One. Over." I knew PBR 52 and Seawolves were monitoring.

"Threadbare One, Whirltop. Over."

"Whirltop, Threadbare One. Ready to extract. Scramble three. Over."

"Threadbare, Whirltop. Roger. Understand ready to extract. Scramble three. Over."

"Roger. Threadbare out."

Immediately the PBR came on the net.

"Threadbare One, PBR fiver two. Over."

"PBR fiver two, Threadbare."

"Threadbare, PBR fiver two. Say status. Over."

"PBR fiver two, quiet and clean. Over."

"Roger. ETA fiver mikes."

That told me that Lieutenant Johanssen was doing his usual good job, and had moved up closer to our extraction point in anticipation of my call. We'd be out of here quickly.

We heard the roar of the PBR in the distance, then, as it dropped from plane, the rumble of its engines as it maneuvered, which then muted even further as he glided in to the bank to pick us up. The prow hit the bank, and we climbed on. Jumpin' Jesus! It was a real struggle for my exhausted body, and Rocky gave me a helping hand. Thanks, guy! The prisoner struggled— she didn't want to climb on no boat—but Gieng controlled her. He was a hardcase, that one. I collapsed on the deck. It was a done deal, man. We'd made it one more time.

Not quite. Oh, the forty-minute trip back was quiet, and I

dozed most of it, waking only to suck down the welcome pollution of cigarette after cigarette. But I was patrol leader, and my work was far from done. I finally got my shit together and called up Whirltop to inform them we had a prisoner, would NILO have someone at home plate to take her when we arrived. Also send a com message to PRU informing them of mission completion and set up a debrief at 1000. Then I really relaxed. Oh God, I couldn't wait for a warm shower, and then write my patrol report.

We arrived at home plate by midnight, because Lieutenant Johanssen, knowing we were wasted, had really laid on the rpm. Once we docked, I handed over my prisoner to two waiting SPs (shore patrolmen, heavy cops), after Gieng pulled the duct tape off her mouth. Ouch. I bet that hurt, but she was too terrified to pay attention. I followed the guys into the barracks, where we unloaded and shed our weapons before heading immediately to the showers. We kept it quiet so that we wouldn't wake the other guys, but we sure didn't waste no time. We had it awful good here; they had a big water tank on top of the building, which was heated by the sun every day. It was far better than washing off in the river or stream. I looked at the guys in the light of the showers and I had to laugh. They were some filthy, fagged-out-looking bunch. Richards saw me grinning.

"All right, Miller, what the fuck you laughing at?" The others looked around.

I spoke without thinking.

"At you dudes. Some sorry-looking bunch. Your eyes look like piss holes in the snow."

Uh-oh, that did it. I got return flak in a double dose, mostly about how they'd had to carry me in, because I was such a pansy that I couldn't make it on my own. Then Rich had his fun.

"At least we didn't smell so bad that a dog noticed us. That son of a bitch zeroed right in on you, I seen his nose wrinkling. He probably wondered what had died out there."

Hmm. No way I'm gonna let him get over on me. "Huh. It wasn't me who attacked some poor defenseless old woman out there and tried to get laid right in the trail. Prisoner? Shit. I seen you gropin' her. You just wanted some, and that was the ugliest old woman I ever saw. At least you coulda picked a decent-looking one."

That brought the laughs, and took the flak off me. Everybody had something to add, and Rich took it with a grin. But he wasn't quite done yet.

I had washed and peeled off my gear, and I was working on my shirt, which was glued to my back. When I saw Rich was watching me, I gave it a good tug to get it over with, and it tore loose. I saw it was bloody, and I turned under the shower to wash off my back. I heard Rich right behind me, but before I could turn around, he said, "Hey, Miller! You got a hole in your back!" And he gave it a poke with his finger.

Yeeoww! Holy jumpin' Jesus! After I peeled myself off the ceiling and climbed down from the rafters, I cussed him out good, but the damage was done. They all had to check it out and wanted to know where I'd gotten it. When I explained, they all busted my chops about my carelessness. Rocky had to add his two cents.

"Hey, Miller. That's good enough for a Heart. I can hear it now. In the face of overwhelming enemy numbers, at great personal risk, Miller did in fact get ambushed in the back by a radio buckle, showing immense courage and love of God and Country above and beyond . . ."

Shit. I was back under the gun, and there wasn't anything I could do about it.

At 1000 that morning, while I was still groggy from too little sleep, we had our debrief, attended by both our officers, NILO, and the PRU Green Beret adviser with two of his people. That part went quick, but then we were grilled for nearly two hours to deliver every smidgen of intell to the people listening. They hung on every word, and were really thrilled to get my written info. I got some good compliments, which were really for us all, before we finally ended for lunch. Mr. Marsh gave me a slap on the shoulder as we left. "Nice op. Real nice." That made me feel good.

The closeout of this op was a real surprise. I mean, we talked some about running another op in the same area, an ambush or prisoner snatch, but we weren't given permission by PRU. That turned out to be good for us, though, because three days later PRU sent in a company on a daylight search and destroy, and they got the shit kicked out of them. They caught Charlie laying up in the ville in a large group, and Charlie fought his way out. PRU had nine killed and eleven wounded, and Charlie lost twenty, with an unknown number of unrecovered wounded. As I'd guessed and passed on in the debrief, the ville had turned out to be a transit point for Charlie's troops. Sergeant Johnson, the Green Beret, shook his head when I talked to him.

"That fucking bamboo thicket you saw to the north of the ville was loaded right to the hilt with booby traps. Charlie zoomed right through it, but we lost three as soon as we entered it, and two more trying to get back out of it."

Man, I shivered, because I had considered the thicket as a way in and out for our recon op. I had only turned it down because of the limited visibility. Just goes to show you.

Chapter
Thirty-five

BASED ON NEW intelligence, we moved to Moc Hoa, where we're quartered on a barge. At Moc Hoa, we would mostly be using choppers instead of our boats, Warrior 10 UH-1D slicks for transport and Seawolf 32 and 36 for air cover, although MST came along with us to do river work on their own and to be available if we needed them. Moc Hoa was in easy reach of Cambodia, and intelligence indicated a lot of VC troop movement coming out of Cambodia to operate in Vietnam, then running back across the border for sanctuary. We wanted to take advantage of this movement if we could, since unlike conventional forces, borders meant nothing to us.

On the twenty-first, we went out on an exploratory day patrol to check our new AO. For the most part the swamps are gone, but not the water. The terrain is open, flat, and grassy, with a zillion waterways cutting it up, mostly small, which meant very little boat traffic except on the larger canals and streams.

We're out here based on intell from Cai Cai Green Berets and the Border Control Center. Nothing specific, but we're to keep our eyes open, and get a feel for the area. We insert normally, recon around, and then we stumble on a fresh trail, and mother, what a trail. This sucker is four feet wide, and it's got cart tracks beat right into it! There's also a shitload of spread-toed foot tracks, sandal tracks, and bicycle wheel marks. Oh lord, then we also see boot tracks, and we get a little edgy, because boots mean NVA. A short way down the line we meet an intersecting trail, just as heavily traveled, that leads to a loading and unloading spot on a large canal. Yowza! This might be more than we can handle, and we start to get really nervous. Lucky for us, it's daytime, so we'll be perfectly safe unless we walk up on something.

Dream on, suckers! About that time a nervous Charlie opens up on us from the treeline about 100 meters ahead, first one weapon, then another and another, until we figure about twenty guns are firing at us. The bullets are snapping, kicking dirt, grass, and mud around us, and I ain't liking that at all. Being totally unprepared and completely surprised, we hesitated for an eyeblink, returned fire full bore, then ran for our lives, because we had absolutely no cover. But that turned out to be okay, because Charlie didn't chase us, he didn't want to venture out in the open either. All right! We ran for about a hundred meters, walked another fifty, and when we saw Charlie wasn't following, we stopped and set security. I got on the horn to call air support to tear up Charlie's ass.

We have SOPed four "scrambles" with our choppers. Scramble four means that no contact has been made, but we have a target of opportunity for the Seawolves, load up your weapons and slide on out to us for some fun. The Seawolves always come a-running anyway, because they love to get the action, and the slicks will follow them to pick us up after the fun is over.

Scramble three is the normal one. It means that we have completed the op with no contact. Fire up your engines, warm them normally, and come give us a ride home.

Scramble two means that we have made contact with Charlie, but we aren't in too much danger, or if we are taking fire, we're at least holding our own. Come and get us, but please don't lollygag around, because conditions could change at any moment. Cock and lock your weapons, though, because we'll probably need them. Scramble two will occasionally get upgraded to scramble one.

Scramble one is the biggy. It means we are in a world of shit. Drop your cocks and grab your socks, get off the ground and get to us ASAP. Naturally we never want to be in a situation that necessitates a scramble one call, and neither do the birds, because taking off without a proper engine warm-up damages the choppers. We don't want to get picked out of a serious action just to crash on the way home; that can ruin your day.

The PRC 25 and 77 radio is supplied with a short flexible ribbon antenna and a long rigid whip antenna, connected in sections. In the swamps and thick undergrowth of our previous AOs, I had used the ribbon antenna, because it didn't snag on everything. But working the Cambodian AO, the Plain of Reeds for example, I always carry the long sectional whip antenna with just the base section plugged in, because I want all the radio range I can get. I mean, we are way the hell out in the middle of nowhere. For patrolling, I simply break down the sections and rubber-band them to the base section, reattaching all the sections the moment we are set up on ambush or laager. Right now I put the antenna together, turn on the radio, and make my call. Since Charlie is chicken to come out and fight, I'll send him to gook heaven.

I say, "Whirltop, Whirltop, this is Threadbare One. Over."

"Threadbare One, this is Whirltop. Over." As usual, home base is alert.

"Whirltop, this is Threadbare One. We have a target. Scramble four. Over."

"Threadbare, Whirltop, understand you have a target, Scramble four, over."

"Whirltop, Threadbare. Roger, I have approx two zero Victor Charles in treeline. Terrain is flat and grass. Over."

"Roger, Threadbare. Wait one. Over." But it's less than ten seconds.

"Threadbare, Whirltop. I have four fast movers available your AO. Can you use. Over."

Can we use jets? Oh boy!

"Roger, Whirltop. We can use. Over."

"Roger. Wait one."

It's about fifteen seconds before Whirltop comes back to me.

"Threadbare One, this is Whirltop. Thunder two six is waiting your call. I say again, Thunder two six. Should we scramble Warrior? Over."

"Whirltop, Threadbare. Roger. Warrior scramble three. Over."

"Roger. Warrior scramble three. Whirltop out." I wait for a second, then I press the button.

"Thunder two six, Thunder two six, this is Threadbare One. Over." I am nervous, excited; this may turn out to be risky, but fun.

"Threadbare One, this is Thunder two six. Over." Ah, good. I went formal.

"Thunder two six, this is Threadbare One. I have a fire mission for you. Coordinates _____ and _____. Target is approx two zero Victor Charles with small arms, terrain flat and level with treeline, suggest you make run east to west on treeline. Friendlies will mark with smoke. What is your load? Over."

"Threadbare, Thunder. Understand coordinates _____ and _____, run east to west on the treeline. Full load. Damndamns, fire, and twenty mike mike, over."

"Roger, Thunder. Fire and twenty mil should do it. Over." Oh boy, oh boy, I'm gonna give Charlie a hotfoot.

"Roger, Threadbare. Understand fire and twenty mil. We are four mikes out. Over."

"Roger. Standing by. Over."

Mr. Marsh got a smoke grenade ready, and we waited for contact with the jets, and right on time, we heard them coming.

I pressed my mike button. "Thunder two six, this is Threadbare One. We can hear you. Over."

"Roger."

It was only another instant and we saw them, two coming in low, and two more higher in the sky. The two down low would do a spotting run, and I nodded to Mr. Marsh, who popped the grenade. Purple smoke billowed, and I talked.

"Thunder, Threadbare. Have you in sight, smoke out. Identify, over."

"Roger, Threadbare. I see goofy grape, over." The jets boomed over us. "Wait, Threadbare, I also see mellow yellow. . . . Over!"

My jaw dropped; Charlie popped smoke too. Hmm . . . those sneaky bastards! But Charlie was playing games with the wrong dudes. As I watched and talked, the fast movers made their turn and came back over us.

"Thunder, we are goofy grape. I say again, goofy grape. Distance to target two fiver zero meters."

"Roger. Goofy grape in sight. Target in sight. Stand by."

The jets moved out of sight, we could only see tiny silver flashes in the blue sky as they joined up. We got flat on our bellies, and we could hear the roar of their engines as they approached. I figure Charlie is writing his last letter home.

"Threadbare, Thunder two six. Starting fire run. Get your heads down. Over."

"Roger, Thunder. Heads down. Roast 'em. Over."

Our world was filled with roaring high-pitched engine whine as the jets flew in, and I couldn't help myself, I had my head raised for a look. I also had my fingers crossed and my asshole clamped tight as a virgin's knees.

I don't know, I guess I expected to hear an explosion, but all I heard was a heavy whooshing sound, like a hurricane wind, and following it, a concussion wave of hot air which dried my eyeballs in a flash. I blinked furiously, unable to tear my eyes away, and a second wave hit me, then a third and fourth. Holy jumpin' Jesus! The treeline out in front of us disappeared in huge columns of red and yellow flame, black smoke billowed, and the heat was intense. I couldn't help it, I hollered in exultation.

All of a sudden there was a tremendous explosion in the flames, sending streamers of firebits out in a umbrella. Son of a bitch! What was that? I notified Thunder.

"Thunder two six, Threadbare. Direct hit. Major secondary explosion. Good shooting. Over."

"Roger, Threadbare. You want another run? Over."

I took a good look, shook my head. "Thunder, Threadbare. Target wiped out. Your choice. Over."

"Threadbare, Thunder two six. Understand target complete. I think we'll save Uncle a few dollars, get 'em next time. Over."

"Roger, Thunder two six, this is Threadbare One. Fire mission is complete. Many thanks for your help. Over."

"Threadbare, this is Thunder two six. Our pleasure. Thunder two six returning to home plate. Thunder two six out."

"Threadbare One out."

Holy mackerel. As we got to our feet we looked out at the devastation, and it was hard to believe our eyes. What had been bright green grass, trees, and foliage with rounded silhouettes was now stark black, and the round lines were gone. Skeletons of trees and brush fingered up out of the ground, trailing streamers of smoke. Even as we watched, the flames died down, but smoke still billowed and the heat was intense. Good God, nothing could have survived in there. Charlie was a gone goose, cooked to a turn. We relaxed and waited for Warrior slicks to arrive.

We went back in the next day to recon and obtain results, and patrolled the edges of the napalm scar, but none of us wanted to walk into it and get all dirty. We averted our eyes when we spotted several lumps of blackened humanity, but they sure didn't look human.

It was one of the nastiest sights I ever saw, and the smell, God, it made us want to puke. It was a thick petroleum smell, flavored with roasted meat and burn odor. We reluctantly counted up the lumps (got to get those numbers for higher-higher), and there were twelve of them. Roughly in the center of the burn was a big hole, about four feet deep and maybe six feet wide. We figure it had probably been a cache of mortar rounds. God knows how many bodies were vaporized when it went up.

Nobody was eager to stick around, so we got the hell out of there. Welcome to the real war.

We all had some heavy thoughts as we flew away. Mike Emerson said it for all of us. "Can you imagine what it would be like to be on the receiving end of that shit? Thank God Charlie ain't got none." Amen, brother.

We knew damn well how good we had it by being on the right side. It was something the civilians at home would never appreciate.

And that brings another thought to mind, about civilians, that is. I still get asked occasionally what it was like to be in actual combat, and I always have to clamp my lips. What can I tell them? The truth? Ain't no way in this world. They'd just gape with disbelief or run with disgust and loathing.

How can I explain to them that battle, lordy lordy, battle is glorious when you are winning, and it is end-of-the-world desperation when you are losing. How can I paint them the picture of the three people encased in one body? Casual Mr. Cool with maybe some slight anxiety before the battle. During the battle? The driving, fierce warrior behind the machine gun guiding his tracers in on target, while only vaguely aware of the empty casings and links flying, who yells in exultation when the enemy falls. The merciless hawk who gives a wounded enemy an extra burst to finish the job. And then, after the battle is over, the quiet, introspective loner, who has shot his wad of adrenaline and wants nothing more than to curl up for a while, and sleep a dreamless sleep.

And the odors of battle, they are unique and never forgotten. Cordite, and the pungent smell of fear sweat. The sharp tang of hot gun oil and metal casings. The coppery smell of spilled blood and torn flesh. And the rank, one-of-a-kind odor of opened bodies and exposed guts.

How do I relate these things to other people? I can't. It's impossible because they're too personal and the telling might reveal too much of the real me. You say that someone who had been there, had done that, would understand if I talked about it? Maybe. But it's much easier for me to make a quick joke instead, avoiding the memories. That way I don't have to re-live them.

The sights of battle, specifically the terrible ones, are much easier to deal with. Within days a healthy mind will have blurred the images of unfaceable sights, and they will dim even more with age and other activities to take their place. Some are immediately rejected, and will only recur in future nightmares or flashbacks. So if you can't remember, you don't talk about them, and if they're blurred or sublimated, you just make a joke about them and get on with your life.

But still you persist. "What's it like to be in combat?" And you expect an answer? Well, okay, if you insist.

"Shit man, I strode through the Nam like Paul Bunyan! I kicked ass and took names! Hey, Charlie see me comin', he'd write his last will and testament, 'cause he knew his ass was a goner!"

See? Nothing to it.

But rarely, and it does happen, I also get accosted by the hostile asshole, almost always a woman, who wants to make me appear the barbarian fool. The question is always the same: "How many people did you kill in Vietnam?" They don't really want to know, the question is posed purely to put me in the role of jerk. What the hell do I say in answer?

"Oh, I was a SEAL, but I didn't kill anyone"? Sure. No one is going to buy that, and I appear the liar.

Or maybe I am hardcore, or I don't give a shit, and I say seriously, "Oh, maybe four (or five or six or ten) that I know of." Then I can be certain what the next question is going to be. "How many of them were women and children?" Now I'm really on the spot.

Postwar, when I was first asked these questions, I stuttered and stammered and became red-faced, especially if I was in a group of listening people. (I was once asked this question in a college class!) But eventually, when I realized that this might happen again and again, I got my shit together and formulated a ready answer.

To answer women? "Oh, I don't know. Fifty or sixty, I suppose, mostly women, because they'd always be yakking or asking stupid questions instead of running." Then I'd give them a shit-eating grin, and it works 'most every time. Puts them right on the defensive. They either flush and fade away, or they go off into a militant harangue that turns everybody off. Regardless, their guns have been spiked.

Men are a slightly different matter. Depending on how big and fierce he is, I may invite him outside to kick his ass, or use a variation of the "woman" statement. Either way, I slough off the question and move on, showing disgust that the question was even asked.

How many people did I kill in Vietnam? That is the one question I will never answer truthfully. For one reason, because I don't know. Who counts? For another, I don't want to know and remember. So if you meet me, please, please don't ask me that question. I will do my best to make sure you won't like the answer.

May 24 we're getting ready to go to our mission briefing, and we pause to admire Jim Richards sleeping on his flowered pillow that his girlfriend sent him. We debated putting his dangling hand in a pan of warm water to make him wet the bed, but we thought of it too late, and besides, "do unto one another." Usually once that joke stuff started it snowballed, and it could happen to you, and you, and you. Not me man. Let me sleep in peace. Dee woke Rich up and we only gave him some verbal abuse. That dude could sleep anywhere anytime, I never saw anything like it. (Except myself of course. I could do the same, but so long as no one brought it up, I wasn't going to say a word.)

Lt. JG John Marsh is leading us on this op, and he takes us through it. We're to recon a suspected VC base camp near Rach Bac Chien. We'll chopper in on the slicks, patrol a couple of klicks, and set up our recon on what used to be a mango grove back when the French were here. The mango grove is described as similar to an overgrown apple orchard, and a VC company is supposedly dug in there and using it as a base camp. Cover is minimal, so we'll approach it only at night, and make certain we're long gone before daylight. This one has been designated as a potential bombing target, and NILO wants confirmation before they send in the fast movers. We chuckle at that, because NILO is the only officer we know who wants to be economical with Uncle's armaments. If it was Army or Marines, they'd bomb first and invent body count later.

Mr. Marsh takes us through the familiar patrol specs and requirements and alternatives, then makes a final point.

"Load up on the water, guys, 'cause there's none out there, and I don't plan on sharing mine."

Then he grins and singles me out.

"I was also gonna mention extra food, but I know I don't have to tell Rad."

The idiots laugh. Huh. The amount of food I carry is a standing joke, and now even the officers want to bust my hump. Hey, I work hard out there, and I need the fuel to be the super SEAL that I am. What do those guys know?

We're done, and we file out to make our preparations. Now is the time to find out any problems with our gear, not just before the mission. We load up on food and ammo, check weapons for function, and we'll do our water just before the op, that way it takes longer for it to pick up that plastic taste from our quart collapsible canteens. (Oh God, what I'd give for some ice!) One change that I make is that I wear my jungle boots this time out instead of coral shoes. Last op Slim Wilkins had found an old punji pit, and since our new op area is comparatively "dry" as compared to the Rung Sat, it only makes sense that we might run into more of them. Punjis would pierce canvas and rubber coral shoes like tissue paper.

We're inserting late to hide our choppers from Charlie, so at 2000 we load onto the slicks, and at 2030 the bird flares hard and then settles, and in the pitch blackness, I hop off into the short grass of the Plain of Reeds. At least I attempted to hop off. Unfortunately the pilot hadn't adjusted his height, so we were off the ground, by how much I didn't know. My expectant feet meet only air, and when my toe hooks over the skid, I go ass over teakettle on the ground, jarring the breath right out of me. Then Louie McIntosh, with the same problem, lands on top of me, and that don't help, especially when the barrel of his M-60 whacks me alongside the head. We do some quiet grunting and cussing, but we soon get sorted out and on the move. (Rocky, that big liar, claims later that, being last man off, he fell at least forty feet, but being the superstar that he is, he did an excellent PLF and was able to save his legs.)

For once the patrol was easy easy, and although I was sweating like a pig, it sure was nice to be dry and have no mud hanging off me. I was able to step right out, and when we finally crossed a stream, I slid right in gratefully; it was a pleasure to cool off a bit. I already liked our new op area a lot. Without the strenuous physical struggle of Rung Sat patrols, I was soon relaxed in a new mode, 10 percent alert and 90 percent daydream. It was pretty cool, because before I even realized it, we had arrived at our objective.

As always, Mr. Marsh had done a previous flyover, and he had selected a broken patch of treeline to set up in. The trees are rooted in thick low brush, and should be an ideal hiding place.

Well, I'm here to tell you, it sure was. With incredible luck, we walked right up to it and settled in, and only moments later Charlie was all around us. Holy jumpin' Jesus! Charlie was home big-time. He was walking around at ease, he was coughing and spitting, he was gabbing up a storm, and I estimated with shriveled dick that he had to be at least a hundred strong. Well, maybe fifty or sixty, but that was about forty or fifty more than I was comfortable with. Man, was I scared.

We were helpless. We couldn't move, we couldn't make a sound, and no way could we take on this many without receiving significant casualties. There was an unseen footpath right by our brush clump, and Charlie was strolling by less than ten feet away. None of us were overly religious, but you can bet there was a fervent funnel of prayers going skyward from five extremely nervous SEALs and one Viet scout. Then things got worse.

It appears that our brush clump was butting Charlie's latrine area, and every few minutes he was taking a leak against one of our bushes, or digging a small hole and squatting over it to take a shit. Some of the odors that wafted over the area were pretty foul, but at least they would cover our own nasty body smells.

Add to that the pungent smell of *nuoc mam* (fermented fish sauce) and a faint drift of marijuana, and we felt fairly secure aroma-wise. But I certainly didn't need my Dexamil pill to stay awake. Fear took care of that.

Then two gooks stopped right by me, not fifteen feet away. One's standing with his weapon across his shoulders, and he's hanging on to barrel and stock. The other is wearing a boonie hat, his rifle is slung from his shoulder with the barrel sticking up, and he's standing hipshot. They must be buds, because they are shooting the breeze at high speed, occasionally laughing. Me, I am shitting bricks. I am breathing through wide-open mouth so as not to make a sound, I am making certain not to drill them with my eyes, and I feel entirely helpless; the pee runs right down my leg. See, my thumper is loaded with an illum round, which makes me extremely uncomfortable. If I was discovered, I was dead meat, because I couldn't defend myself, but if worse came to worst, one of those dudes would eat a flare round if that was the best I could do. The other one better be fast, 'cause I was gonna snap his spine. But then, once I got over my initial fear, I realized I was worrying over nothing. Why? Because I wasn't here alone. My buds would take care of me, as I would them. I knew without question that both Mr. Marsh and McIntosh had Charlie under the gun, ready for any emergency. They'd save my life so that I could do my job, lighting up the action with my flare. I relaxed, and soon got my shit together. Supported by my friends, I could do this.

We all could, because this is what we were about, being SEALs and sneaking and peeking around. Charlie never in this world expected that anyone would have the balls to set up right in among him, and we remained undetected simply because Charlie wasn't looking for us. He strolled around the rest of the night completely at ease, going about his life without a thought of close danger. He squatted in groups of four or five and shot the shit, he started a couple of small fires and cooked some food, making my stomach growl. He took a leak, he took a shit, he scratched his balls and put his arm around his friend's shoulder, and he told war stories to his buds and laughed at theirs. All under our silent, watchful eyes.

Around 0400, Charlie stirred into activity. He loaded up his meager gear, he wriggled in his field pack until he was comfortable, he formed up into squads of about ten, and he moved out in an orderly manner, headed west. Oops. Not quite all. About twenty stick around and disperse to the edges of the mango grove, apparently to set up daytime security. We shift uneasily. This is a danger time for us. If Charlie stepped on one of the SEALs...

But again we lucked out. Apparently Charlie wasn't any different than us, and none of them wanted to spend a hot day lying next to an odorous latrine area. As the morning light strengthened into light gray, we moved out. I mean, first I loaded an HE round in my thumper with a huge sigh of relief, then we got cautiously on our feet, turned 180 degrees, and ran for our lives. Radio gear or not, I was right on Mr. Marsh's heels, and Flak Body was breathing down my neck. At 100 meters we slowed, and at 200 meters we dropped back into normal patrol mode. Man, we are out of there!

We are patrolling along, and when I hear eating noises, I look back at McIntosh. He's eating some kind of green fruit! I look at him questioningly and he offers me one. It's about the size of an apple, and is mushy soft. It must be a mango, which I had never seen before. Trust Flak Body to get the fruit while the rest of us are shitting our pants. I bit into it, and lordy lordy, it was heaven. It was warm, soft, and incredibly sweet, almost puckered my mouth, it was so sweet. And it was messy and sticky, the juices ran right down my chin and got all over my hand. It sure was manna for my dry mouth.

But then, after about fifteen minutes, I started to feel pretty uncomfortable. My mouth was burning up, and I took a quick swig of water, but that didn't help. The burning got worse, and my mouth got all dead. I couldn't even feel my tongue. My hand was itching like crazy. Goddamn McIntosh! He'd poisoned me! When I turn to glare at him, I don't, because he looks to be hurting a lot worse than me. Good! Serves him right. I feel a little better mentally as I continue to suffer, my stomach rumbling like a volcano.

As we approach and enter a treeline, we slow almost to a halt, because Rich is ranging around like a bloodhound. We soon see why. There are three bare dirt hard-pack trails there, and they intersect at one of the strangest sights I've ever encountered. We stop to take a breather and marvel at the sight. We're in church.

It's Charlie's temple, and it's an amazing sight. It's mud-brick walls, the rear one about five feet high, the side walls lower, tapering down to ground level, a patch in front that is worn almost shiny where people have been kneeling or standing. It contains several shelves, and arranged neatly on these shelves are a prayer stand holding incense sticks, several hand-made bowls with flowers in them, and a bunch of candles. I notice that the monkeywood prayer stand has two bullet gouges in it and a couple of the urns have been patched. Looks like Charlie can't even worship his god without being shot at.

I am resting on one knee gazing at this display and I feel very strange. I think the other guys do too. We're hardened warriors, and none of us are particularly religious, but seeing this, I kinda feel for Charlie. He's a guerrilla, he's far from home, and this is the best he can do for a church. Must be tough.

We never think about stuff like that; I mean, that Charlie could be human like us, that he might have parents, a girlfriend or a wife and kids and a home life waiting somewhere. We found several black-and-white snapshots on Charlie's bodies that we'd killed, family portraits and the like, but we always put them out of our minds, even as we collected them for intelligence to peruse. That was dangerous ground, thinking of Charlie as human, and although we didn't hate him, we also didn't want to like him or have too much sympathy for him, because that might create problems doing our jobs. But I'm telling you, this temple out in the middle of nowhere really threw us for a loop, it being so unexpected. It wasn't much as far as material goods—in fact it was next to nothing, but to Charlie we figured it was pretty important, and in an unusual attempt to show some respect, we didn't touch or take anything. Let Charlie have his place of worship; he didn't have much else. I only wish I could have gotten a picture of it, but that's not a problem. I have it pictured plainly in my mind as I write these words.

Wow! Away from the gloom. We moved out of there and patrolled a klick or so to be well away from the area, then called up our slicks for extraction. We might have been under Charlie's eyes as we left, but he didn't give a sign of it. No shots, no action of any kind. We flew away to our American good life—showers, hot meals, and dry racks.

Four days later a fast-mover group out of Saigon wiped the mango grove out to bare dirt. CIDG went in to check it out, and found eight bodies and a minimal amount of equipment. That's the trouble with Charlie: trying to catch him in a sizable group with his pants down. Because he's always on the move, it's extremely hard to do. You've got to respond immediately to hot intell, not a couple of days later. Flak Body McIntosh (when he could talk again) swears we should have called in an air strike while we were there; he, at least, is so tough that the bombs would have bounced right off him. Sure. We shake our heads. Somebody's gonna have to sit that boy down and give him some strong counseling, and soon. ("Boy"? I know I didn't hear you say "Boy"!)

Oh, by the way, about the famous "mangoes." Doc told us, after everyone had laughed loud and long at me and McIntosh for being such chowhound dummies, that it was the citric acid in the mango that burned us so bad. Seems that here in the tropics, fresh fruit is loaded with concentrated citric acid, and us unaccustomed Americans must eat the stuff only in small pieces along with plenty of fresh milk to neutralize the acid, or else age the fruit before eating it. Fresh milk? In the Nam? Are you shitting me? Uh-huh. Doc also said we were really lucky that we didn't get the shits real bad from the mangoes. They'd do a number on your intestines. I nodded wisely, but kept my mouth shut. So that was why I had felt like a dog shitting peach pits for two days. Live and learn.

Chapter
Thirty-six

ONE NIGHT ON our barge we are doing what we do best, sleeping, when we get a rude awakening—a mortar round hits the watch shack. Damn, Charlie wants to play. Lou Hyatt yells, we roll out of our racks, and as my feet hit the floor another round impacts and particles dust my head as I hear my air mattress hiss flat. As the third round hits, I *di di mau* outside away from it, toward the boats. No time to cover our naked asses or to grab our gear and weapons, but I know the boats have guns. The other guys have headed for the bank of the river that the barge is moored to, but I spot Espinoza and holler to him. The boats are firing up to get the hell out of there, and as they pull out we jump into them. Well, I jump in like Tarzan, but Espi doesn't quite make it, and hangs on the rail as the boat drags him through the water. While the boats beat feet, I haul Espi aboard, and we no sooner get stood up than the fourth (or fifth—who's counting?) round hits, right in the water pretty close to us. We've been able to hear the *"chunk . . . boom!"* of the mortar clearly, and we know it's close, so we fire up the riverbanks with the fixed .50 cals. Ya-hoo! Although we're probably not hitting anyone, we are having a great time playing.

Things quiet down a bit and Espi says, "Hey man, I think I'm hit."

Caught by surprise, I say, "What?"

"Yeah, I ain't lyin'. I think they got me."

I'm all concerned, so we check him out, and sure as shit, he's got a shrap hole in his thigh.

He says, "C'mon man, give me some help here. Put on a bandage."

Hey, I ain't working on his crotch. I tell him, "Put it on yourself. You ain't crippled."

But he's a bud, so I do it, and thank God there's no audience. I never would have heard the end of it. When we get back to the barge, we find out Emerson has been hit again; he's gotten some shrap in the armpit. ("Armpit? What the hell were you doing, Mike, giving them the finger?") My air mattress also wins the Purple Heart; it's flatter than a board. Luckily the Big Pack Rat has another, and I get it out. Then I pick a couple of tiny chunks out of my scalp with my fingernail.

Before going back to sleep, we all gather in the mess hall to watch Doc "operate," and it's pretty interesting, except maybe to Mike and Espi. Naturally we were all grave and concerned, and didn't make any disparaging comments. I didn't say one word. Ain't gettin' me under the knife.

May 27: Mr. Marsh led a four-dayer, this one a multipurpose op. We'll be working with a group of Air Cav, the intelligence is from Cai Cai Special Forces, and we plan to sweep-search an area that, according to electronic listening devices, has had a lot of nighttime enemy activity. Sweep-search? Are you shitting me? But we'll let the Air Cav do the sweep and we'll monitor from the rear. At the end of the first day, Air Cav will extract, we'll stay, laager nights, and recon patrol during the day. Basically Cai Cai wants a concise mapping of the area, and they'd like any enemy sign to be interpreted by eyeball. Hey, that part we can do.

The sweep nets us zilch. The Air Cav are good soldiers, but there's just nothing but grass out here. It's dry, sign is minimal, and so far it's been a nothing op, so we are glad to see the Air Cav guys extract. We set up laager, and it's very strange, because it's just like camping on your front lawn. We do not like to be without some kind of cover to hide in, but we're not nervous, because there ain't a soul within a hundred miles, seems like. We sleep peacefully through the night, and at first light we move out toward a distant treeline. Man, it's a Sunday stroll, except for the fact that we are loaded down with gear, you know, supplies for four days of patrol. It's hotter than a bastard in the direct sun, and we have to take several salt pills, which also means we use more water than we like. We're just not used to rationing. At least I can smoke without restraint, but the cigarettes seem to make me drier. Our water concern mounts.

We're walking on a football field when we see something odd out in front of us. Looks like a bunch of sticks stuck in the ground, and our curiosity is aroused. Then, out of the blue, we stumble onto a stream cutting the field and we can't believe it—there's not a twig or plant of any kind on its banks. Although the water is a nasty green, piss-warm, and has wigglers in it, we fill our canteens (we're all carrying two) and put in the water conditioning pills. We'll have to wait thirty minutes for the chemicals to work before we can take a drink.

We approach the sticks we've had in sight for quite a while, and we are totally amazed. They are booby traps! Our AOs had all kinds of booby traps, and we thought we'd seen them all, but here is something entirely new. Charlie, you sneaking bastard! These are booby traps for choppers. They are sticks planted in the ground in big circles; there are eight circles, and attached to each stick about three feet high is a Chicom grenade with trip wires crisscrossed all over the place. Goddamn! It's sure death for a chopper and its landing force. Man oh man, we keep our distance, and move cautiously around this area, shaking our heads. How in the devil do you negate this setup? We sure can't destroy it with what we're carrying, so we don't even try. This is one for the record books, and all we can do is map the location as best we can.

We keep going, and as the afternoon wanes, we're finally approaching the treeline. We become more alert, because in this kind of terrain, any cover at all is bound to be Charlie country. We stumble on another stream, no different from the first, and as I crawl up on the far bank and get to my feet, something foreign in the grass catches my eye, and I move toward it for a better look. Then I halt and my jaw drops a foot. Lying there in the grass, all by its lonesome, is an AK-47 and five magazines! Man, I look around, but that's all there is. No pouch, no rig, no bodies or bones, just nothing, and the damn thing is hardly rusted! I can't believe my eyes, and neither can the rest of the guys when I call them over and point it out. After checking it very carefully for trip wires, I tie a string to it, walk away and drop flat, and give my string a good yank. When nothing happens, I pull the weapon closer, to make sure it is not trip-wired. We get to our feet, and before anybody can stop him, Lou Hyatt picks up the weapon, jacks the cocking lever, and fires a burst of about ten. Jesus! We all cringe, but Lou doesn't blow up, so we relax. (Hand me that weapon, son, that's my war trophy.) Like many things we ran into in Vietnam, it is a total puzzler, but who cares? At least now I have me an AK.

The rest of the patrol was an anticlimax for me while I fondled my new weapon possessively. We saw nothing, found nothing, but after we had extracted and talked it over, all agreed that we didn't like extended ops. We also agreed that other units who ran them regularly, like the Army's LRRPs and the Marine Force Recon and Recon Battalion teams and such, were probably brain-damaged. Extended ops were just too much like hard work for us.

The final op of May, our luck turned and we had a bad one. It was another trail recon near the border, a three-dayer based on electronic surveillance intell.

A word about electronic listening devices—we thought they were great! What happens is, if you want to monitor a particular section of country without disturbing Charlie, you install hidden electronic listening devices in that area. Our slang term for them was "black ears," and they were simply battery-powered transmitters. They were incredibly expensive and (I'm not sure why) rated Top Secret. In some cases ground troops hid them by tying them to tree trunks or brush, and we had to put out a bunch of them during our tour. Others were dropped from aircraft and just lay there on the ground. These units were extremely sensitive, and any time Charlie came around, the monitors would hear the sounds of his troop movements, and based on what they heard, and how often, ops could be scheduled to take advantage. When you were operating in the wide-open spaces of the Plain of Reeds, for example, it was damn nice to know that Charlie had at least been there recently, so that we wouldn't just wander around with our thumb up our ass, hoping for contact.

On this op, we inserted without problem, found the trail, and it appeared to be recently used. These dry trails were really difficult to read, but it was the best we could do, so we found a nice brushy hump along the trail and set up on it. The hump was about twelve feet by thirty feet, and maybe five feet high, with two spider holes in the center. I appropriated a nice spider hole (my body protection always comes first—you know, the radio guy is key), stripped off my gear, and set up the radio, running the extended antenna up through a small tree where it couldn't be seen. I did a radio check ("loud and clear") and got comfortable. This might be a long three days.

Not quite. About 2000 we hear voices, and watched about four bodies walk through the gloom in front of us. Mr. Marsh didn't initiate, rightly figuring them to be the point element, so we stayed put, but our new LDNN—he was gung ho, I guess— yelled at the VC and initiated. We had no choice now, so we all opened up, but the VC had moved out of the kill zone, and none were hit.

They ran like deer, and we immediately started taking heavy fire from the north, obviously the main body. They are some distance away, but one of the weapons is a heavy machine gun, probably a .51 cal, and there are also lots of green and yellow tracers from AKs and M-16s arcing in. As leaves and twigs start showering down on me, and we start receiving fire from a circle all around us, I don't need to be told. I shrivel down in my spider hole and get on the horn. We need help, and we need it yesterday.

"Whirltop, Whirltop, Threadbare One. Over!"

"Threadbare One, this is Whirltop. Over." I give a big sigh of relief.

"Whirltop, Threadbare One, contact, contact. Scramble one! Over!" My voice breaks and I immediately think, calm down, Miller, do your job, and don't be such a coward.

"Threadbare, Whirltop. Understand scramble one. Wait, over." Shit, he's nice and calm. He comes right back. "Threadbare One, Whirltop. Outlaw two six (our slicks) not available at this time. (What? I don't believe it!) Seawolf three fiver and three six in the air. Scramble one. Over."

I replied, "Whirltop, Threadbare. Roger." Mr. Marsh is right there listening.

What is going on, and where the fuck are our slicks? I find out later that an Army captain had "borrowed" them for a milk run, overriding the pilots' complaints with a direct order, but right now, with hundreds of tracers coming in on me, I am shitting my pants. Oh lordy, I'm too young to die.

The only other fire support I had available to me was South Vietnamese artillery. Oh no. That's almost as bad as the Viet Cong, but I had no choice. I rang them up, gave them firing coordinates, and crammed myself deeper into my spider hole. I crossed my fingers, eyes, nuts, and toes, took a deep breath, and prepared to get blown up. ARVN were notorious bad shots, but the group at Cai Cai must have had a good American adviser, because their spotting rounds didn't wipe us out. They didn't hit the enemy either. In fact I had no idea where they landed. I tried two more salvos, adjusting cautiously, but never saw a round, so I gave it up while I was still alive. Suddenly the radio blared in my ear.

"Threadbare One, Threadbare One, this is Seawolf three fiver, say status. Over."

Oh, you lovely guy. "Seawolf three fiver, Threadbare. Taking heavy fire from all sides, no casualties, estimate Charlie company strength and larger. Over."

"Roger, Threadbare. We are one zero mikes out. Prepare for firing runs. Over."

"Roger, Seawolf. Threadbare is color true blue. I will guide when I hear you. Over."

"Roger."

Then I hear the sweet chopping sound of rotors from the east. "Seawolf three fiver, I hear you. Bear five degrees north. Over."

"Roger five."

After another minute I say, "Seawolf three fiver, Threadbare. Go five more north. Over."

"Roger. Five more." I love this guy.

"Seawolf three fiver, you will be overhead in approx one mike. Over."

I pointed the blue-lensed strobe light at the birds, and I called it. "Seawolf three fiver, you are overhead . . . now! Charlie all around, range approx two zero zero meters."

I had a momentary flash picture of myself as a high-flying bat looking down at our action, and I shriveled. In the vast bowl of impenetrable Vietnamese darkness, our pulsing pinpoint of blue light must be tiny indeed, especially when contrasted with the hundreds of tracers flying around, but those eagle-eyed chopper pilots never seemed to fail us.

"Threadbare, Seawolf. We see color true blue. Maintain. Starting run."

As I kept the lens of my strobe light pointed to them, the choppers made their runs and fired them up around us, but much to our discomfort, the enemy fire didn't stop, it only decreased a bit as Charlie started shooting at the choppers. But since we haven't returned fire, the enemy has lost exact track of us, and the fire is no longer centering on our position. We like that a lot. There is a hole in the tracers to the southeast, and we discuss running through it, but it's a little too inviting, and might be a trap to entice us out. Shit, looks like we don't have much of a choice, so we decide to run. Let's pull in our claymores and get the hell out of here.

When Emerson went out to retrieve his claymore, our new LDNN saw him moving and shot him. Damn! Down goes Mike. This is some nightmare. The guys rush out, but thank God, he's only got a slight wound in the arm and is stunned by a round that clipped his hatband. He's scared and so are we, and we vent our fury verbally on the LDNN. That dude came awfully close to being killed by friendly fire.

We are packed up, we're ready to make our move, and I am just about to notify Seawolf, when he comes up on the horn.

"Threadbare, Seawolf three fiver and three six. Ammo expended. Get ready, we're coming in to get you. Stand by to load."

Well, we just can't believe it. We're certain that Seawolves are designed to carry like three or four people, and even split up, there are eight of us on the ground. But those crazy suckers had dumped all their gear, everything that ain't nailed down, and they swoop in to get us. This ain't never gonna work, but beggars can't be choosers, so we move out into the open and drop down. I step forward and kneel on one knee, pointing the strobe light. I guide them in, bringing the enemy tracers with them. I can sense the bullets tearing up the ground around us, and I expect any second to get hit. As Seawolf three fiver's hood settles about ten feet away, the guys get up and run for them, with me right behind. Not only can I see all the tracers, I can hear them ticking into the sides of the bird, and that's scary.

Don't ask me how we got off the ground. It ain't possible, and yet they did it. I'm telling you, I rode home on a skid, and I was damn glad to have it. We land on a rotor and a prayer, and before we can even shove off those chopper dudes are out there counting the bullet holes in their birds, and bragging about who had the most. Incredible.

And this is the time for me to say a respectful and admiring "Thank you!" to all the support guys we worked with in Vietnam. Our support guys, and I'm sure many others we didn't work with, were unsung heroes. The boat people, MST, although sitting ducks on their boats, never failed or refused to come in and get us, seemed like no op was too dangerous for them to respond to. And those chopper guys, holy shit! I will always believe that you have to be a little brain-damaged to fly a chopper. Talk about being a sitting duck! There was no easier target in the world than a slow-moving chopper, tied by an invisible string to the troops they must pick up. Mostly young warrant officers, chopper pilots and their enlisted crewmen displayed a kind of courage I certainly don't have. For us, it became a given that when it was time to leave, the choppers would come and get us. I never heard a balk, I never heard a refusal. It was always, "Stand by. We're coming in." Sweet music to my ears.

Chapter
Thirty-seven

WE'RE WELL VERSED in the routine of SEAL ops now, and we carry them off with casual expertise. It is now a matter of pride to run smooth, trouble-free patrols, and the urgency for spectacular results has eased a lot. Our attitude is simple: We're here, we're confident, and we take pride in doing our job with a high comfort level. We enjoy the small things, and most important, we're beginning to take time to recognize those small things.

One of those things that I pick up on is that the damn country is beautiful! Take away the war, and this would be a great place to live. The primary color, green, is so vivid it hurts your eyes, and that is contrasted with a sky that's as magnificently blue as I've ever seen. And growth? Man you never saw anything like it. Rich black dirt, so fertile that if you cut off a stick and used it, then threw it on the ground, it would root and grow again. If you ever introduced modern farming methods to this country, you could make a frigging fortune, to say nothing about supplying the world with crops. Granted, it's hot and humid, but we have adapted to that physically, and it's no worse than America's east coast in the summer. Hey, if you get too hot, just take a few steps and slide into the nearest water to cool down. We do it all the time. Monsoon season sucked, but so did winter snows and cold in the U.S. If I missed anything at all, it was the spring and fall seasons. But I tell you what, I daydreamed about what it would be like to be a farmer or planter in Vietnam in peacetime, and my thoughts were pretty attractive. I could live here. (Naturally, I was kidding myself. With all the unexploded ordnance laying around this country, booby traps, unexploded bombs, shit like that, farmers were going to be blowing themselves up for the next fifty years, and I definitely was not gonna be one of them.)

Another thing I pick up on is that I like the regular Vietnamese people, especially the kids. A lot of the poor bastards have mixed blood, because there's always been other nationalities around trying to conquer their country. The kids don't care. Like kids anywhere, they live each day for the enjoyment they can get out of it. I know one thing for sure, they want nothing to do with the fighting going on around them, and their parents feel the same.

I mean, they're just regular country people like mine, fishers and farmers struggling to make a decent living for their families. I feel for them. And I must have heard a hundred stories about how the kids are so dangerous, they throw grenades and such, but I never bought it. Every time I got near a friendly ville, it was always the kids who came running out and surrounded you, close packed, curious, and friendly, and I always got a big charge out of them because they momentarily relieved the reality of war. They reminded me of my home and family, and it's only as they grow up that they become reserved and less friendly, as they learn about "face" or learn to hate Americans.

Once you adjusted to the Oriental "opposites," and stopped judging them through American eyes, you found out that they were a decent, religious people. But that was the trick, wasn't it, not making comparisons. Most Americans found it impossible to do, and held the Viets in contempt.

We were huge in body size compared to them. We were boisterous and friendly, they were reserved and formal. If you wanted to have a Viet come to you, and you gave him the American "come here" motion, then you could shoot him in the back when he didn't obey you, because to the Viets, that "come here" motion means go away. The Vietnamese "come here" is expressed by waving him away from you with a limp-wristed shooing motion. Opposites. Americans shake hands and touch. Viets bow and never touch strangers. Americans smile and laugh to show they are friendly, Viets smile and laugh if they are nervous or uncomfortable. Viet males walk around with their arms around each other in friendliness, and hold hands. They must be fags, because American males would never do that. Viets will drop trou and shit in a gutter in the cities, or take a leak right out in the open. They must be lowlifes, because Americans would never do that. And so on and so forth. Opposites. Pity the Viets such as our LDNN scouts who had to live with Americans and behave exactly opposite to their heritage.

In fact, I got a real shock when I unthinkingly questioned Gieng about his culture.

I said, "Hey Gieng. Does it ever bother you that you have to fight against your countrymen, you know, the Viet Cong?"

Holy mackerel! He got really mad. "The NLF are not my people! They are Northerners, and they want to make us slaves. My people are not like them!"

I apologized immediately. "Hey, sorry, man, I didn't know."

He calmed a bit. "Well, yes, some of them are South Vietnamese, but those have been brainwashed by the VC or NVA. If I have any feelings about fighting them, it's only for the ones who have been conscripted by the VC against their will, or the ones who fight only to keep their families from being butchered by the VC. But you know, Mr. Miller, that in a fight, there's no way to tell the difference. If he is my enemy, trying to kill me, I must kill him without regard as to who he might be."

Well now. That was a real shocker. Even with all my attempts to get to know the Vietnamese, I hadn't even considered that. It's easy for me. Any enemy I ran into was just that, the enemy. I could wipe him out in total comfort. But Gieng and the other Allied South Vietnamese had a much bigger mental burden than I. It must be tough, and I'm glad I ain't in his shoes. As usual, I tell him don't call me mister, but these guys are that polite as a way of life. It's kinda nice, but it takes some getting used to.

But if you could open your eyes and modify your arrogant American viewpoint, you also discovered that your ordinary Vietnamese was real easy to get along with because he was so laid-back. They had none of the hustle-bustle, frantic pace of us Americans, and that also takes some getting used to. Personally, I like their style, but when I talk it over with the guys, they mostly disagree, and give me abuse. Their thoughts are those of all the foot soldiers: I was forced to come here, I don't want to be here, let's get on the stick, get the job completed, and get back home. Home? Now that I think more about it . . . Could we have won the Vietnam War? Hell, we SEALs did win our war—we didn't sit around and wait for Charlies' attack; we took it right to him.

We start June with a fun op. River Division 532 has a downed chopper, a slick, and they want us to blow it up so that the gooks can't take it to pieces and use the material. We can hardly wait, and we all volunteer, but it's only a squad-size op. The chopper has crashed on a riverbank, and its nose is in the water, with the body of the bird tangled in some bushes. We reach it by PBR. The footing is kind of shaky, but we overload the bird with sixty pounds of C4 so we can get a decent shot. Oh boy, it goes up with a huge bang and concussion, and shit showers all over the place. It's fun time in the combat zone.

But there the fun ends. Intell has dried up. Charlie appears to have gone on R & R, and unless we want to go out and wander around foolishly hoping for contact, we have no work. Surprisingly, we're not real happy about our new status, because we'd all gotten used to being busy, and now time seems to drag. We simply don't know what to do with ourselves, so we look around for stuff. Espi traded for a pet hawk, and that was pretty interesting for a while, but mostly we did a lot of reading, a lot of talking and speculating about life back home, and a lot of horsing around.

One night we're gathered around our little TV—and no, no one remembers after all these years where it came from or how we got it; we probably stole it—and we're watching some student demonstrations in the U.S. against the war in Vietnam. It's strange that the Armed Forces Channel even showed that stuff, but among us there was a lot of gritted teeth. It started a firestorm of conversation and soon the TV was forgotten.

Lou Hyatt spoke his mind firmly, as usual.

"Fucking whiner draft-dodging pussies! We're putting our asses on the line over here so that they don't have to, and the motherfuckers don't even appreciate it! Send me back there with some claymores, and I'll stop their fucking demonstrations. And that bastard waving the Viet Cong flag, I'll hang that son of a bitch by the balls!"

Espi adds, "Fuckin-A! Go get 'em, Lou," and we all grin.

But Lou ain't grinning. "Son of a bitches need a good boot in the ass! That'll straighten them out!"

Then Dee says, "Now Lou, you know that they're just speaking their minds. You know, the Constitution guar—"

"Fuck the Constitution! Those bastards . . ." and then Lou was off and running, he was gonna bomb, he was gonna unman the boys and stick his foot up the ass of the girls, and he listed several other atrocities that he was gonna commit, until the paint was blistering right off the walls of our Quonset. Man, when Dee lit his fuse, Lou was on the rise, and me, I wasn't gettin' in his way.

But then I had to open my mouth. I said, "But Lou, I spent a lot of time last year at UC Santa Barbara, and I went to four of those demonstrations with my girlfriend."

Oh my. Before I could continue, Lou pounced.

"I might have known! A fucking Commie!" Lou said, and then he started to say a lot more, but I cut him off.

"No, listen, what I'm trying to say is that those demonstrations, they were led by a few assholes who were professional agitators, and some others who were just trying to build a rep. The students, they were just there for the partying and hanging out. You know what I'm saying?" He sure did.

"Fuck them and their partying! They should get their asses back to their classes and stop encouraging the Commies!"

But, and it's a huge but, we all agreed with him. They had no right. For the most part we believed that those demonstrations were 97 percent ignorant sheep following the mob instinct, 2 percent professional agitators, Communist or not, and 1 percent "filthy, greasy-haired, faggy creeps" who were taking advantage of ignorance to try to pass themselves off as leaders.

It's interesting that a while back, only last year, A.J. and I got into a conversation about Jane Fonda, who had gone on to fame and fortune.

A.J., he's so easygoing, he says, "You mean to tell me after all these years you still hold it against her that she was playing and posing with the North Vietnamese? C'mon, man, that was a long time ago, and besides, the NVA were probably just manipulating her like a puppet."

I nodded agreement.

"True and true. But if you play the game, and you get the name, you got to suffer the fame. Anytime I think about forgiving or forgetting people like Jane Fonda, I remember the black wall with fifty thousand names, or I see a vet in a wheelchair or missing arms or legs, or I see a guy my age with a reconstructed face. As far as I'm concerned, she should have been charged with treason, or at the very least fraternizing with the enemy. It was only because of her family and fame that she wasn't. Forgive Jane Fonda? Sure, when I can restore the missing and the dead to their families."

We also played a lot of cards, using monopoly money. Monopoly money was MPCs, military payment certificates, that's the scrip the government issued to us instead of greenbacks, to control black marketeering and prevent devaluing of the Vietnamese currency. I played cards in my usual conservative style, and I always had this huge stack of MPCs in my locker. It looked like a million dollars, but was "penny paper," worth only a few dollars.

Business-wise, I got myself a new uniform of black PJs to wear in the bush, and they were very comfortable. I know now why the Viets wear 'em. With my body size, there was no way I was gonna pass for a Viet at close range, but at long range, hey, you never know. I shined up my AK, and had all kinds of plans for it, until one of the guys mentioned that a few years before, the U.S. had brought a shitload of booby-trapped AK ammo into Vietnam. Instead of being loaded with gunpowder, the rounds were loaded with explosive, and would wipe out your face if you fired one. Damn, that ended my AK plans, because I was still a big chicken. I didn't want to believe what I heard (it was true though), but I liked my face the way it was.

I did get a good trade on some M-1 carbines, though. I did some research in Saigon, and found a SeaBee who had a case of

them. I traded him a couple of "the real thing" VC flags that I'd
had made for me in the ville outside Moc Hoa, which I had
smeared with chicken blood, along with my authentic Ho Chi
Minh sandals. That dude was thrilled, and let me assemble five
excellent carbines from all the ones in the case. Right out of the
cosmoline, yet!

June 9 we got some decent intell from Tuyen Nhon NILO
and ran an op. It was an observation post kind of thing, to
monitor traffic on a large canal. We sat out all night, and would
you believe it? Zilcho. Not a single boat. We're resigned, until
about 0200, we spot a firefly unit approaching down our canal.
A firefly unit is a slick with a spotlight, flying low to draw fire.
Above and behind him will be some Cobra gunships, ready to
blast any VC foolish enough to fire on the slick. My pulse rate
goes up, because although we are well camouflaged at ground-
level, we are completely open and vulnerable from the air. For
once, we're in Charlie's sandals. The adrenaline pumps, and
you can almost hear the sighs of relief as the spotlight misses us
by twenty-five yards, and continues on without pause while we
curse the Army.

One of our SOP premission tasks is always to reserve our
AO. That reservation would put the province on notice: SEALs
are in the area on such and such a date, don't violate our space,
but if you must, don't shoot us. Through carelessness, incom-
petence, but mostly obstinacy, our AO would occasionally be
violated, putting us in great danger. I overheard an Army colonel say it once: "SEALs? Fuck them! That's my AO."

June 14 we lost Toung, one of our best LDNNs, through
carelessness. Rarely, booby-trapped areas would be marked
with signs—TU DIA, which loosely translated means "dangerous ground"—and when you saw one, you'd better get your
shit together, because the area was bound to be loaded with
traps. Sure enough, on this particular op, we run into a Tu Dia
sign, and for some reason we'll never know, when Toung
spotted the sign, he kicked it over. The booby-trapped sign went
boom and we hit the ground, but Toung received shrap wounds

in his chest and legs. U.S. dustoff refused to pick him up (orders from higher-higher, the lousy bastards) and ARVN dustoff took over an hour to come and get him. We were pretty upset.

I led another "interesting" op on June 16, one that still gives me the shivers. It was a stream checkpoint/ambush, and intelligence believed the stream was heavily used by the VC. We went loaded for bear. The brief, insertion, and patrol went well, and the guys even thought I knew what I was doing. When we arrived at the objective early, around 1400, I was amazed—I'd been goddamn sure I was lost, though I never let on. The site was the "U" of a stream, our favorite kind of ambush site, but the U was heavily overgrown with brush and dried cane. It's excellent for cover, but noisy as hell and murder to try and travel through if we got into some hot shit.

We start in, but the point man runs into some trip-wire booby traps, first two together, then another, and another. It's encouraging, because I think Charlie has set up protection for his travel route, but it's also discouraging, because it's way too dangerous for us to filter into the area, and maybe have to move around in after dark. I'm reluctant to switch sites, because this one's so good for our purposes, and Mr. Woodard is encouraging me to take a chance.

Well, I don't want to, but I make a decision. Since it's so early, we'll set the site on fire, recon patrol around for a time while it burns, and then move into the site at dusk. The fire should clean out the cane and set off all the booby traps, and if Charlie hears them go, he might come around later to see what damage had been done. So that's what we did, set the place on fire. Sure enough, as we patrol away, we get three or four explosions, and hopefully the rest of the traps, if any, have been negated. To our delight our recon patrolling uncovers a lot of VC sign, and we even find a little cache of six mortar rounds, so we immediately booby-trap them. Let's give Charlie a little surprise when he goes to use them.

At dusk we move back to the ambush site, and oh Lord, I get the shakes. The burnt-off ground was covered with cooked snakes, hundreds of them! (Well, maybe twenty or thirty.) I ain't sitting on that ground, and I'm all for choosing another

site. But we're out of time, so we set up anyway, cleaning up the
snakes in our spots by moving them with sticks. Brrrr! According to Gieng they're cobras, but I don't care what they are, I
ain't touching them. Damn! All I can think about is what if we
had moved in and set up, and all these snakes started crawling
on me and biting me. They would have killed us all, and no one
would ever have found us. I was almost an MIA.

Since I'm more worried about the snakes than I am about the
VC, I say to myself, "Oh Charlie . . . here boy, here we are.
Come on in and get us so we can get this shit over with and get
the fuck out of here."

And Charlie must have been listening, because shortly after
we set up, here comes a sampan, paddled by one woman. I give
her a "lai dai" call as quietly as I can, and wave my fingers in a
shooing away motion, which is the Viet sign for come here, and
very reluctantly, she paddles in to us. The minute she lays eyes
on us she is terrified, and she actually pees her pants. I have
never seen a human being so scared. Well now, I have a six-inch
goatee and a Fu Manchu mustache, and of course, my face paint
and black PJs. I think I look pretty sharp, but I don't believe she
agrees with me.

Anyhow, this is a farm girl, she's wearing shabby black PJs,
and her hands are callused, with broken nails. And she is a
knockout. She must be a French mixture, because no pure Vietnamese is built that way. But she sure don't like the way I'm
admiring her, and she never takes her eyes off my face. She's
ready to rabbit at any second. Her terror of me soon makes me
very uncomfortable though. Jesus, woman, I'm not a monster!
But she obviously thinks I am, and it bothers me to no end. I put
the cuffs on her just to be safe, although I'm sure she's no VC.

Pretty soon here comes another sampan, and this one also has
a woman paddling it. We scratch our heads, but we finally think
we know what's going on. Charlie's no fool, and he's sending out these women as decoys. They're probably the local
farmer's wife and daughter. Shit.

We wait there for another two hours, but nothing else happens and we expect we're compromised, so we pack it in,
release our prisoner, and *di di* out of there. You always wonder,

though. Were the women the innocents they appeared to be? Or were they VC spotters? Had we been seen, or was Charlie just testing the waters? Maybe if we had let the women go by, Charlie might have followed.

Man, who knows? There were never any easy answers in Vietnam, but I am convinced of one thing. Any time we violate noise discipline, Charlie the pro is not gonna come around. Sneak and peek in absolute silence is the only way to go.

June 22, 1969, Mr. Woodard leads one, and for me, it was the weirdest of all my ops in the Nam, because of the feelings I experienced while on it. A hoi chan who had just recently surrendered from the VC was to lead us into a large ville, where he said there was a VC dispensary and medical center. I volunteered to be point. I mean, I wanted to attempt all the positions so I could be the perfect SEAL. You know how it is.

We chopper in at 2400, patrol, and at 0200 we are approaching the ville. As soon as I see it, I am impressed—the ville is a big one, and I wonder momentarily if we've bitten off more than we can chew. But it really doesn't matter. I've got to earn my pay.

The ville is set right against a large stream, almost a river, and there are about twenty hootches, some quite large. I look the place over, and decide the best way in is by a ditch coming off the river that heads into the center of the ville. It's me, followed by the hoi chan who's guiding me, then Tich, who is guarding the hoi chan and interpreting. I ease into the stream, staying close to the bank, and carefully wade through chest-deep water to the beginning (end?) of the ditch. At the intersection there is a platform and railing about fifteen feet overhead, and I keep my eye on it, because it's a Vietnamese shitter.

It's dead quiet and dark, with pinpoints of oil lamps scattered throughout the ville, and the odor of a Vietnam ville is filling my nostrils. It's a foreign odor, one I will never forget, and is composed of fish-and-rice diet, human sweat, human and animal waste, damp swamp smell, a faint drift of marijuana, a whiff of incense, and over it all the pungent fumes of *nuoc mam*. *Nuoc mam* is the "spice" sauce of Vietnam, and it is made by laying fish on a rack to rot in the sun, funneling the drippings into clay pots, and burying the pots in the ground for a while to ferment.

The Viets put the sauce on and in everything they eat, and although it's quite tasty when you get used to it, the odor of *nuoc mam* will put Limburger cheese to shame. It was always a dead giveaway that there were Vietnamese around. Even today, if I smell something similar, it will raise my head and put me on the alert.

Nothing's stirring except my pulse, but then suddenly there is something. I spot motion, and I quickly hand-signal the patrol to freeze. I see a woman coming down the walkway hawking and spitting, and I quick-move under the platform, because I'm right out in the open. The rest of the patrol dropped neck-deep in the water and leaned tight against the stream bank. The woman stopped right over me, dropped trou, grabbed the railing, and squatted. Oh no. I squinch right down in the water, because I'm only wearing a headband, and I expect the worst. I want to look up, but I don't quite dare. When the water splashes a few feet from me, however, I'm sure relieved.

Once the woman is done and gone, I motion the patrol forward and turn up the shitditch, easing into the ville. It's pretty nasty. The shitditch is waist-deep, it's pig shit, water buffalo shit, human shit, and God knows what else. It penetrates my PJ pants immediately, gluing them to my legs, and grits in my coral shoes and groin. As I stir the gooey mixture up by wading through it, the fumes rise and make my nose wrinkle and my eyes water. I know one thing. Charlie ain't never gonna expect us to come in this way.

Once we are well into the ville, I consult quietly with the hoi chan, and he points out the hootch that contains the dispensary. I crawl up out of the ditch trailing slime and move several yards ahead to squat and let the rest of the patrol form up behind me, and when I get the go-ahead sign, I move out. As I walk silently crouched through the hootches, I am on full-awareness alert, but the ville remains quiet, except for the sounds of people in deep sleep—a cough, a snore, and an occasional dream groan or whimper.

Each hootch has a night-light, a small oil lamp, and because of the hootch half walls or no walls, I can see most of the occupants clearly. They're grouped up, several on sleeping mats, and two or more in a sort of bed, and they're mostly women and children. Most of the males have been conscripted, and are now fighting for one side or the other. Some of the beds have mosquito nets hanging over them, which blurs the outlines of the sleeping occupants.

I am feeling very strange indeed. Here we are, painted up and armed to the teeth, filthy and stinking, their very worst nightmare, and they are completely unaware of our presence, even as Instant Death silently steals among them. Unknowing, they lay with eyes closed and faces relaxed, free of all expression and at their most vulnerable. I feel just like a burglar, and I feel very powerful. If only one person wakes up, I know this place will explode with emotion. It's like the Twilight Zone, you know?

As I approach the target hootch and carefully scan the interior over the half wall, I spot movement. I raise a fist to stop the patrol, go to one knee, and freeze. I can see three beds in there, all with mosquito nets, and in one of them two males are moving, looks like they're playing grab-ass. I can't see them well, and I'm just about to motion the patrol forward into assault formation when dogs start barking. The target hootch instantly comes alive with movement and I holler, "Chieu hoi! Chieu hoi!" (Hey guys, surrender, will ya?)

But Charlie ain't no slouch, and reacts instantly. I see three or four guys crash right through the solid grass rear wall of the hootch and we open up on them, but they're gone like a puff of smoke. Around us the ville has come alive, women screaming and kids crying, but they're old hands at this sort of thing, and nobody's stepping out.

We quickly sweep through the hootch and grab a wounded dude, and another hiding under a bed, and a field pack. Then without pause we move right out the back of the ville, and circle to hit the stream and main trail we'd entered on. As the rear guard crossed the trail, three unarmed women came racing down it, and were taken prisoner.

All this time we are expecting to take fire, but so far there isn't any. We form up, patrol out, extract, and talk it over. The ville has been typical for this area. The occupants are just ordinary Vietnamese, but the VC move in and use them for cover. Charlie don't give a shit for the people.

When we get back, Lou Hyatt busts my ass. "Fuckin' Miller! You just had to take us through that shitditch, didn't you?" I just grin. Who, me? But I guess by the time several SEALs waded through it, the ditch got pretty nasty.

Well, that was all for June. Seven ops. Hardly seemed worth it.

Chapter
Thirty-eight

BECAUSE OF THE scarcity of intell, we move bag and baggage once again, to Tuyen Nhon, a base camp, and they quarter us in a big Quonset with, of all things, housemaids! These Viet women are locals, older women, and not at all attractive. Still, it takes time to get used to having them around, especially since we spend a lot of our time naked. It isn't long, however, before we learn to ignore them, as they do us. It sure is nice to have clean floors and laundry done for us.

We will mostly be operating in the Plain of Reeds, occasionally running a water op near Moc Hoa to keep our hand in. The "Plain of Reeds" is hundreds of miles of open grassland, flat as a football field, and broken only by the inevitable streams, ditches, and canals. There are occasional humps of raised ground four to six feet high—either the remains of old dikes or maybe old hootch sites. These humps are covered with sparse brush and trees, and are the only reliefs in the area. They are also the only cover, so they will be key points as far as enemy movement. All the permanent trails lead to and from them, and also to ditches and small ponds. All these things had to be carefully searched and checked, because Charlie kept buried supply caches in the humps, and mortar tubes and other weapons under the water in the ponds. See, metal needs oxygen and wet to rust, but anything kept underwater without oxygen didn't. Charlie was a true guerrilla, he used what he had.

And suddenly we couldn't do anything right. We only ran eleven ops during July, because we just weren't getting decent intell. It seemed that Charlie wasn't just on R & R, he was on permanent vacation. Naturally, the more our frustration mounted, the worse things went. It got so bad that we even ran a platoon-size sweep, not once but three times, one of them with CIDG troops. Negative results. Oh, we'd find stuff—small caches, empty base camps, and lots of sign, but no warm bodies to shoot up. It would blow our minds to be patrolling along in the middle of nowhere, and stumble on twelve mortar rounds lying in the grass, waiting Charlie's next action. Or find prepped booby traps and no other sign of enemy activity. You always wonder what kind of action had gone on in this empty area, and how long ago. Some of the shit we found appeared to have been lying there for months or years. If we could, we destroyed everything we found, hoping that Charlie would come back and replace it, giving us indications on future ops that he had been there, but it just didn't happen. The Plain of Reeds was just too big and empty to support SEAL operations without specific intelligence, and we soon deserted it, going back to tried and true territory, the waterways. At least there, even though there was no intelligence, we had some chance of running into Charlie.

July 4 we wanted to set off our own brand of fireworks when we were on ambush and spotted a lighted sampan with four armed males in it. We used borrowed junks to insert, and it looks like we made a good decision, because here comes Charlie. Oh boy: I am M-60 man this op, and I am ready to burn 'em up.

I'll be a son of a bitch! The sampan is just out of range, when suddenly it turns sharp left and goes down another stream. I'm telling you, I almost cried with frustration. Naturally, we saw nothing else that night.

Another time we are as usual set up on a stream, when we see Spooky (or is it Puff?) coming toward us. Oh man, now we are dead. He is firing up the stream to our north, and working his way slowly south. We can plainly hear the sustained groan of his miniguns and see the solid lines of his tracers connecting the plane to the ground. Finally he breaks off just north of us and disappears. One more close call.

We just couldn't seem to be in the right place at the right time, because we were mostly guessing. Mr. Woodard said it best on one of his last op reports, under lessons learned/recommendations: "Nonintelligence ops have little or no chance of succeeding." I hear that.

As July crawled by we watched three sampans with eight males approach our ambush, then veer off on another stream before they entered our kill zone. We never got to fire a shot.

When we were coming out of another ambush on our LSSC, we stumbled across a sampan, which immediately evaded. We fired them up anyhow, and watched the VC beach their boat and run, apparently unhurt. We were so desperate by then that we carelessly put ourselves in danger by landing and chasing them, but those light little suckers easily outran us, and we were damn lucky that's all they did.

Another night we watched a VC tax collector collect money and goods from a bunch of fishermen only 150 meters away from us, and then disappear into the crowd.

We eventually started getting really desperate, and changed tactics, but still had no success. We tried boat ambushes. We'd get on the larger streams and rivers in small boats—LCPLs, PBRs, Boston Whalers (we even "borrowed" a junk)—and float, looking for the enemy. We stopped and searched numerous sampans and junks, but nothing was happening.

For the first time we were regularly dumping ammo in the river instead of using it on the enemy. You see, it was SOP for us that we carry the same ordnance on no more than three ops. Since we lived in water and mud, you couldn't trust the stuff after so many wettings, and we'd have to replace it with fresh. What a waste, but hey, it might mean our lives.

July finally closed out, and as we entered August, we were hopeful, because our bad luck just couldn't continue.

Chapter
Thirty-nine

FINALLY! THE VERY first op of August produced Charlie and some action, otherwise we might have assaulted ARVN just for fun. We had moved again, to Cat Lo, which is a big Navy base and another Quonset for us, leaving the empty Plain of Reeds forever. We quickly got some hot intell, so four of us went out on an overnighter stream ambush, taking along some visiting Australian Special Air Service guys. Wow. These guys are excellent, maybe as good as us. They are gung ho, disciplined, and very professional. We really like working with them, and we admire their FLN rifles, but they won't trade for any of them, regardless of what I offer.

Thank you God, at 0300, along comes seven Charlie in three sampans. For form's sake we hailed them, but our LDNN's words hadn't even ended when we opened up. We poured out our frustration on the poor bastards, and when Mr. Woodard finally got a "cease fire," we had very little ammunition left, but there was a shitload of shell casings all around us. The stream was completely empty now except for a single head floating, and the matchsticks of the sampans. The head, when we retrieved it, turned out to be the only survivor, and he was so badly wounded that he only lasted a few minutes. We pushed his body back out into the stream. Hey, fishes gotta eat too. . . .

The SAS guys looked at us with amazement and concern, because they didn't know about our frustration, and didn't understand our strange enjoyment of the "sampan massacre." We didn't tell them, either, let them believe what they wanted.

Mr. Woodard is leaving us. We are near the end of our tour, and San Diego has decided to pull him back to attend some officers' school. We are sorry to see him go. He has been a good officer, and has done right by us, so we give him a send-off beach party. Lordy lordy, do we get drunk. For some unique chemical reason, I never get hangovers, but I sure had one the next day. Must have been that warm Carling Black Label beer.

I am cheered up considerably, though, when Mr. Marsh receives his "survival" pack from his wife. (Mr. Marsh had shown me some pictures of her, and eeyow! She was a knock-out! Blond and gorgeous—Mr. Marsh, how did you ever capture her?) Anyway, she wanted to do her part for the war effort, so she had sewed together a survival pack for her husband to use in the field. When Mr. Marsh opened the package we were at first incredulous, but then we rolled on the floor laughing when he told us what it was. It was a nice belly-pack full of goodies like white face tissues, laundry soap, face soap, underarm deodorant, and cologne, stuff like that. And it was made of pillow cloth! You know, the white-and-blue-striped pillow envelope that you put your pillow cases over. We laughed ourselves sick, and dared him to wear it out in the bush, Charlie would love to see that coming. It would contrast nicely with his faded and nasty-looking camos and web gear. In reality, I think we were all a little envious that he had someone who cared enough about him to go to all that trouble. Once our laughter died it was replaced by wistfulness, truth be known. At least those were my feelings. Maybe it was time to go home.

Chapter Forty

SHIT. AUGUST IS turning out to be no different from July. We run op after op, and we aren't seeing the enemy. Maybe Charlie himself has given up and gone home? We didn't know, but when we finally did get contact, it was bogus. Produced by the Dexamil diet pills that we used to stay awake (Somebody just called me an idiot and told me "Dexadrine, dummy, not Dexamil." Man, how the hell do I know, I ain't no doctor. They worked, so I don't give a shit what they're called.), we had various enemy sightings that were nothing but illusions. I had two of those sightings, and I was as hard to convince as the others that it was just the drug, and not reality. I'm telling you, those visions were real to me!

One night we were lying on a hump, and after I blinked my eyes, I could see a whole battalion of NVA soldiers spread out in front of me. I mean, I saw groups of NVA squatted around their fires shooting the shit, I saw stacked arms, uniforms, the whole works. It took Dee ten minutes to convince me that I was dreaming, and there was nothing out there but darkness.

Another time we sat up on Football Island in the middle of the Mekong River. I am sitting on the lower point of the island, armed with a Stoner that's just begging to be emptied at Charlie. Only problem was, we hadn't taken the tides into account. At 1600 I'm sitting high and dry on ambush, at 1800 the river has risen to my waist, and by 2000 I'm chin-deep, with my weapon laid across my head. It's uncomfortable but not unbearable, until something swims up my pantsleg.

Now, I didn't always believe everything I was told, and one of the advice items I had ignored was that of tying off the bottom of my pants. So far, we hadn't seen a leech, and I hated it when we would wade into water, my pantslegs would fill, and I'd have to slosh along noisily until they emptied. So I didn't tie off my pantslegs, just left them loose and flopping, and now my time had arrived to regret it.

Whatever it was that swam up my leg (and I had no doubt whatsoever that it was a big old snake) decided to explore its new home, and Lord above, the thing nuzzled my dick! Of course I don't dare grab the intruder; if I do it will bite me. All I could do was sweat and pray, and long after I had lost my sanity, whatever it was swam back out the bottom of my pantsleg. Yowda! I had to have lost ten years off my life span.

My relief is short-lived though, because I can't tie up my pantslegs to discourage other visitors, and the tension letdown brings drowsiness. I try and I try, but my eyelids want to drop closed, and when ducking my head under the water several times doesn't help, I pop another Dexamil pill. It takes an hour of hard struggle before the Dex kicks in. The tide has turned and the water is receding down my body before I am alert again. Good thing, because here comes a sampan with several VC in it. I can see them plainly, so when they get in range, I open up and wipe them out with my Stoner.

Richards grabs me. "What the fuck you shooting at?"

I told him, righteously, "It was a sampan! Right full of VC!"

He gives me a punch. "You idiot! That was a log. Nothin' but a log."

Then he looks at me suspiciously, "How many Dexes did you pop?"

I say, "Hey, man, only two." But I can tell he don't believe me.

I defend myself, but when the others ask what's going on, Rich tells them that Miller the fool had shot up a VC log. Damn. I knew I'd never live that down.

But on other ops, nothing's happening, and we have mixed feelings about it all. On the one hand, our time in country is getting short, and we're glad things are quiet. On the other hand, we were SEALs, and the inactivity was driving us crazy. The monotony of sitting out night after night with no action finally affected our attitudes. I admit it, we soon became sloppy and careless, prime candidates for a wipeout. But I get saved by R & R.

Hey, it must be time for some heavy partying. I've gotten R & R to Australia, and what a fabulous place that turns out to be. God, round-eyed women, with pink nipples instead of brown, and friendly, too. These are nice girls, the "girl-next-door" type, and they meet you at the airport and invite you to stay with their family while you are there. For some strange reason they really like Americans, unless of course you are a typical American asshole, behave badly, and ruin it for everybody else. I meet Jessie, or rather, she meets me, and invites me to stay at her house. It is a mixed bag: pure pleasure at spending time with and wooing a sweet lady, but it also reminds me of what's waiting at home, and I want to get back there, soon. I know I will be leaving her forever in too short a time, but while I'm here, she makes me a whole new person.

At first I was uncomfortable dealing with a nice girl, my "smooth-dog" manners were rusty, and I just didn't know how to act like a normal human being, but I'm a SEAL, Mr. Adaptable, and after a short recon, I reach my objective and complete the mission. God, how I hated to leave, and after way too short a visit, I came back renewed to the same old shit. But I definitely don't mind it as much now.

One day some of us decide to make a trip to Saigon and hang out. I am looking to trade a load of lumber that I have "found" for a decent .45 pistol for the old man. We whip on our civilian clothes, and catch a ride on a slick. The pilot is, as usual, a warrant officer, young and redheaded, and he decides to have some fun with the SEALs. He starts hedge-hopping. This is a fun game where the chopper rockets along the ground at high speed, and when a treeline appears, the pilot "hops" over it with minimum clearance. It's guaranteed to stimulate your heart rate. But we are SEALs, with nerves of steel (Hey, "I'm a poet, and I do know it, 'cause my big dick shows it, it's a Longfellow."), so we pay no attention and act unconcerned. Pretty soon this hot-rod joker tires of the game and flares the chopper hard, up to 2,000 feet, and flies on. Pretty quick I smell something, and when I look around, there's smoke coming out of the engine. Being Mr. Helpful, I tap the pilot on the shoulder and yell, "Uh . . . say listen, man, there's smoke coming out of your engine."

His eyes flare a look at me to see if I am bullshitting, and about that time the engine stops dead. If ever I saw a guy turn white it was that pilot, but he was no slouch. Both pilots start flipping switches and pushing buttons and talking up a storm on their mikes. Me, I quickly sit down and get a good brace for the crash.

Now, you've got to understand, our slicks were set up for combat. Nylon bench seats, no seat belts, no doors, hell, half the time we sat on the floor and dangled our legs out. Not this time, though. Well, that guy may have been a hotshot, but he was also a damn good pilot. We started spinning in rapid circles like a top, and finally landed on the skids with a pretty good thump. It's called autorotating, and now I like it a lot. Since it has worked, we scrambled out quickly, but everything was cool—nothing caught on fire.

Hmm . . . this was pretty interesting. Here we were in the middle of nowhere, in enemy territory, dressed in civilian clothes, no gear, no weapons, and no place to hide. Were we in the shit? Nope. No way. We couldn't even attract Charlie by offering ourselves as an inviting target. As we waited for rescue, not even a bird stirred. It was Dead City.

Eventually another slick arrived, and so did a Chinook. The Chinook picked up the downed chopper on a cable and flew away with it. As for us, we went back to base. Liberty would have been an anticlimax. Besides, we had to go clean out our pants.

Chapter
Forty-one

AND THAT PRETTY much did it for us. It appeared that Charlie was nonexistent in our AO, so we gave it up, and moved to the big Navy base at Vung Tau. In fact, Vung Tau was reputed to be an R & R town for Charlie and we hoped we might catch him going back and forth. No weapons were allowed to be carried in the city (except for SEALs, of course; we all carried concealed handguns) and it was live and let live, a place of unofficial truce for conventional forces. But once Charlie was outside the city, or before he entered, we figured he was fair game.

Sorry, GI, it's numba ten. We don't see shit, and I mean absolutely nothing. We finally threw up our hands, said, "Xin loi," and made preparations to go home.

First we got a stereo catalog and all of us ordered stereo gear from it. I knew absolutely nothing about stereo stuff, so I just ordered the most expensive model of each component, figuring I couldn't go wrong that way, and I didn't. The Sansui tuner lasted seventeen years, the Akai reel-to-reel tape deck lasted twenty years, and the Pioneer studio turntable and speakers are still part of my system to this day. I spent $1,000, and I figure the system was worth at least three times that. I directed the company I ordered from in Japan to send my system directly back to my parents' address, where I could pick it up next visit.

We also had to pack our trunks. Because of our unique equipment, and because of our Top Secret clearance, our gear traveled with us at all times, and didn't go through customs. To facilitate this, we had been issued fiberglass trunks. These trunks were about two feet by two feet by five feet, and we

stood them on end and lived out of them instead of lockers.
They turned out to be ideally suited for our mobility as a platoon, and as the Big Pack Rat, I could easily have filled three
of them, but I did my duty and packed all my goodies in just
one. It took me several tries, though, and I had to force it closed
with the banding tool, but finally it was ready. I mean, it was all
good stuff, you know, not junk. I had a few rifles (eleven), a
couple handguns (eight), and of course, plenty of ammunition
for them. I had also obtained eight poncho liners and twelve
quarts of Chivas Regal. Plus, I couldn't leave all my books and
war trophies behind, could I? When we loaded the trunks on the
truck, I got a lot of bitching and moaning, just because it took
four men to carry mine, and two men for everyone else's.

Mr. Woodard had left for the States early, and Mr. Marsh and
Tom McDonald were staying behind to break in our replacement platoon, so as the ranking petty officer, I'd be taking our
platoon back. On September 8, 1969, our plane took off from
Saigon, and our tour was over.

It had gone very well for us. In six months, we had run
ninety-four ops, and I had had the privilege of leading nine of
them. For all you officers out there (and you know who you
are), we'd killed forty-three enemy, wounded sixteen, and captured thirty-one, all confirmed. Balanced against that we had
five U.S. wounded (poor Emerson three times) and none killed.
Our primary contribution, as expected, was to military intelligence. Our observations, the info we'd taken from prisoners,
and the documentation we'd captured had fueled numerous ops
by conventional and airborne forces. We'd earned our pay.

Final footnote: I liked being a SEAL so much that I planned
to re-up and stay in the Teams, but after I got back to the World
and took my final leave, civilian life was just too attractive.
American girls, driving my new Chevy, my reunion with my
brother, A.J., and my family, all these things made me change
my mind. Add to that the fact that I had my former IBM job
waiting for me, and on January 19, 1970, I took my Honorable
Discharge and left the military forever.

I never really looked back, until SEALs started getting publicity, and then it was usually just to laugh at the way I saw Special Forces and other military portrayed in books and movies. I kept waiting for someone to get it right. Hopefully I now have. One thing that has always been difficult for me to deal with was when my friends, family, and acquaintances gave me this look of awe and respect because I had been a SEAL. It's okay, but in my mind, I was just a normal person, nobody special, who had done the job required, as well as I was able. All the SEALs I knew were like that.

In 1996, when I met Gary Linderer, a former LRRP who now publishes *Behind the Lines* (a special operations forces magazine), he suggested I write this book. I was very reluctant at first, because I just didn't believe that there was any interesting story in my military career. But now I say, "Thank you, Gary," because this has been great fun for me, remembering and reliving the old memories and putting them down on paper.

It only remains for me to make two apologies. One, if I have neglected any of you that lived those former days, or have not given full or proper credit, I sincerely apologize. Twenty-seven years is an awful long time ago and tends to fade your memory.

And to those of you who are disturbed by the humorous way I have treated a very serious subject, war, I can only say, life is lived one of two ways: You can shrug off the bad and go on to enjoy the good, or you can worry too much about everything and develop ulcers. I've never had an ulcer in my life, and do not anticipate getting any.